POWER AND INNOCENCE

A Search for
the Sources of Violence

By the same author

LOVE AND WILL
MAN'S SEARCH FOR HIMSELF
THE MEANING OF ANXIETY
THE ART OF COUNSELING
PSYCHOLOGY AND THE HUMAN DILEMMA
SPRINGS OF CREATIVE LIVING
DREAMS AND SYMBOLS (WITH LEOPOLD CALIGOR)
EXISTENCE: A NEW DIMENSION IN
PSYCHIATRY AND PSYCHOLOGY
(WITH ERNEST ANGEL AND HENRI F. ELLENBERGER)
EXISTENTIAL PSYCHOLOGY (ED.)
SYMBOLISM IN RELIGION AND LITERATURE (ED.)

POWER AND INNOCENCE

A Search for the Sources of Violence

ROLLO MAY

W · W · Norton & Company · Inc ·

NEW YORK

Library of Congress Cataloging in Publication Data
May, Rollo.
    Power and innocence.
    Includes bibliographical references.
    1. Violence.   2. Aggressiveness (Psychology)
HM291.M393   301.6'33   72–5432
3. Social history—1945–   I.   Title.
ISBN 0–393–01065–1

1 2 3 4 5 6 7 8 9 0

To Ingrid

Contents

Part III

Contents

Preface

As a young man, I held innocence in high esteem. I disliked power, both in theory and practice, and abhorred violence. I came down with tuberculosis in my early thirties, a time when there was still no medication for the disease. For a year and a half I did not know whether I would live or die. As best I could, I tried to do what my doctors instructed me to do. This meant, as I then interpreted it, accepting the program of rest and giving my healing over to others. I could only lie in bed, tracing with my eye patterns of light on the ceiling of my room, waiting for the monthly X-ray which would tell whether the cavity in my lung had enlarged or decreased.

But I found, to my moral and intellectual dismay, that the bacilli were taking advantage of my very innocence. This innocence had transformed my helplessness into passivity, which constituted an open invitation to the bacilli to do violence to my body. I saw, too, that the reason I had contracted tuberculosis in the first place was my hopelessness and sense of defeatism. My then present lack of self-affirmation and self-assertion, conveniently rationalized by the innocence, could only lead in one direction. I could see in the apparently innocent patients around me in the sanatorium that passively accepting their powerlessness in the face of the disease meant dying.

Not until I developed some "fight," some sense of personal responsibility for the fact that it was *I* who had the tuberculosis, an assertion of my own will to live, did I make lasting progress. I learned to listen to my body with an inner concentration like meditation, to get guidance as to when to exercise and when to rest. I learned that healing and cure are active processes in which I myself needed to participate.

This truth, though experienced by me in my getting well, was not very useful since I could never formulate it. I was later forced to think about it at length, however, when I found my patients in psychoanalysis describing similar experiences. Practically all of them had come for help because they felt or were powerless. They had no effective bridge to the significant people in their lives; they could only remain passive while others (like the t.b. bacilli in my analogy) did violence to them. This bridge to significant others was never directly confronted by Freud. Sullivan pointed to it, but had never elaborated on the nature of this bridge. It is, in fact, power. But it is power analogous to the healing power by which one overcomes tuberculosis, not analogous to the military power of a general on the battlefield or the economic power of the head of a corporation.

I had, then, to confront my own relationship to power. No longer could I conceal behind my own innocence my envy of those who had power. This, I found, only follows the general procedure in our culture: power is widely coveted and rarely admitted. Generally, those who have power repress their awareness of this fact. And it is the dispossessed in our society, represented by such movements as "women's power" and "black power," who, when they are able, force a direct confrontation with the issue.

When we join in this confrontation, as we obviously must, we find ourselves immediately up against the issue of violence. Can violence also have something to do with innocence—or, as I ask later in this book, does innocence invite its own murder? This leads us to difficult, if fascinating, questions. We can only agree that Jacob Bronowski's words (in *The Face of Violence*) are true:

> Violence is here,
> In the world of the sane,
> And violence is a symptom.
> I hear it in the headlong weeping of men
> who have failed.
> I see it in the terrible dreams of boys
> Whose adolescence repeats all history.

As these weeping men and dreaming adolescents, however, become able to actualize their power, they are able, to some extent, to turn their violence to constructive use and their dreams and visions to the social and their own good. I hope to suggest ways not *around* the problems of power and violence, but *through* them.

To understand power and the sources of violence, we must ask more profound questions than are customary. We must probe the problem of what it means to be a human being.

The difficulty and the loneliness of writing this book were lightened by the companionship of several friends who discussed the topics with me or read chapters or both. Anthony Athos, himself involved in the theme, discussed the subject with me far beyond the call of friendship. I am grateful also to Alberta Szalita, Daphne Greene, David Bazelon, Leslie H. Farber, and Stanley Kunitz for valuable ideas. The students in a seminar on this topic which I taught at Yale, through their insights, uncovered other dimensions in the psychology of power. My patients have been—here, as always—my richest source of learning, and I am indebted to them.

Rollo May
Holderness,
New Hampshire

PART I

ONE

MADNESS AND POWERLESSNESS

Wherever I found the living, there I found the will
to power.
— Friedrich Nietzsche,
from *Thus Spake Zarathustra*

Power is essential for all living things. Man in particular, cast on
this barren crust of earth aeons ago with the hope and the require-
ment that he survive, finds he must use his powers and confront
opposing forces at every point in his struggle with the earth and
with his fellows. Insecure as he has been through the ages, buf-
feted by limitations and weakness, laid low by illness and ultimately by death, he nevertheless asserts his powers in creativity.
One product of this is civilization.

The word *power* comes from the Latin *posse*, meaning "to be
able." We can see the vicissitudes of the emergence of power as
soon as a baby is born into the world—in his cry and in the wav-
ing of his arms in demand that he be fed. The cooperative, loving

side of existence goes hand in hand with coping and power, but neither the one nor the other can be neglected if life is to be gratifying. Our appreciation of the earth and the support of our fellows are not gained by abdication of our powers, but by cooperative use of them.

The infant's capacity to cope with necessities becomes, in the growing adult, the struggle for self-esteem and for the sense of significance as a person. This latter is his psychological reason for living in contrast to the infant's biological one. The cry for recognition becomes the central psychological cry: I must be able to say *I am*, to affirm myself in a world into which, by my capacity to assert myself, I put meaning, I *create* meaning. And I must do this in the face of nature's magnificent indifference to my struggles.

In Nietzsche's proclamation of the "will to power," it is important that we remind ourselves that he meant neither "will" nor "power" in the competitive sense of the modern day, but rather self-realization and self-actualization. If we are freed from thinking of power only in the pejorative sense, we are better able to agree with Nietzsche.

Far from treating power only as a term of abuse, one which is to be applied to our enemies (i.e., *they* are power-driven, but *we* are motivated only by benevolence, reason, and morality), I use it as a description of a fundamental aspect of the life process. It is not to be identified with life itself; there is much in human existence—like curiosity and love and creativity—that may be and normally is related to power but is not to be called power in itself. But if we neglect the factor of power, as is the tendency in our day of reaction against the destructive effects of the misuse of power, we shall lose values that are essential to our existence as human.[1]

A great deal of human life can be seen as the conflict between power on one side (i.e., effective ways of influencing others, achieving the sense in interpersonal relations of the significance of one's self) and powerlessness on the other. In this conflict our efforts are made much more difficult by the fact that we block out both sides, the former because of the evil connotation of "power drives," and the latter because our powerlessness is too painful to confront. Indeed, the chief reason people refuse to confront the whole issue of power is that if they did, they would have to face their own powerlessness.

As soon as powerlessness is referred to by its more personal name, helplessness or weakness, many people will sense that they are heavily burdened by it. "Indeed, no social emotion is more widespread today than the conviction of personal powerlessness," Arthur M. Schlesinger, Jr., writes, "the sense of being beset, beleaguered, and persecuted." [2] Hans Morgenthau gives the political comment: "Majority rule, for which men have struggled for centuries, has produced a situation in which men are more impotent, more powerless to influence their government than 150 years ago." [3] The juggernaut of the state grinds on with no attention paid to you or me. And now multitudes are having to get used to living without their usual confidence that "America is the world's most powerful nation," a confidence to which, inadequate as it was, many people clung for their past sense of personal status.

To admit our own individual feelings of powerlessness—that we cannot influence many people; that we count for little; that the values to which our parents devoted their lives are to us insubstantial and worthless; that we feel ourselves to be "faceless Others," as W. H. Auden puts it, insignificant to other people and, therefore, not worth much to ourselves—this is, indeed, difficult to admit. I cannot recall a time during the last four decades when there was so *much* talk about the individual's capacities and potentialities and so *little* actual confidence on the part of the individual about his power to make a difference psychologically or politically. The talk is at least partially a compensatory symptom for our disquieting awareness of our very loss of power.

It is, therefore, understandable in this transitional age, when we have at our fingertips the power to blow each other off the face of the planet, that certain persons should propose we give up the human experiment. In his presidential address to the American Psychological Association, Dr. Kenneth B. Clark argued that "we live in times too dangerous to trust to human individual mood or choice. . . . We can no longer control the men in power, and we therefore must resort to pacifying drugs to control our leaders." [4] We can appreciate this despair, considered against the background of Dr. Clark's intimate knowledge of Harlem and the powerlessness of the blacks, out of which the impetus for this proposal arises. But this does not prevent our also realizing, as we read with sinking heart of the new discoveries of chemicals that purport to cure modern man of his aggressiveness and develop in him a "cooperative" personality, that use of them goes with depersonalization and loss of our sense of personal responsibility. This alternative would mean, indeed, a gradual abdication of man's humanity.

Other psychologists, noting that we have not done very well in controlling ourselves, propose to do the controlling for us in the form of operant conditioning. We hear of new methods of bringing up our children which will train out of them aggressive tendencies and make them docile and placid. Has everyone forgotten in this despair, I ask myself in alarm, H. G. Wells's "The Time Machine," in which the people are polarized into two groups, the majority domesticated into docile, cowlike passivity, their flesh soft and tender, who are then eaten by the tougher group, the engineers?

The failure-of-nerve theories arise out of the true observation that the exercise of power has done colossal harm in the modern world. The proposals have the double attraction of expressing the reaction against power and promising a utopia in the same breath. They will have a strong following among people threatened by impotence and hoping against hope for some substitute for power. As David McClellan says: "America's concern about the possible misuse of power verges at times on a neurotic obsession." [5] The important question, however, is not whether these theories are right or wrong. Rather it is whether or not we would, by trying to rid ourselves of our tendencies toward aggression, be discarding those values essential to our humanity—our self-affirmation and self-assertion, just to mention two. And would we not then be adding greatly to our feeling of powerlessness and thus setting the stage for an eruption of violence that would dwarf everything so far?

For violence has its breeding ground in impotence and apathy. True, aggression has been so often and so regularly escalated into violence that anyone's discouragement and fear of it can be understood. But what is *not* seen is that the state of powerlessness, which leads to apathy and which can be produced by the above plans for the uprooting of aggression, is the source of violence. As we make people powerless, we promote their violence rather than its control. Deeds of violence in our society are performed largely by those trying to establish their self-esteem, to defend their self-image, and to demonstrate that they, too, are significant. Regardless of how derailed or wrongly used these motivations may be or how destructive their expression, they are still the manifestations of positive interpersonal needs. We cannot ignore the fact that, no matter how difficult their redirection may be, these needs themselves are potentially constructive. Violence arises not out of superfluity of power but out of powerlessness. As Hannah Arendt has so well said, violence is the expression of impotence.

1. POWERLESSNESS CORRUPTS

The relationship of powerlessness and psychosis was impressed upon me a number of years ago when I started work as a psychotherapist. In the mentally troubled person psychotherapists are able to see the extremes of the behavior and the experience of us all. It bears out the words of Edgar Z. Friedenberg: "All weakness tends to corrupt, and impotence corrupts absolutely." [6]

A young musician, Priscilla, was one of my first patients. According to the person who administered her Rorschach, she had "one foot in schizophrenia and the other on a banana peel." In her sessions with me she would give long, involved comparisons of the colors of the musical notes made by the train from Newark in contrast to those made by the train from New Brunswick. I had not the slightest idea about what she was talking much of the time—and she knew it. But she seemed to need me as a person who listened, wanting and trying to understand her whether I succeeded or not. She was also a woman with considerable dignity and a sense of humor, which helped us immeasurably.

But she could never get angry. Not at me or her parents or anyone else. Her self-esteem was so shaky and vague as to be almost nonexistent. Once a young man in a chorus to which she belonged asked her to go to a concert with him. She accepted. But the next day, in a surge of self-doubts, she phoned him to say: "You don't have to take me if you don't want to." She could not affirm or assert herself enough to conceive that someone might *like* to go to a concert with her. When, at the age of eight or nine, she would play football with a boy slightly older than she, he would run into her hard enough to hurt her. Another child might have yelled at the boy, or started a fight, or cried, or abandoned the game; these are all, good or bad, ways of coping. But Priscilla could utilize none of these methods; she could only sit there on the ground, looking at him and silently thinking that he shouldn't hit her so hard.

When she was exploited, as she often was, sexually and financially, she had no defenses, no way of drawing a line beyond which she could firmly say "no," no anger to support her. (One gets a feeling that such persons almost invite exploitation—it at least gives them some relationship and significance.) Along with her inability to get angry, there went, as a necessary corollary, a deep experience of powerlessness and an almost complete lack of capacity to influence or affect other people in interpersonal relations.

But such a person has another side which, as I have confirmed in working with many borderline patients since, is completely different. Priscilla's dreams were of cut-up bodies put in bags, of blood and battles—in short, as *violent* as her conscious life was docile.

Since that time and partly due to this young woman, I have frequently reflected on the relationship between powerlessness and madness. I am purposely stressing both meanings of the word *mad:* its personal sense of enragedness to the point of violence; and its historical psychiatric sense of psychosis. There is a relationship between the two, and this double use of the term may lead us to the center of the problem.

We know that a common characteristic of all mental patients is their powerlessness, and with it goes a constant anxiety which is both cause and effect of the impotence. The patients' insignificance is so firmly assumed by them that they accept it as a given, often going through life making sad and pitiful gestures to get whatever bit of significance they can. An adolescent girl came to consult me in the middle of the day wearing a crinoline evening dress, possibly one of the prettiest things she had, as a gesture of how much she needed my attention and concern, unaware that it was likely to be regarded as out of place.

When a person like Priscilla can no longer support this way of life, something "cracks" within her and she may then move into a state in which she is nothing but mad. The person then seems to be the exact opposite of what she had been. The violence of dreams like Priscilla's then becomes the content of her waking life. The person seems *all* madness, which is surely why psychosis through the centuries was called madness. Mad now at everybody, including herself, the person threatens or attempts suicide, cuts her wrists, smears blood over the doors in hospitals to dramatize her need of the attendants and interns. She does overt violence to herself and whoever gets in the range of her projections.

We see the same movement in other patients. In the autobiographical novel on her own schizophrenia *I Never Promised You a Rose Garden,* Hannah Green was admitted to Chestnut Lodge at sixteen. She was the epitome of docility and placidity, never showing any anger at all. Whenever she needed to, she withdrew into the mythology of her private spirit world and talked with mythical figures. Dr. Frieda Fromm-Reichman, the psychiatrist at Chestnut Lodge who treated her, dealt with this mythology with respect, assuring Hannah that she would not take it away as long as the girl needed it. But when Dr. Fromm-Reichman went to Europe one summer, another, younger doctor was assigned to the girl. He charged in, blithely courageous, to break up her mythological world. The results were disastrous. In her explosion of violence, the patient set fire to herself and to her belongings at the Lodge, scarring herself for life. The error of the young doctor was that he did not appreciate that the mythology was what gave significance to Hannah's existence. The question was not whether it was theoretically right or wrong, but its function for her. This placid patient, who seemed incapable of any aggressive act, swung from docility into outright violence.

This may seem and feel like power to the hospital attendants, but it is a *pseudo*power, an expression of impotence. The patient may now be spoken of as "mad," which means that she does not fit the accepted criteria in our society which, like all societies, prefers docile, placid "face." It is important to see that the violence is the end result of repressed anger and rage, combined with constant fear based on the patient's powerlessness. Behind the pseudopower of the madness we can often find a person struggling for some sense of significance, some way of making a difference and establishing some self-esteem.

When Priscilla was in treatment with me, she received a newspaper from her home town in which it was reported that a certain man in her village had committed suicide. She said to me: "If only one other person in that town had known him, he would not have committed suicide." Note that she did not say, "If *he* had known someone," but "if someone had known *him*." She was telling me, I believed, that she would not put a violent end to her life so long as I was related to her. But she was also describing something critically important for a human being—*the necessity of having somebody listen, recognize, know him.* It gives a person the conviction that he counts, that he exists as part of the human race. It also gives him some orientation, a point where he can find meaning in an otherwise meaningless world.

It would be a red-letter day when Priscilla could get angry with me, for I knew that she could then begin to protect herself in her contacts with other people in the wide world. And what is more, she could dare to live out her considerable capacities as an original and lovable as well as loving human being.

2. MADNESS AND SOCIETY

What relation does this pattern of passivity/madness that we have seen in Priscilla have to do with the violence in our society, which has become such a critical problem for contemporary men and women?

A friend of mine, not in analysis or psychotic in any way, tells us how it feels to be in a rage after a quarrel with his wife:

How close this rage is to a temporary psychosis! As I walk down the street on a sidewalk that seems very far away, I cannot think; I am in a daze. But it is foggy only externally—inside I am hyperalive, hyperaware of every thought and feeling, as though I am in an illuminated world, everything very real. The only trouble is that this inner illumination has practically no connection with the outside world.

I feel slightly ashamed in relation to the outside world
—ashamed and defenceless. If people made fun of me or suddenly demanded something important of me (say an accident
occurred on the street), I wouldn't be able to respond. Or if I
did respond, I'd have to get out of my "mad"; it would be
broken through.

The streets are foreign; they seem empty though people are
walking on them just as always. I do not know the streets very
well (though I have seen them thousands of times).

I walk on as though I'm drunk, picking up my feet and self-
consciously putting them down. I go into a restaurant, afraid the
cashier girl will not recognize me—I am in a different skin—or
she'll think something is wrong. (She does recognize me and is
friendly as always.

I go to the men's room; I read the graffiti over the urinal
without any emotion. I am still afraid someone will require something of me, attack me, and I couldn't defend myself. I come
back to my seat, staring out the window at the far end of the
restaurant. I feel only a vague relation to the world. Food is
brought me; I'm not much interested in eating or taste; I go
vaguely through the motions.

I try to recall the details of our quarrel, without much success
—two or three things stand out with great vividness; the rest is
a jumble. I eat a little.

A waiter comes up, a middle-aged Chinese, and he says to me:
"I can see you think too much," he pointed to his forehead. "You
got some problem?" I smiled and nodded. He went on: "These
days everybody got some problem." His words were strangely
comforting. He went away, shaking his head. This was the first
breakthrough of the outside world. It made me laugh to myself,
and helped me much more than one would think.

I could understand how, when this state is relatively permanent,
people do themselves harm, step in front of a motor car for example. They do this mostly out of a lack of awareness of the
real world about them. They do it also out of revenge. Or they
get a gun and shoot somebody.

The experience of being caught up in such a rage is very close to
the historical experience of being "mad."

What, for example, is the meaning of "mad" in such statements as the following made by a young black in Harlem:

> The white cops, they have a damn sadistic nature. . . . We don't need them here in Harlem! . . . They start more violence than any other people start. . . . When we're dancing on the street because we can't go home, here comes one cop, he'll want to chase everyone. And he gets mad. I mean he gets mad! . . . He comes into the neighborhood aggravated and mad.[7]

This black is saying that there is a relationship between the "mad" of the policeman and violence in Harlem. Does the policeman, by inciting a violent reaction, use his own rage as a stimulus to preserve what he feels is law and order? Is this one of the reasons a man would choose to become a police officer in the first place? Does he seize upon a culturally accepted psychosis and use it to ally himself with the status quo, thereby giving himself the right, in line of duty, to carry a club and gun with which to let out his own violence?

In the verbatim reports in *Violent Men*, by professor of criminology Hans Toch, we can consider these questions in greater detail. Toch believes, for example, that

> The black kids and the white cops—their pride, their fear, their isolation, their need to prove themselves, above all their demand for respect—are strangely alike: victims both, prisoners of an escalating conflict they did not make and can't control.[8]

As shown by their own reports, the policemen feel they have to uphold "law and order," and they identify this with their own individual self-esteem and masculinity. Time after time it is clear that the policeman is fighting an impotence-potency battle within himself that he expands and projects on the concept of "law and order." Affronts to themselves the police interpret as affronts to the law of the land. They have to insist, then, that the "suspects" respect their authority and power. They feel their manhood is being challenged and their reputation, on which their self-respect is based, is at stake. A typical instance is the officer who, responding to a call of a family fight, sees a black man sitting in a car who he thinks can tell him something about the altercation:

> The officer asks the black to step out of the car. The black responds, "You can't do this to me, I'm on private property." He seemed obnoxious, the officer reported, his "attitude bothered me."
>
> The black eventually got out but kept his hands in the pocket of his trench coat. This continued to bother the officer, who asked him to take his hands out. Meeting with continued refusal, he called another policeman and they forced the hands out.
>
> The policeman sees this as an unforgivable defiance of his authority. He must assert police authority at all costs. . . . ("I felt it was imperative that I take the man's hands out of his pockets. . . . He became abusive as we took hold of him. . . . We arrested him and put him in the back seat of the patrol car, where he threatened to urinate on the seat, kicked and pounded on the glass.") [9]

The black man in this case believed that the policeman, whom he sees as the arm of the white establishment and the enemy of the whole black race, humiliated him arbitrarily. And, indeed, he is right in the sense that the policeman must cow him to preserve his own authority. Both are "violent men." Blue Power in this instance is the opposite side of the coin of Black Power. Each is engaged in protecting his own self-image, his own sense of being "a man." But the policeman, by virtue of his identification with law enforcement and his gun and badge, has a special advantage. The "violent men" in the police force, writes Toch, "are experts in escalating interpersonal encounters into explosive situations." The "suspect" regularly feels that the cards are stacked against him; his opponent in the "duel" hides behind his badge and gun, and often the "suspect" will challenge the officer to take off his badge and settle differences "man to man."

The placing on of hands, the physical contact, and the other aspects of *touching* are especially significant. The "suspect" has to protect the inviolability of his body. The policeman feels that he has to violate the "suspect's" body, to push him around with unnecessary roughness, in order to make the "suspect" bow to his authority.

It is important to note that this type of policeman almost always reports that he asks the blacks for identification. Now identity is a highly personal thing. Psychologically, demanding identification is like requiring a person to undress physically; it gives a person who has already been told he is inferior an added feeling of personal humiliation. It provokes the black's sense of outrage, and the policeman finds he has pushed the situation to the brink of a riot over simple proof of identity.

Noteworthy in these violent acts is that often the man who ends up in jail was simply trying, through his act, to defend his self-image or his reputation or his rights. Almost everyone is struggling in some form or other to build or protect his self-esteem, his sense of significance as a person. Both police and "suspects" are fighting an impotence-potency battle within themselves. Each interprets this in his own, though diametrically opposite, way. True, this power battle can be blown up to paranoid proportions, the offense simply being imagined; or it can take the infantile form of bullying or some other deviation. But in order to see the roots of violence we must go below these psychological dynamics and seek its source in the individual's struggle to establish and protect his self-esteem. This is, in essence, a positive need—it is potentially constructive. Prisons don't deter criminals, according to Toch's data, for "violence feeds on low self-esteem and self-doubt, and prison unmans and dehumanizes; violence rests on exploitation and exploitativeness, and prison is a power-centered jungle." [10]

There seems to be growing evidence that the police and guards on one side and the incarcerated men on the other are of the same personality type. Toch writes, "Our research indicates that the ranks of law enforcement contain their share of Violent Men. The personalities, outlooks and actions of these officers are similar to those of the other men in our sample [i.e., the men who have been arrested]. They reflect the same fears and insecurities, the same fragile, self-centered perspectives. They display the same bluster and bluff, panic and punitiveness, rancor and revenge as do our other respondents. . . . And whereas much police violence springs out of adaptations to police work rather than out of problems of infancy, the result, in practice, is almost the same." [11]

The need for potency, which is another way of phrasing the struggle for self-esteem, is common to us all. We see its positive form in the rebellion at the Attica, New York, prison, where the leader of the revolting inmates proclaimed: "We don't want to be treated any longer as statistics, as numbers. . . . We want to be treated as human beings, we *will* be treated as human beings. . . ." Another inmate, older than the first, took a more realistic view: "If we cannot live as people, we will at least try to die as men." History records that twenty-eight of them did die several days later when the troopers charged into the prison, shooting. But—such is the strange partnership between guards and prisoners, both being "in prison" and both being of the same personality types—history also records that some prisoners died using their bodies to protect their prison guards from the shots.

3. POWERLESSNESS AND DRUGS

Drug addiction is another possible effect of powerlessness. The conviction of powerlessness is especially profound with young people, and this is also where drug addiction is most prevalent. Their addiction is a form of violence, first of all, in that the individual violates his own mind—which, indeed, is the purpose of the drug; and there follows later all the petty crime and greater crime that drug addicts get into.[12]

The basis of addiction is a "lot of weakness" and a "blocked anger." [13] The weakness takes the form of "I can't meet the demands of my family"; "I can't get a job"; "I am sexually impotent"; "I am a 'no person.'" The anger takes the form of the addict's revenge upon his family and the world for forcing him into this painful position of powerlessness. Sexual impotence is present before taking the drugs; a large majority of addicts report that they had suffered from premature or quick ejaculations or had great difficulty in getting an erection at all. Their fear is that they are "not man enough" to satisfy a woman.

The heroin wipes away all this discomfort of perpetually feeling weak. It anesthetizes the person, partly through chemical and partly through psychological means, and gives complete relief in place of the original profound and continuous pain. No more inferiority, no more worry about being a failure in the working world, no more fear of being a coward in battle, no more disappointing one's parents—all these oppressive feelings evaporate.

A typical case of a white drug addict is roughly as follows: he grows up in the suburbs, where his mother quells her own anxiety by feeding him (the "Eat, baby, eat. It's a proof you love me" syndrome). His father is successful financially but otherwise weak; he has two Cadillacs but can only throw his weight around the house by boisterous profanity or some other such cover for weakness. The son is drafted and goes to Vietnam where he becomes somewhat familiar with drugs. On his way back, he throws his medals into the Pacific as a symbol of his conviction of the utter uselessness and insanity of the war. Back home he cannot get a job and for six months hangs around the house, becoming more and more out of tune with his parents. Feeling increasingly worthless, he takes his shot of heroin. Finding it gives him great comfort, he soon also finds he has a purpose in life, chiefly that of stealing money from his parents for the drug. His father ultimately finds out that his son is a drug addict and throws him out of the house, telling him not to come back until he is "clean."

Throughout the whole sorry account, there emerges most clearly the young man's powerlessness and lack of sense of purpose.

The origin of this sense of powerlessness is generally the young person's lack of a relationship with a strong father. (Sometimes it is attributable to his relationship with the mother, but not as often.) Having no male figure with whom he can identify, he has no direction, no structure which the father is supposed to bring in from the outside world, no set of values by which to direct himself or against which to rebel. In the case of the black man this lack of a strong father is taken for granted. Blacks have more realistic reasons for taking heroin—their problems are externalized, and hence drug addiction does not represent such a serious illness as it does for whites. The white drug addict seems not to have the oedipal motive of striving to surpass his father, which can give a constructive dynamic for development; but the son will take revenge upon the father by means of the addiction.

Heroin addiction gives a way of life to the young person. Having suffered under perpetual purposelessness, his structure now consists of how to escape the cops, how to get the money he needs, where to get his next fix—all these give him a new web of energy in place of his previous structureless world.

The treatment method comes out of this situation of powerlessness. At the Phoenix House treatment center, as at Synanon, a great deal of power is let loose in encounter groups, power that is directed toward the demand for absolute authenticity. Living together, these groups are encouraged to be as direct as possible with each other (without physical violence) in insisting on honesty. The phrase "dope fiend" is used, for example, because there is no euphemism in it; they attack each other verbally for any slight covering up of the cold truth in how they take care of their rooms, etc. Obviously this gives a structure that cannot be evaded; the strong substitute father comes out in the leader or someone in the group. Each person is required to hold a position in the resi-

dency; they can move upward, and they are very sensitive to re-
wards and punishment.

This seems to boil down to a rediscovery of one's power and
how to use it. The notorious permissiveness that was so completely
followed a few decades ago is out, and what is in is what gives personal power. Even the words that were anathema, *striving* and
competition, are back again. On the anvil on which the treatment
is hammered out, all things are used that will recover some sense
of power in the addict, which is necessary for his cure. The addict's anger and his energy are connected; the angrier he can become—which means direct, not expressed in revenge or in other
indirect ways—the more likely he is to get cured. The addict is a
person of much energy, but it has been blunted by his drugs.
When he comes off drugs, he is apt to have a good deal of anger;
it is on this "angry energy" that his rehabilitation depends. But
it is the social side of power that is stressed. The desired emphasis
seems to fit Alfred Adler's concept of "social interest."

4. THE CRY FOR SIGNIFICANCE

Power and the sense of significance, I have said, are intertwined.
One is the objective form and the other the subjective form of
the same experience. While power is typically extrovert, significance
may not be extrovert at all but may be shown (and achieved) by
meditation or other introvert, subjective methods. It is nevertheless experienced by the person as a sense of power in that it helps
him integrate himself and subsequently makes him more effective
in his relations with others.

Power is always interpersonal; if it is purely personal we call it
"strength." Hence Hannah Arendt holds that Bertrand Juvenal was
right when he argued that power was social and consisted of persons in groups acting "in concert." This is why the interpersonal

viewpoint of Harry Stack Sullivan, the tap root of the cultural school of psychoanalysis, is so important. Sullivan believed that the feeling of power in the sense of having influence in interpersonal relations with significant others is crucial for the maintenance of self-esteem and for the process of maturity. When the sense of significance is lost, the individual shifts his attention to different, and often perverted or neurotic, forms of power to get some substitute for significance.

Our particular problem in America at this point in history is the widespread loss of the sense of individual significance, a loss which is sensed inwardly as impotence. A situation in our day more tragic than the violence about us is that so many people feel they do not and cannot have power, that even self-affirmation is denied them, that they have nothing left to assert, and hence that there is no solution short of a violent explosion. Consider a recurring nightmare from a radical student at Columbia University. In this dream, the student, Carl,

> came home from school and rang the bell to his house. He was told by his mother that she didn't know him and that he didn't belong there. He went to his cousin's house and they told him the same thing. Finally he walked across the country to his father's house in California and was told by his father that he didn't know him and he didn't belong there. The dream ended with him disappearing into the Pacific Ocean.[14]

Judging from how often this kind of dream—"My parents didn't recognize me; they closed the door in my face," "I don't belong any place"—comes up in therapy, it seems to be an important clue to understanding our times. The student who had that dream was a member of the revolutionary movement not by accident. Violence, or acts close to it, gives one a sense of counting, of mattering, of power (whether the feeling be ersatz or not is unimportant at the moment). This in turn gives the individual a sense of significance.

No human being can exist for long without some sense of his own significance.[15] Whether he gets it by shooting a haphazard victim on the street, or by constructive work, or by rebellion, or by psychotic demands in a hospital, or by Walter Mitty fantasies, he must be able to feel this I-count-for-something and be able to *live out* that felt significance. It is the lack of this sense of significance, and the struggle for it, that underlies much violence.

Writing in the Report to the National Commission on the Causes and Prevention of Violence appointed by the president after the assassinations of Robert Kennedy and the Reverend Martin Luther King, Jr., the historian Richard Maxwell Brown makes sobering statements about American violence:

> The first and most obvious conclusion is that there has been a huge amount of it. We have resorted so often to violence that we have long since become a "trigger happy" people. . . . It is not merely that violence has been mixed with the negative features of our history such as criminal activity, lynch mobs, and family feuds. On the contrary, violence has formed a seamless web with some of the noblest and most constructive chapters of American history. . . .[16]

The aftermath of the 1968 political assassinations saw a bevy of opinions and researches spring up on the causes of violence and its cures, consisting largely of debates between those emphasizing *nature* and those emphasizing *nurture*. The former (stemming back, in the main, to Freud) held the general viewpoint that aggression is instinctive, part of the genetic equipment of man, and that human beings are inherently aggressive. According to this view, it is a cross we must bear, an expression of the old Adam inevitably tainting human beings, and the most we can hope for is to control this evil in our hearts or let it out in wars and other culturally approved forms of violence.

The other chief view, *nurture*, claims that aggression is a cultural phenomenon, caused—or at least augmented—by mass communication, faulty education, and especially TV. It is to be attacked and gotten rid of by changing our educational methods and controlling programs on TV.

What all too often is tiresomely ignored is that these two approaches are not mutually exclusive. Aggression *is* part of the basic equipment of man, but it is also culturally formed, exacerbated, and can be, at least in part, redirected. Our culture is not simply a given, but is also *us*. We "homo *called* sapiens," as Edna St. Vincent Millay put it in her sonnet, are the kind of creatures who *create* a vast TV and other forms of mass communication and, using these means, covertly teach aggression to our children. At the same time we endlessly sermonize against aggression. The contradiction this creates adds to the impotence everyone feels and to the hypocrisy with which we surround the issue of power in our culture.

But the real argument against many of these either/or explanations is that they leave out of the discussion exactly what is most important in the problem—that is, the question of the values, rooted in both nature and nurture, that link the two and are bound up with aggression and violence.

Richard Maxwell Brown concludes his part of the Report to the Commission on Violence by citing two problems which confront us: "One is the problem of self-knowledge. . . . When that is done . . . we must realize that violence has not been the action only of roughnecks and racists among us but has been the tactic of the most upright and respected of our people. Having gained this self-knowledge, the next problem becomes the ridding of violence, once and for all, from the real (but unacknowledged) American value system." [17]

But is there not a flagrant contradiction in this? If violence has been part and parcel of "our highest and most idealistic endeavors" and has been the tactic of the "most upright and respected" people, should we not inquire whether these people find something, perhaps unconsciously, in violence that they value? Furthermore, one can never change a value system by willing it changed or by other conscious means, as though plucking weeds from a garden. The roots of values lie deep in the archetypal and unconscious symbols and myths of the society. Changing the value system first of all requires a probing into the questions: What does violence *do* for the individual? What purposes does he achieve through aggression and violence?

In the utopian aim of removing all power and aggression from human behavior, we run the risk of removing self-assertion, self-affirmation, and even the power to be. If it were successful, it would breed a race of docile, passive eunuchs and would lay the groundwork for an explosion in violence that would dwarf all those that have occurred so far.

Thus oversimplifying the issue, we talk as though our choice were only between aggression on the one hand and a race of eunuchs on the other. Caught in the contradiction which this breeds, it is not surprising that we wake up with bad dreams, sensing that the essence of ourselves, the self-affirmation and self-assertion that makes us persons and without which we have no reason for living, is taken from us. What we have failed to see is that aggression has been, on the positive side, in the service of those values of life which would, if discarded, leave us bereft, indeed.

It has long been my belief that understanding aggression and violence requires that *power* be seen as basic to the problem. I believe, also, that the data given to us by depth psychology cast an especially revealing light on the springs of human power and on aggression and violence. In my concern with power, I am trying to reach a level below *both* the nature and nurture theories, below *both* the instinct and culture arguments. I am seeking the answer to the question: What does the individual person *achieve* through aggression and violence?

5. THE ARGUMENT OF THIS BOOK

I propose that there are five levels of power present as potentialities in every human being's life. The first is the *power to be*. This power can be seen in the newborn infant—he can cry and violently wave his arms as signs of the discomfort within himself, demanding that his hunger or other needs be met. Whether we like it or not, power is central in the development in this infant of what we call personality. Every infant becomes an adult in ways that reflect the vicissitudes of power—that is, how he has been able to find his power and use it—indeed, how to *be* it. It is given in the act of birth, not by the culture as such but by the sheer fact that the infant *lives*. If the infant is denied the experience that his actions can get a response from those around him—as shown in René Spitz's studies of the pitiable infant orphans in Puerto Rico who were given no attention by nurses or other mother substitutes —the infant withdraws into a corner of his bed, does not talk or develop in other ways, and literally withers away physiologically and psychologically. The ultimate in impotence is death.

The power to be is neither good nor evil; it is prior to them. But it is *not* neutral. It must be lived out or neurosis, psychosis, or violence will result.

The second phase is *self-affirmation*. Every being has the need not only to be but to affirm his own being. This is especially significant for the human organism, for it is gifted with, or condemned to, self-consciousness. This consciousness is not inborn but begins to develop in the infant after a few weeks, is not fully developed for several years, and, indeed, continues developing throughout his life. The question of *significance* then emerges, and the long and crucially important quest for self-esteem or substitutes for it, accompanied by grief with the lack of it. With human beings, mere physical survival is now no longer the main issue, but survival *with* some esteem.

The cry for recognition becomes the central cry in this need for self-affirmation. If significance and recognition are granted as a matter of course in the family, the child simply assumes them and turns his attention to other things. But if—as is too often the case in our disrupted day when parents as well as children are radically confused—self-affirmation is blocked, it becomes a compulsive need which drives the person all his life. Or the child's affirming of himself may be made difficult in the face of his parents' pattern of "We love you *only* if you obey us." The child thus gets caught in the destructive aspects of competitiveness, the buying and selling of himself and the world: his self-affirmation is taken by others to be a diminishing of them, and he is diminished in turn by theirs. In these or many other ways his self-affirmation is distorted or blocked outright.

When self-affirmation meets resistance we make greater effort, we give power to our stance, making clear what we are and what we believe; we state it now against opposition. This is *self-assertion*, the third phase. It is a stronger form of behavior, more overt than self-affirmation. It is a potentiality in all of us that we react to attack. We make it unavoidable that the others see us as we cry: "Here I am; I demand that you notice me!"

The speech of Willy Loman's wife in Arthur Miller's play, *Death of a Salesman*, is a good example of this: "Attention must be paid. . . ." Even though "Willy Loman never made a lot of money. His name was never in the papers . . . he's a human being. . . . So attention must be paid." The fact that her assertion was nominally for someone else does not change the fact that *she* was doing the asserting. Some of us can assert ourselves more firmly when we are doing it for someone else. That is merely another form of self-assertion—often made necessary by canons of politeness or not "blowing one's own horn."

The fourth phase is *aggression*. When self-assertion is blocked over a period of time—as it was for the Jews for many years, and as it is for every minority people—this stronger form of reaction tends to develop.

When I spent three years in Salonika, I found that the 100,000 Sephardic Jews living there—one third of the population of the city—actually made up the cultured intelligentsia of the city. There was a complete absence of anti-Semitic prejudice such as existed in the rest of Europe and America. There was also a complete absence of the aggressiveness associated in this country with Jews. Indeed, the motto in Salonika was: "It takes two Jews to outwit a Greek, and two Greeks to outwit an Armenian." The Armenians, the group at the bottom of the totem pole, were the ones in whom aggression and a sharp bargaining sense had developed.

In contrast to self-assertion, which is drawing a line at a certain point and insisting "This is me; this is mine," aggression is a moving into the positions of power or prestige or the territory of another and taking possession of some of it for one's self. The motives may be righteous enough—to right an ancient wrong, as with the natives in Africa about whom Frantz Fanon, in his book *The Wretched of the Earth*, writes; or passion for liberation; or pride; or any one of a thousand other things. Motive does not concern us at the moment; we only emphasize that this is a phase of behavior that in every person exists as a potentiality, and in the right situation it can be whipped into action. When aggressive tendencies are completely denied to the individual over a period of time, they take their toll in a zombielike deadening of consciousness, neurosis, psychosis, or violence.

Finally, when all efforts toward aggression are ineffective, there occurs the ultimate explosion known as *violence*.[18] Violence is largely physical because the other phases, which can involve reasoning or persuasion, have been *ipso facto* blocked off. In typical cases, the stimulus transmitted from the environment to the individual is translated directly into the violent impulse to strike, with the cerebrum being bypassed. This is why when a man erupts in a violent temper, he often does not fully realize what he has done until afterward.

It is tragic, indeed, when whole peoples are placed in a situation where significance becomes almost impossible to achieve. The blacks are, of course, the most ready illustration. The central crime of the white man was that he placed the blacks, during several centuries of slavery and one century of physical freedom but psychological oppression, in situations where self-affirmation was impossible. In physical slavery, and later in psychological slavery, every one of the nonviolent phases was difficult or impossible. They were permited to affirm themselves only as singers, dancers, and entertainers for the titillation of the white man, or as tillers of the white man's fields and, later, in the construction of the white man's automobiles. That this would lead to widespread apathy and, later on, to radical explosions should no longer surprise anyone. An illustration comes from the remark of a black man in Harlem:

> When the time comes, it is going to be too late. Everything will explode because the people they live under tension now; they going to a point where they can't stand it no more. When they get to that point . . .[19]

He dangles the end of the sentence, correctly letting us simply imagine what might come, because—as indicated above—before the violent explosion we cannot realize what may happen. For as long as people feel forced to remain in such a semihuman state, there will be aggression and violence.

If the other phases of behavior are blocked, then explosion into violence may be the only way individuals or groups can get release from unbearable tension and achieve a sense of significance. We often speak of the tendency toward violence as building up *inside* the individual, but it is also a response to outside conditions. The source of violence must be seen in both its internal and external manifestations, a response to a *situation* which is felt to block off all other ways of response.

The five phases above are *ontological* ones—that is, they are part of the human being as human. It is the endeavor of ontology to describe the characteristics of being as being—in our case the human being as human. A child of three may erupt in violence that takes the form of a temper tantrum as may a man of sixty; and although we may judge the latter more harshly, the action is potentially present in both. The ontological view does not deny development, but takes its inquiry down to a deeper level. It is not to be identified with the "nature" theory of violence any more than with the "nurture" theories discussed earlier. Ontological inquiry is directed at the structure in which both nature and nurture are rooted.

I believe that the psychotherapeutic approach provides one of the most fruitful avenues for the investigation of violence and aggression. We can see the seeds and roots of the "madness" and the violence in our nation when pondering the condition of Priscilla, or Carl, or Hannah Green. I am aware of the dangers of identifying too closely the society with the individual, but to entirely avoid a relationship between the two is just as erroneous. Social problems and psychological problems can no longer be isolated from each other. I believe it is valuable to try to understand modern social aggression and violence in the context, for example, that Priscilla and other persons in dire need of power taught me long ago.

TWO

INNOCENCE AND THE END OF AN ERA

> It is always and forever the struggle: to perceive somehow our own complicity with evil is a horror not to be borne. [It is] much more reassuring to see the world in terms of totally innocent victims and totally evil instigators of the monstrous violence we see all about. At all costs, never disturb our innocence. But what is the most innocent place in any country? Is it not the insane asylum? . . . The perfection of innocence, indeed, is madness.
> —Arthur Miller,
> from "With Respect for Her
> Agony—but with Love"

We live at the end of an era. The age that began with the Renaissance, born out of the twilight of the Middle Ages, is now at a close. The era that emphasized rationalism and individualism is suffering an inner and outer transition; and there are as yet only dim harbingers, only partly conscious, of what the new age will be.

Recall those towering individuals of the Renaissance, explorers of the earth like Columbus and Magellan, and explorers of the heavens like Copernicus. Our comparable exploration is the recent trips to the moon. But practically no one remembers the names of the astronauts who walked on the moon. What we do remember is the machinery; the hero of the moon trip was not an individual but a projectile, and the men were tenders of this projectile.

Let no one conclude from this, however, that in the new age man will be subordinate to technology. It may be just the opposite: the development of technology, filling a role similar to that of the ancient slaves, may force us to find intellectual and spiritual content to fill the vacuum of our days and nights.

In the present gap between ages, power is disengaged from its hereditary lines, confused, and "up for grabs." Those who have occupied the numbing position of subordinate groups—the blacks and Chicanos, women, students, mental patients, convicts—are springing to life, announcing their existence, and presenting their demands. Power becomes a new and urgent issue not only for those groups, but for every individual in our culture who is trying to get his bearings and find his place amid the turbulence. Powerlessness in such periods—often called by its alternate names, alienation and helplessness—becomes very painful.

There is one way, however, of confronting one's powerlessness by making it a seeming virtue. This is the conscious divesting on the part of an individual of his power; it is then a virtue *not* to have it. I call this *innocence*. The word is derived from the Latin *in* and *nocens*, literally, *not harmful*, to be free from guilt or sin, guileless, pure; and in actions it means "without evil influence or effect, or not arising from evil intention."

To start with, we must distinguish between two kinds of innocence. One is innocence as a quality of imagination, the innocence of the poet or artist. It is the preservation of childlike clarity in adulthood. Everything has a freshness, a purity, newness, and color. From this innocence spring awe and wonder. It leads toward spirituality: it is the innocence of Saint Francis in his Sermon to the Birds. Assumedly it is what Jesus had in mind when He said: "Only as ye become like little children shall ye enter the kingdom of heaven." It is the preservation of childlike attitudes into maturity without sacrificing the realism of one's perception of evil, or as Arthur Miller puts it, one's "complicity with evil." This is *authentic innocence.*

Such innocence can be a real protection in time of need. A woman who grew up in war-torn Germany related that the conquering French and Moroccan troops which took her town had several days of "freedom" in which they raped whatever girl they could find. Though thirteen years of age (and they were raping nine-year-olds) she could walk unmolested through a group of soldiers because she knew nothing about sexual intercourse or what men did. Her complete innocence, she believed, saved her; if she had had any kind of experience, the flicker of her eyelash or an unplanned glance, perhaps of fear, would have been enough enticement—as a dog bites the person whose fear it smells—for the rampaging soldiers to grab her also.

There is another kind of innocence, already hinted at in Melville's novella *Billy Budd, Foretopman.* Billy's type of innocence is that which does not lead to spirituality but rather consists of blinders—*Pseudoinnocence,* in other words. Capitalizing on naïveté, it consists of a childhood that is never outgrown, a kind of fixation on the past. It is childishness rather than childlikeness. When we face questions too big and too horrendous to contemplate, such as the dropping of the atomic bomb, we tend to shrink into this kind of innocence and make a virtue of powerlessness, weakness, and helplessness. This pseudoinnocence leads to utopianism; we do not then need to see the real dangers. With unconscious purpose we close our eyes to reality and persuade ourselves that we have escaped it. This kind of innocence does not make things bright and clear, as does the first kind; it only makes them seem simple and easy. It wilts before our complicity with evil. It is this innocence that cannot come to terms with the destructiveness in one's self or others; and hence, as with Billy Budd, it actually becomes self-destructive. Innocence that cannot include the daimonic becomes evil.

This parallels the innocence in neurosis. It is a fixation in childhood, never lived through but clung to as the only protection against hostile, unloving, or dominating parents. A young man in therapy, who had developed an intricate pattern of capitalizing on such weakness, once dreamed of himself as a rabbit being chased by wolves. But the rabbit suddenly turned the tables and chased the wolves. It turned out that he had been a wolf in rabbit's skin. Often the only strategy available to such persons, learned by necessity in childhood, consists of accepting the overt powerlessness their situation requires and then getting their power by covert means.

This is the sense in which Arthur Miller's statement heading this chapter is true: "The perfection of innocence, indeed, is madness." But Arthur Miller also has a sentence, omitted from this quotation (and with which I disagree), in which he says, "There [in the insane asylum] people drift through life truly innocent, unable to see into themselves at all." As will be clear from the preceding chapter, I do not believe it is an inability "to see into themselves." Nor is it being "truly innocent." It is an innocence only when viewed from the outside. In their detached innocence, like Hannah Green, they talk with spirits because they cannot find anyone else who is willing and able to understand them.

I will be using the term in this book generally meaning pseudo-innocence, for that is the common defense against admitting or confronting one's own power.

1. THE GREENING AND THE PARCHING OF AMERICA

In America, pseudoinnocence has a history as long as the country's. A "Chosen People" set sail from England, turning its back on a

Europe that, for it, stood for sin, injustice, aristocratic exploitation, and religious persecution. These people sought to establish
in America a land that would embody the opposites: righteous-
ness, justice, democracy, and freedom of conscience. The very
founding of the new nation was an enactment of the myth of the
New Jerusalem, not in some distant future but already an actuality before the eyes of the "Chosen." America began with a "belief
in perfection," as Richard Hofstadter puts it, and then became
devoted to progress. But how do you progress beyond perfection?

What about the religious persecution that soon sprang up even
in New England? What about the beginning genocide of the Indians? Necessarily, then, there began the long struggle between
ideals and reality, a battle in which the idealistic America, which
was the approximate of the perfect state, the new Garden of
Eden with no snakes in the grass, was pitted against the reality of
persecution and extermination of the Indians. An ethical dilemma,
indeed! The confusion and hypocrisy to which this led is shown
ironically in Benjamin Franklin's writings: "If it be the design of
Providence to extirpate these savages in order to make room for
the cultivators of the earth, it seems not improbable that rum may
be the appointed means. It has already annihilated all the tribes
who formerly inhabited the seacoasts." Franklin shows how the
citizens identify the design of Providence, the will of God, with
their own and their countrymen's self-interest. Americans are the
"cultivators of the earth," and the genocide of the Indians—an
enterprise the guilt for which we have not yet confronted—is the
will of God. This is the hallmark of pseudoinnocence: always
identify your self-interest with the design of Providence. As Dr.
Hugh Davis Graham and Ted Robert Gurr conclude:

> Probably all nations are given to a kind of historical amnesia
> or selective recollection that makes unpleasant traumas of the
> past. Certainly Americans since the Puritans have historically
> regarded themselves as a latter-day "Chosen People" sent on a
> holy errand to the wilderness, there to create a New Jerusalem.[1]

The framers of the Constitution were, furthermore, deathly afraid of exploitative power, as Americans have always been. They formulated their Articles with the intention that no group would ever gain this power; so afraid were they of being exploited that, in the Articles, they stretched its meaning to include *all* power. Americans now had the difficult ethical task of believing overtly that they did not want power, that their capacity for moral thinking and for serving their fellow man obviated their need for power. They saw themselves as the saviors of the needy from Europe. The Statue of Liberty still promises, through the inscription on its base:

> Give me your tired, your poor,
> Your huddled masses yearning to breathe free,
> The wretched refuse of your teeming shore,
> Send these, the homeless, tempest-tost to me.
> I lift my lamp beside the golden door.

In this country the Garden of Eden myth, along with the open denial of power, has continuously coexisted with a great amount of violence. The homicide rate here is three to ten times that of European countries; we have had one of the bloodiest labor histories of any of the large powers; the majority of Americans in the large cities seem to be afraid nowadays to walk on the streets at night. D. H. Lawrence wrote when he traveled in America: "The essential American soul is hard, isolated, stoic and a killer." [2] John Lukacs's discussion of the problem is entitled, "America's Malady Is Not Violence but Savagery." [3] This violence exists, oddly enough, side by side with a remarkable tenderness and warmth in the American character. We cannot escape the conclusion that some special conflicts must be present in the consciousness of Americans to account for the simultaneous existence of violence and tenderness.

I propose that, primarily, the violence and, second, the tenderness are connected with our conscious denial of power and the

pseudoinnocence that accompanies this denial. Violence comes
from powerlessness, as I have said; it is the explosion of impotence. The denial of our desires for power, when it occurs in the
endeavor to cover up an actually high degree of power, sets up an
inner contradiction: power then does not allay our *feelings of
powerlessness.* It does not lead to the sense of responsibility that
actual power ought to entail. We cannot develop responsibility for
what we don't *admit* we have. We cannot act upon our power
directly, for we always carry an element of guilt at having it. If
we were to admit it, we would have to confront our guilt. That
is why power is customarily translated into money in America. At
least money is external. "Cold cash" we can give to other people
and nations; we share it profusely with charities, indicating our
guilt in possessing it. So we behave like a nation of wolves in
rabbits' skins.

As a nation America has also failed to develop a viable sense of
tragedy, which would serve, through making for empathy with our
enemies, to mitigate our cruelty. One has only to read the reports
of the men who fly the bombers over Indochina ("I do not think
of the women and children below," the fliers say. "I think only I
have a job to do, and I get a joy out of doing it well.") to find
proof of our insulation from the evil of the world. "Two world
wars have not induced in [Americans] either a sense of sin or that
awareness of evil almost instinctive with Old World peoples.
. . ." [4] Lacking this sense of our own complicity, most Americans
also lack the element of mercy, which may well turn out to be a
sine qua non of living in this world with an attitude of humanity.

That this innocence is as influential as ever can be seen in
Charles Reich's book, *The Greening of America.* To criticize this
book places me in a dilemma, so much am I in sympathy with its
aims and the spirit that informs it. I believe that the first half of
it, containing Reich's analysis of the corporate state, is rich and
important. He rightly sees the American dream and even the problem of innocence in the first centuries of America's history. He

appreciates the manner in which the sense of powerlessness eats away at the confidence of our people and their capacity to act, the "wilful ignorance in American life," and our tendency to try to "get rid of evil by forbidding it."

But, ironically, the promise to the young people and to all of us in the second half is pseudoinnocence writ large. "There are no enemies. . . . There is nothing on the other side. . . . Nobody wants war except the machine. . . . And even businessmen, once liberated, would like to roll in the grass and lie in the sun. There is no need, then, to fight any group of people in America." [5] Woodstock is cited as a myth of the new age now realized in all its ease and splendor, with no recognition at all of its aftermath, namely Altamont, where Hell's Angels, brought in as bodyguards for singers, committed murder. It is an impressionistic painting of the Garden of Eden, with all of the glow of innocence and the ease and delight of children romping in the fields to rock music, the age before the fall, before the sense of anxiety or guilt intruded. But alas! It is for children and not for adults. Far from Consciousness III being an answer, it would be no consciousness at all, for it lacks the dialectic movement between "yes" and "no," good and evil, which gives birth to consciousness of any sort. Reich writes: "The hard questions—if by that is meant political and economic organization—are insignificant, even irrelevant." [6] All will be done by Consciousness III, which "will not require violence to succeed, and it cannot be successfully resisted by violence." We are then lulled into a blissful ease that is remarkably similar to those pictures on ancient Greek vases of gods lolling on Mount Olympus.

Are there really no enemies? Can we call to mind the Berrigan brothers and think that? Or the Soledad brothers? Or Angela Davis? Or the convicts at Attica, who, after the slaughter, were forced to run the gantlet naked? Or Vietnam—yes, the defoliation and the dehumanized cruelty of Vietnam? Reich has no understanding of the creeping fascism already discernible in our country: the turning of youth against their fathers, the anti-intellectualism, the growth of violence coupled with the sense of powerlessness of the mass of people, the tendencies of bureaucracies to make decisions on the basis of what works mechanically with all human sense drowned in opportunism.

There is also in Reich no understanding of the isolation, the loneliness, the despair that motivates many young people, especially in the drug scenes. At Big Sur I once went to a hippie wedding; everybody was as colorfully dressed as a stage set for the opera *Carmen.* But I could not escape seeing the isolation in practically everyone's eyes, each young person seeming alienated and lonely even in the crowd devoted to innocence and joy. Reich's book has been said to be part of the "prophetic" literature and to give us a vision that America needs. But prophetic literature, for example in the Old Testament where it abounds, always includes a sense of evil, which is totally absent here. The danger in the book lies in its reassurance that the new world "cannot be successfully resisted by violence," which will increase the tendencies toward apathy that already are so obvious in our nation.

This book reminds me of an incident that occurred a few years ago at a conference in California. I was sitting at breakfast with a young man, one of a group of flower children, perhaps nineteen or twenty, with a clear, open face and guileless blue eyes. In the course of our talk he showed me a letter he had written and was sending to his draft board chairman in his home state, confident that he would thereby be excused from the draft. Addressing the draft board chairman by his first name, the letter stated: "I do not believe in killing"; then several more sentences to the same effect; and finally the signature, "Larry." I asked Larry if he had made a copy of the letter. "No, I don't think it is necessary—the draft board chairman will read this one." As I looked at him now, his eyes and face seemed too clear and too open—I felt the doom toward which he and his comrades were marching; I felt the heavy boots under which they would be crushed, crushed like flowers indeed, with the wearers of the boots feeling no more than the boots themselves could feel. I saw the crushed heads of these young men, and I felt like crying out: "Harmless as doves you are, but where is your wisdom of serpents?"

The crux of these errors, again, is illustrated in Reich's denial of power. He uses the word often but almost every time negatively: it is the power of the corporate state, the power of the military; totalitarianism is defined as pure power. There is no "good" power; it always corrupts. Reich finally waxes so enthusiastic in his condemnation of power that he writes: "It is not the misuse of power that is the evil; the very *existence* of power is an evil." Again we see the parallel between innocence and the denial of power. And since this comes from a forty-four-year-old professor of law, we must conclude it is pseudoinnocence.

Innocence in our day is the hope that there "are no enemies," that we can move into a new Garden of Eden, a community characterized by freedom from all want, guilt, and anxiety. But this also means freedom from responsibility; it means going back *prior* to the birth of consciousness, for guilt is only the other side of moral consciousness—we have "eaten of the tree of knowledge." We valiantly try to persuade ourselves that if we only find the "key," we can easily create a society in which nakedness, guilt, anxiety will all be things of the unmourned past.

Unmourned and unstudied—here lies the contemporary uninterest in history and the refusal to study it. To hang on to this picture of innocence, you *must* deny history. For history is the record, among other things, of man's sins and evils, of wars and confrontations of power, and all the other manifestations of man's long struggle toward an enlarged and deepened consciousness. Hence so many of the new generation turn their backs on history as irrelevant; they do not like it, they are not part of it, they insist we are in a brand-new ball game with new rules. And they are completely unaware that this is the ultimate act of *hubris*.

Such innocence is particularly tempting in America because we actually lack a long history. We have very little sense of the sacredness of place, of roots, of homeland. De Tocqueville, in *Democracy in America*, made a perceptive remark in this connection: "In the United States a man builds a house in which to spend his old age, and he sells it before the roof is on. . . . He settles in a place, which he soon afterwards leaves to carry his changeable longings elsewhere . . . he will travel fifteen hundred miles to shake off his happiness." This, in contrast to Europeans who have lived in the same city for a thousand years, and whose very walls around the city bespeak the centuries of struggle by which they earned their convictions and their culture.

2. OTHER FORMS OF INNOCENCE

Let us pass in review several reasons given for our present predicament, reasons that themselves illustrate this innocence. One is the common explanation of the contemporary unrest as due to a failure to preserve "law and order," the favorite rallying cry of conservative politicians. It illustrates our innocence in two ways. One, that each act of violence or aggression can be dealt with by the tried-and-true method, following the nineteenth-century myth in America, of throwing in more hardware and personnel in the form of policemen, national guardsmen, and soldiers. The naïveté of this is shown by our experience in Vietnam, to the continual shock to our own narcissism.

The second and more important expression of innocence lies in the bland identification of "law" with the particular "order" that happens to exist at that moment in the society. My *order* becomes, therefore, *right*; it is as eternal as the law with which it is coupled; it is God's will—whether this means white supremacy, Indian genocide, or any other kind of parochial moral arrogance.

Law can also be used, when coupled with "justice," as a creative set of principles unfolding continuously toward greater public good. But "law" coupled with "order," in the shibboleth "law and order," becomes regularly a justification of the status quo. And in a transitional age such as ours, the one thing that must, at all costs, be avoided is rigid adherence to the status quo; for that is just what has to be changed and reformed by the transition. The only way to live out a transitional period is with flexibility to adapt to change—and, unfortunately, that is what most people, in their anxiety at the dizzy speed of change, feel they do not have.

Emphasis on "law and order" can be destructive to a person's self-esteem and self-respect. When President Johnson proposed greater effort to get "crime off the streets" in his final State of the Union address (February, 1968), he received the largest and loudest ovation of any time in the whole speech; which means that "law and order," which is the meaning of Johnson's phrase, appeals tremendously to congressmen of both houses. But let us note how getting people off the street works. The following is written by a black man in Harlem:

> Last night the officer stopped some fellows on 125th Street. . . . The officer said, "All right, everybody get off the street or inside." Now it's very hot. We don't have air-conditioning in . . . these houses up here. . . . Now where were we going? But he came out with his nightstick and wants to beat people on the head . . . he arrested one fellow. The other fellow said, "Well, I'll move, but you don't have to talk to me like a dog." . . . I think we all should get together . . . every time one draws his stick to do something to us, or hits one of us on the head, take the stick and hit him on the head, so he'll know how it feels to be hit on *his* head, or kill him, if necessary. Yes, kill him if necessary.

The emphasis on "law and order" can itself contribute to violence and can be one of the things that makes an ultimate revolution more bloody.

Human pride and esteem are offended by a show of force. One of the things that can abet a riot is precisely the lining up of a hundred policeman on a street. It offends both those who are being protected and those who are protected against; for it makes us all "faceless Others." I have never been in a riot, but when I see a mass of policemen I feel a strange urge to riot, as though it is somehow called for, expected. There is an incendiary quality to this act: an increase of policemen beyond a certain point can only add to people's conviction that something must explode.

The bitterness that goes into the phrase "law and order" often has as one of its sources a reaction formation to one's own guilt. For example, I may have acquired my money by questionable quasi-legal means, and now I come out as a staunch citizen for "law and order" to prevent others from taking it away from me.

In its best sense and by itself, order ought to mean the forms and conventions by which we live and work together; order ideally is freedom from disturbing interruption of peace, physical safety which in turn gives the psychological security for the pursuit of intellectual, emotional, and spiritual aims. But when coupled with law, it implies a rigid clinging to old forms of acting, a prevention of the very changes made necessary by our transitional age.

It is primarily the older generation that adheres to law and order so innocently. But innocence is obviously used by the new generation as well, as a way to avoid facing its powerlessness. There are so many absurd aspects of the so-called battle between the generations—youth's continuous confession of the sins of teachers and parents, the endless blaming of others, the "over thirty" shibboleth—that one is in danger of overlooking the deeper meaning of the conflict. Not that the younger generation hasn't plenty of reason for accusing its elders. As Hannah Arendt, writing of the younger generation, states:

> They inherited from their parents' generation the experience of a massive intrusion of criminal violence into politics—they learned in high school and in college about concentration and extermination camps, about genocide and torture, about the wholesale slaughter of civilians in war. . . .[7]

But does it not confuse the whole picture to make this a conflict of youth versus age? What would they have done in their fathers' place, given the historical situation in which their fathers were born and working with what they had to use? It is an antihistorical viewpoint to insist that the *mere* fact of having been born a generation later guarantees any rightness in itself. Furthermore, it is a taking over, in masqueraded form, of one of the least noble of our culture's myths—the adulation of youth, the falsehood of believing that "everything is better in earlier years than later." [8]

When young people are pressed for a statement of their values, and one asks what they would make the center of a new world, one is often left with picayune or self-revolving items like never stepping on insects or never throwing away anything made of plastic. This is a blatant use of innocence. We look—often in vain—for a serious, responsible confrontation with the real problems: power, organization in national groups, fidelity in personal life.

One feels that the younger generation gets particular gratification out of simply attacking the establishment as such. Is it a reaction-formation to their own unease at the affluence of their parents and to their own guilt at their dependency on their parents for sustenance? But this is an unnecessary battle, if for no other reason than that the establishment is dying anyway. The present college generation was born in an era when practically all mooring posts—i.e., in sex, in marriage, in religion—are threatened or already lost. We have a new morality, most obviously in the areas of sex, marriage, and the role of women. No one can doubt that a new electronic technology is fast revolutionizing our economic and communication systems. Religious practices are also involved in profound change, what with ersatz Buddhists, Yogis, and Hindus springing up on all sides. One age is dead and the other not yet born—ours, which includes both youth and age, is in limbo.

To what extent, we must finally ask, is technology used as the scapegoat for our present situation and, therefore, an escape from responsibility? A student who participated in the protests at the time of the Cambodian invasion told, in his therapy sessions, of milling around the park at his university at the moment when the protest hovered on the edge of riot. One of his fellows had shouted: "Let's get the computer!" The student then remarked to me: "All my life I've wanted to smash a computer." Now, on my college tours, when I tell that story, the students unfailingly burst into laughter, and it is the kind of laughter that indicates that some unconscious urge in them has been released.

Why this animosity, this spirit of *revenge*, against technology? For one thing, young people are entirely aware of the disastrous effects of technology—as, for instance, in the galloping pollution of air, earth, and water. They see that "technological progress seems in so many instances to lead straight into disaster; that the proliferation of techniques and machines, far from threatening only certain classes with unemployment, menaces the very existence of whole nations and conceivably of all mankind." [9] This is surely true. But a serious citing of it would also lead to the opposite statement, that technology has far-reaching values for nations and conceivably all mankind. Why, then, the refusal on the part of young adults to accept, or at least see, the latter?

I believe that this refusal is used to protect their own consciousness. Technology consists of a complex system of tools that ought to extend human consciousness. A simple example of this may be illustrated by a chimpanzee fastening two sticks together to pull into his cage a banana that he cannot reach with one stick. But in our day—so the younger generation feels—technology does just the opposite: it shrinks, dries up, depersonalizes human existence. Young people have discovered in their own bitter experience how the juggernaut of technology overrides them without paying the slightest attention to their protests. They find themselves crying, both silently and aloud: "Stop the machinery!" It is interesting that this metaphor from Charles Reich is identical with that of Mario Savio back in the first rebellion in 1964 in

Berkeley: "You've got to put your bodies upon the gears and upon the wheels, upon the levers, upon all the apparatus, and you've got to make it stop. . . ."

There are various ways of accomplishing this arresting of the machinery: meditation, communes, movements back to nature. But most important of all, there has arisen a new understanding of the value of subjectivity, to redress our gross overemphasis upon objectivity. This accounts for Yoga, Zen Buddhism, and partially for the Jesus freaks; and it is the constructive side of the vast interest in the occult now occurring on all sides. As Werner Heisenberg wrote, quoting an old Chinese parable, dedication to the machine makes us tend to act

> in a machine-like manner. Whoever does his business in the manner of a machine develops a machine heart. Whoever has a machine heart in his breast loses his simplicity. Whoever loses his simplicity becomes uncertain in the impulses of his spirit. Uncertainty in the impulses of the spirit is something that is incompatible with truth.[10]

Many members of the new generation are discovering for themselves that "impulses of the spirit" are more precious than the worldly goods they inherit from their parents. Their discovery is of tremendous value indeed, and no one would argue with it. But here, again, a kind of trading on innocence comes in to confuse the picture. To a greater or lesser extent, youths of today, like the rest of us, use and enjoy the benefits of technology, no matter how simplified their lives may be. Our culture's affluence, often to be found in the life styles of parents of the more radical young people, is what makes it possible for them to indulge in their radicalism and, many times, form communes. Here they get into such absurd contradictions, as Peter Fonda, in *Easy Rider*, scattering wheat on unploughed, hard, dry ground, insisting: "It will grow." All he proves is that without some knowledge of agriculture, all the good intentions in the world cannot prevent the members of the commune from starving when winter comes. Th fact, of course, that many of these communes fail and all have a difficult time does not lighten their moral value as a testimony to the voice of nature; and they are a sharp reminder to all our consciences of the divisive baggage of worldly possessions.

But "high purpose" is not enough. One observer of a number of communes says that those doomed to failure are the ones with no other purpose than the self-improvement of the group, whereas those that succeed have some goal or value—a special religious commitment, for example—that transcends the members themselves. This saves them from the innocence of believing that what they want will come out of their wanting it, that nature will renounce its age-old neutrality and fit their morality (as it was in the Garden of Eden), and that somehow one escapes the tragedies and complexities of life simply by being simple.

We have seen that innocence cuts across the generations. Faced with the multitude of choices and sensing our essential impotence, we cry for some shield, for some protection from this insoluble dilemma, for someone or some technique to take the impossible responsibility from us. One defense is innocence. Innocence is real and lovable in the child; but as we grow we are required by the fact of growth not to close ourselves off, either in awareness or experience, to the realities that confront us.

Innocence as a perpetuation of earlier attitudes—the innocence of the flower children, of the too easy program of loving everyone, of nakedness without anxiety or guilt, of oversimplification of honesty and sincerity as though one were still a child—all these may be charming but they are also radically nonadaptive in our contemporary world. It is an innocence that shows itself in the clear, open, pure visage of a Larry, an innocence that expects nature to hear our need and forsake her ancient condition of neutrality in order to protect us from harm. It is an innocence without responsibility.

This type of innocence is a defense against having to confront the realities of power, including such external forms of power as the war machine or such inner forms of power as status and prestige. The fact that innocence is used for such extrainnocent purposes is what makes it suspect. Innocence as a shield from responsibility is also a shield from growth. It protects us from new awareness and from identifying with the sufferings of mankind as well as with the joys, both of which are shut off from the pseudo-innocent person.

THREE

LANGUAGE:
THE FIRST CASUALTY

As a poet, there is only one political duty, and that
is to defend one's language from corruption. And
that is particularly serious now. It's being so quickly
corrupted. When it's corrupted, people lose faith
in what they hear, and this leads to violence.

—W. H. Auden

When an age is in the throes of profound transition, the first
thing to disintegrate is the language. This, as Auden rightly says,
leads directly to the upsurge of violence. Billy Budd, at his trial
after he had killed the master-at-arms with his fist, exclaims:
"Could I have used my tongue I would not have struck him.
. . . I could say it only with a blow." Not being able to find his
tongue (becaue of his severe stuttering), he could only speak by
means of the physical expression of his passion.

Violence and communication are mutually exclusive. Put simply, you cannot talk with someone as long as he is your enemy, and if you can talk with him he ceases to be your enemy. The process is reciprocal. When a person feels violent toward another—in a surge of rage, say, or a hurt pride that demands immediate revenge —the capacity to talk is automatically blocked by neurological mechanisms that release adrenalin and shift the energy to the muscles in primitive preparation for fighting. If the person is of the middle class, he may rapidly pace back and forth until he can control his violence enough to put it into words; if he is of the proletariat, he may simply strike out.

Speaking of the origin of power in infants, Harry Stack Sullivan points out that

> the infant has as his mightiest tool the cry. The cry is a performance of the oral apparatus, the lips, mouth, throat, cheeks, vocal cords, intercostal muscles and diaphragm. From this cry is evolved a great collection of most powerful tools which man uses in the development of his security with his fellow man. I refer to language behavior, operations including words.[1]

We can see the reasons for these phenomena when we consider what makes language possible. Language arises from an underlying web of potentiality for understanding, an empathetic tie between people, a shared structure, a capacity to identify with another. This potentiality for understanding is much more than mere words: it implies a state of we-ness, a bond that potentially unites people, the prototype for which are the facts of gestation in the mother's womb and then the process of birth. If there had been no womb in which we first grew as embryos, language would not be possible; and if there had been no birth, language would not be necessary. From this dialectical bond with others, into and out of which we can move, there has evolved in profound and complex ways over the centuries the capacity for language. The individual is both bound to others and independent from them at the same time. Out of this double nature of man are born the

symbols and myths which are the basis of language and serve as a
bridge over that chasm between human beings to establish the
bond again.

The "bridging" function of the symbol can be seen more clearly
when we recall that *symbol* comes from two Greek words, σύν,
"with," and βαλλειν, "to throw." It means literally "to draw together." It pulls together the different aspects of experience, such
as consciousness and unconsciousness, individual and social, historical past and immediate present. The antonym of *symbolic* is
diabolic, "to tear apart." The "devilish" functions are thus separating, alienating, breaking relationships, in contrast to bringing together, connecting, uniting. Ancient peoples knew as well as
modern ones do of the dangers in the corruption of language. As
Plato has Socrates say in the *Phaedo:* "The misuse of language is
not only distasteful in itself, but actually harmful to the soul."
And modern critics of the social malaise similarly say: "A strong
society depends on common language and concepts, and it is clear
to us that the black and white communities in America no longer
speak the same language or share the same understanding of what
is happening." [2]

Since symbols carry a confluence of meanings, they also release
great energy. The long hair and hippie-type clothes of the younger
generation, for example, are symbols of its opposition to the whole
competitive, acquisitive economy of America. Hence Nixon and
Agnew, and some other people in this country, react with such
fury to this form of hair and bluejeans. The hair and jeans are
harmless enough in themselves, but as symbols of the reaction of
youth against the values which the president and vice president
identify with America, they are powerful indeed.

When the bond between human beings is destroyed—i.e., when
the possibilities for communication break down—aggression and
violence occur. Thus distrust of language on one side and aggression and violence on the other arise out of the same situation. [3]

1. THE DISTRUST OF WORDS

The deep suspicion of language and the impoverishment of ourselves and our relationships, which are both cause and result, are
rampant in our times. We experience the despair of being unable
to communicate to others what we feel and what we think, and
the even greater despair of being unable to distinguish for ourselves what we feel and are. Underlying this loss of identity is the
loss of cogency of the symbols and myths upon which identity and
language are based.

The breakdown of language is graphically pictured in Orwell's
1984, in which the people not only go through the "doublethink"
process but use words to mean exactly their opposite—e.g., *war*
means *peace*. In Beckett's *Waiting for Godot*, we are similarly
gripped when Pozzo, the industrialist, commands his slave Lucky,
the intellectual, to "Think, pig! . . . Think!" Lucky begins to
orate a word salad of lengthy phrases strung together without a
period that continues for three full pages. He finally collapses in a
faint on the stage. It is a vivid portrayal of the situation that exists
when language communicates nothing at all except empty eru-
dition.

The breakdown is shown in the students' protest against the
"words, words, words" to which they must listen, in their sickness
of heart at hearing the same things mouthed over and over again,
and in their readiness to accuse faculty and others of "word garbage" or "verbal masturbation." This is generally meant as a
criticism of the lecture method. But what they really are—or ought
to be—talking about is a particular *kind* of lecture that does not
communicate "being" from one person to another. It must be
admitted that all too often this has been a characteristic of academic life, which makes the student protest against irrelevant ed-

ucation distinctly more relevant. The shelves of college libraries
are weighed down with books that were written because other
books were written because still other books were written—the
meat of the meal getting thinner and thinner until the books
seem to have nothing to do with the excitement of truth but only
with status and prestige. And in the academic world, these last
two values can be powerful indeed. Small wonder the young poets
are disillusioned with talk, and they hold, as they did in the San
Francisco love-in, that the best poem is a "blank sheet of paper."

At such a time, in our alienation and isolation, we long for a
simple, direct expression of our feelings to another, a direct relation to his being, such as looking into his eyes to see and experience him or standing quietly beside him. We yearn for a direct
expression of his and our moods and emotions with no barriers. We
seek a kind of innocence that is as old as human evolution but
comes to us as something new, the innocence of children in para-
dise again. We long for a direct expression through our bodies of
intimacy to short-cut the time of knowing the other that intimacy
usually takes; we want to speak through our bodies, to leap immediately into identification with the other, even though we know
it is only partial. In short, we yearn to bypass the whole symbols/
verbal-language hang-up.

Thus the great trend toward action therapies in our day in contrast to talking, and the conviction that truth will emerge—if it
ever will—when we are able to live out our muscular impulses
and experiences rather than get lost in dead concepts. Hence encounter groups, marathons, nude therapy, the use of LSD and
other drugs. This is, in short, the bringing of the body into a relationship when *there is no relationship.* Whatever relatedness there
is is ephemeral: it springs up multicolored and bright today, and
often will be but a damp place where sea foam has evaporated
on our hand tomorrow.

My aim is not to derogate these forms of therapy nor to disparage the use of the body. My body remains one way in which my self can express itself—in this sense I *am* my body—and surely it is to be appreciated. But I *am* my language as well. And I wish to point out the destructive trend represented in action therapies precisely in their implicit attempt to bypass language.

For these action therapies are closely related to violence. As they become more extreme, they hover at the edge of violence, both in the activity within the group itself and in the preparation of the participants for anti-intellectualism outside. The longing for them really has its seat in despair—the despondent fact of not being understood, of not being able to communicate or to love. It is the endeavoring to jump over that period of time required for intimacy, the trying to immediately feel and experience the other's hopes and dreams and fears.[4]

But intimacy requires a history, even though the two people have to create this history. We forget at our peril that man is a symbol-making creature; and if the symbols (or myths, which are a pattern of symbols) seem arid and dead, they are to be mourned rather than denied. The bankruptcy of symbols should be seen for what it is, a way station on the path of despair.

The distrust of language is bred into us by experiencing the "medium is the message" phenomenon. Most of the words coming over TV are lies not in the sense of outright falsehood (that would imply a still remaining respect for the word) but in the sense that the words are used in the service of "selling" the personality of the speaker rather than in communicating some meaning. This is the more subtle form of emphasizing not the *meaning* of the word but the *public-relations value* of it. Words are not used for authentic, humanistic goals: to share something of originality or personal warmth. The medium is then the message with a vengeance; as long as the medium works, there is no message.

The phrase "credibility gap," which is conspicuous in wartime but is present in other times as well, goes much deeper than anyone's mere intention to deceive. We listen to the news dispatches and find ourselves wondering where the truth really lies and why we were not told. In our day it often seems that deception has been accepted as the means of communication. In this confusion, there is a more serious ailment in our public life: language bears less and less relationship to the item being discussed. There is a denial of any relationship to underlying logic. The fact that language has its roots in a shared structure is entirely ignored.

An illustration of this will be helpful. Half a dozen days after the invasion of Laos, while the event was as yet unannounced in this country, Secretary of Defense Laird came out of a meeting with the Armed Services Committee and was accosted by the usual group of reporters:

REPORTERS: Sir, it is rumored on all sides that we have been making plans to invade Laos. Is this true?

SECRETARY LAIRD: I have just come from a meeting of the Armed Services Committee, and I wish to say our discussion of the draft was valuable and harmonious.

REPORTERS [*protesting*]: That's not the question, Sir. [*Also*] *Izvestia* has already reported the invasion.

LAIRD [*smiling*]: You know *Izvestia* does not write the truth.

[*Reporters ask the first question over again.*]

LAIRD: I will do whatever is necessary to protect the lives of our boys in the fighting field. No more comment. [*He walks away.*]

Now no one could say that Secretary Laird spoke any untruth: obviously, everything he said was factual. The only point is that his language denies the whole structure of communication. There is no relationship in his answers to the question asked. In extreme and persistent form, this is one species of schizophrenia; but in our day it simply is called politics.

2. OBSCENITY AND VIOLENCE

There is a halfway stage in the disintegration of words. This is obscenity. It gets its power from the using of words to do violence to our unconscious expectations, to destroy our mooring posts, and to undercut the forms of relationship we are used to. The words threaten us with the insecurity of formlessness. Obscenity expresses what had previously been prohibited, reveals what previously was not revealed. Thus it insists on and gets our attention.

This can be constructive or destructive. When Ezra Pound writes,

> Winter is icumen in,
> Lhude sing Goddamm. . . .
> Damm you, sing: Goddamm,[5]

he catches our attention immediately because of the shock value: our expectations were set to hear something like the lovely Middle English lyric. This kind of language can be entirely justified: the poet has to develop a language that has "guts." Obscenity is the process of attacking what has been sacred and occurs when the word is losing its holy character. It is often factually true that words have already lost all roots to their meaning and have become nothing but empty forms.

The same is true in modern art. By showing blood and gore and using sensational colors that carry these impressions, many painters are crying out: *"You must look, you must pay attention, you must see in a new way."* This can, indeed, teach us, shocked as we are, not just to look but to see.

The breakdown in language has become very clear to the extremists on the left. Jerry Rubin says in his book *Do It*: "Nobody really communicates with words anymore. Words have lost their emotional impact, intimacy, ability to shock and make love." [6] "But there is one word," he goes on, "Americans have not destroyed. One word which has maintained its emotional power and purity." As you have guessed already, that is the word *fuck*. It has kept its purity only because it has been illegal, says Rubin—so now it has some freshness, some impact left.

I agree that the word does have emotional power. But is its power connected with what the word *means?* No, it is connected with just the opposite—not its original meaning of a relationship between two people characterized by physical and psychological abandon combined with tenderness and gentleness, but rather an exploitation, an expression of aggression. Indeed, the word *fuck* proves precisely my point, that words have been twisted into *opposite* meanings. A word becomes aggressive as a stage in its deterioration: it loses its original meaning, takes on the aggressive form in obscenity, and then may pass into oblivion.

Language can be as violent as physical force when it is used to incite people's aggressive emotions. The masses of students who protested on Wall Street in New York after the invasion of Cambodia had a special chant: "One, two, three, four./We don't like your fucking war." They seemed to be totally oblivious to the fact that if you keep chanting that to an upper-middle-class stock broker, you are going to make him mad, and in the irrational, explosive sense of the first chapter—as mad as if you had struck him over the head with a billy club. And his rage will have nothing to do with the war. It will be because of the term *fucking*, a word about which he has fairly rigid beliefs in using and not using in public.

Obscenity is a form of psychic violence and can be used with great effect, a weapon that can excite people to lethal physical violence. One should know this when one is using it. It is a mark of our time that each side in a disagreement uses violent language.

This amounts to using violence to defeat violence—which never works, whether it is done by police and administration or by young people themselves.

3. WORDS AND SYMBOLS

The importance of language in an evolving culture is that it provides *symbolic forms* by means of which we can reveal ourselves and by means of which others stand revealed to us. Communicating is a way of understanding each other; if there are no such ways, each of us becomes like the man who, in a dream, finds himself wandering in a foreign country where he can understand nothing of what is being said around him nor feel anything from the person next to him. His isolation is great, indeed.

During the week end of the moon landing, a TV reporter interviewed members of the crowd in Central Park just after the landing. One answer to his question of what they were waiting for was: "To see the extravehicular activity." Now this phrase "extravehicular activity" gives one pause. Its main word consists of six syllables and is highly technical; it tells, like many technical phrases, what the astronauts are *not* going to do (*extra*vehicular) rather than what they are going to do. The word "activity" may mean any act under the sun—swimming, flying, crawling, diving, etc. There is no poetry in the sentence, no meaning that is not technical, nothing personal. We finally discover the polysyllabic phrase means "to walk on the moon." But that is a *poetic* phrase. No word of over one syllable, coming straight out of our own lives (from the age of one when we learned to walk), a phrase associated with all the romance of the moon. It is actually more truthful than its scientific parallel in the sense that it reveals not an abstraction but an act that will be done by human beings like you and me.

The more technical we become without a parallel development

in the meaningfulness of personal communication, the more alienated we also become. Communication is then replaced by communiqué.

The breakdown of communication is a spiritual one. Words get their communicative power from the fact that they participate in symbols. Through drawing meanings together into a Gestalt, a symbol gets a numinous quality which points toward a reality greater than itself. The symbol gives the word its power to carry across to one some meaning from the emotions of another. Symbolic breakdown is, therefore, spiritual tragedy. The symbol always implies more than it states; it is essentially connotative. Thus words, in so far as they are symbolic, point to more than they specifically can say; what counts is the afterglow, the ripples of meaning that appear like a stone being dropped in a lake, the connotative rather than the denotative aspect of the words. It is a Gestalt similar to that which the poet uses. A form emerges out of the very speaking of words—which is why people tend to become more poetic when they report something under stress.

All this, of course, is exactly contrary to what we have been taught. We are taught that the more specific and limited a word is, the more accurately we talk. More accurately, yes, but not more truthfully. For we tend, with this point of view, to make our language more and more technical, impersonal, objective, until we are talking in purely scientific terms. This is one legitimate way of communicating, and certainly the way that thrives in a technological age. But it ends up with computor language; and what I really want to know about my friend as he walks beside me in the country is as absent as though we were in two vacuum tubes.

4. WORDS AND EXPERIENCE

A crucial problem is the distinction between *experience* and what the younger generation calls "mere thinking" or "mere words."

This is particularly important for us here since historically "experience" has also been set in opposition to innocence. An "innocent" girl is a virgin, whereas a girl or woman who has had sexual intercourse is experienced.[7] Experience is set over against "ideas." Existentialism, for example, is often mistaken for a denial of thinking; and new adherents are often surprised when they read Sartre and Tillich to find that these existentialists are thinkers and logicians of great power.

Experience puts the accent on action, living out something, or feeling it "as a man tastes apple in his mouth," to quote Archibald MacLeish. By experiencing something, we let its meaning permeate through us on all levels: feeling, acting, thinking, and, ultimately, deciding, since decision is the act of putting one's total self on the line. The passion for experience is an endeavor to include more of the self in the picture; one experiences as a totality. Experience is set over against any partial view of man. Behaviorism, for example, is certainly a part of experience, but when behaviorism is turned into a total way of understanding man and a philosophy of life—which amounts to intellectual naïveté—it becomes destructive.

One can, and ought, to *reflect* on experience. This not only gives power to thinking but also communicates being. In my education the most important and engulfing experience was the lectures of Paul Tillich. Tillich, a German and a scholar of the first order, believed in lecturing. But he was also a man committed to life and to truth and a thinker of great logical ability which he did not hesitate to use. Thus every lecture was an expression of Tillich's being, and it awakened my being. It became my ideal of what a lecture ought to do.

It is arbitrary and confusing to say that reflection is also part of experience; we must keep the thinking function in its own right. The error is in using experience as a way to shut out thinking or in using "immediate" experience to evade the implications of history. The younger generation is right in its attack on "mere" thought, "mere" words, and so on; but it makes the same error when, under the guise of "experiencing life," it seizes on "mere" feelings, "mere" actions, or any other partial function of man. The "experience" then becomes intellectual laziness, an excuse for sloppiness of execution.

Culture is a result of communication between men, a slow building process, a hard-won gain, that takes tens of thousands of years. In it, communication and conceptual thought go together: one implies and aids the other. Konrad Lorenz states:

> Culture can die even though men survive, and that's what threatens us today, because the growth, the expansion, of this immense body of cumulative knowledge requires brains, books and traditions. Culture is not something that soars over men's heads. It is man himself.[8]

Rousseau, with his noble-savage delusion, can do enormous harm, says Lorenz. This noble savage would have been a cretin at best. Young people who wish to cancel out everything and start over had best realize that this means going back before the Stone Age to Cro-Magnon man.

> Traditional languages take thousands of years to evolve. Language can be lost in a few generations. In our own day it is already becoming impoverished, and, as a result, so is the faculty for logical expression.[9]

In a period like ours, when concepts become emptied of being, there is an understandable tendency to throw out conceptual thinking. But there is no authentic experience without a concept, and there is no vital concept without experience. The concept gives form to the experience; but the experience has to be present to give content and vitality to the concept.

PART II

FOUR

BLACK AND IMPOTENT: THE LIFE OF MERCEDES

> The real tragedy for the Negro is that he has not taken himself seriously because no one else has. The hope for the Negro is that now he is asserting that he really is a human being, and is demanding the rights due to a human being. If he succeeds in winning these rights he will respect and trust himself, but he cannot win the right to human dignity without the ability to respect and cherish his own humanity in spite of pervasive white rejection.
> —Kenneth Clark, from *Dark Ghetto*

This chapter is an account of the development in psychotherapy of a young black woman from almost complete impotence to self-esteem and the capacity for aggression. She was born and raised in a state of powerlessness. It is not by accident that she is both a black and a woman, two conditions that decisively increase the usual feeling of powerlessness.

An extreme form of powerlessness can be for a woman the inability to bear a child. Mercedes, as we shall call her, was conscious of only one real desire, a desire her husband shared—to have a baby. But every time she got pregnant, she would have a miscarriage or, for various reasons, have to have an abortion. Whatever else may be said about procreation, it is a special demonstration of one's power, an extension of one's self, a production of a new member of one's kind, a new being. This is especially obvious with women; many a woman blossoms with confidence only when she has a baby. But there is also in men the experience that their manhood is affirmed. The sense of pride of paternity is a cliché, but should not for that reason be derogated.

When I first saw Mercedes, a thirty-two-year-old woman, she looked like a West Indian, striking and exotic in appearance. She explained that she was one-quarter Cherokee Indian, one-quarter Scotch, and the remaining half Negro. She had been married for eight years to a white professional man, whose therapist had referred her to me. The marriage was on the edge of collapse, partly because of Mercedes's so-called frigidity and complete lack of sexual interest in her husband.

She had no active belief that she deserved to be helped, but seemed to accept her problems fatalistically, each hardship being taken as another expression of inevitable doom. The only problem she did recognize and feel with any strength was the already mentioned inability to carry through a pregnancy. Eight experiences of miscarriage or abortion had occurred up to this time.

She had been judged unanalyzable by two other therapists on their belief that she did not have enough motivation, could not generate enough inner conflict about her problems. They felt she was unable to be introspective enough or to feel enough about her problems to engage in the long-term process of working them through. She seemed not to repress her problems, but just to find it inconceivable that she could do anything at all about them.

I accepted her as a patient partly because of my conviction that the label "untreatable" refers not to a state of the patient but to the limitations of an individual psychotherapist's methods. It is important that a psychotherapist try to find the special kind of treatment that will unlock the door to the problems of this particular person.

In the first session Mercedes told me that her stepfather had used her as a prostitute from the time she was eleven until she was twenty-one. The stepfather brought men in to her several times a week after school, before her mother got home from work. Ostensibly the mother knew nothing about this.

Mercedes was not aware of anything she got out of this prostitution; with rare exceptions, she had no sexual excitement, only a feeling that she was being desired. Whatever money was exchanged, none of it ended up in her pocket. But she could not say no to her stepfather and, indeed, could not even fantasy refusing to go along with his expectations. She later went to a community college—an I.Q. test, which she remembers somewhere along the line, gave her a score of 130 to 140. At college she joined a sorority where she went through all the proper motions and emotions. The prostitution continued all the while. It was only when she went to nursing school after college and lived out of her mother's house that she broke away from her stepfather.

Mercedes seemed like a "nice" person, docile, who had adopted the role of harmonizer in the family. Brought up in a Negro section, she had learned almost with her first breath in life that it was her function to please everybody, to be passive, and to accept whatever form of victimization life might bring her. She had taken faithful care of her grandmother, who lived with the family. Not at all a sissy, however, she had learned, like everyone else in her environment, to fight. She had fought not only her own battles at school and on the street—in which she would go into a wild fury—but had also protected her younger brother as he grew up.

My assumption that on some level she must have hated the prostitution was borne out by a childhood memory she was to recount later in the therapy. When visiting relatives in Virginia she had watched a donkey keep trying to get its penis into a mare which stood there apathetically. "I *hated* that donkey!" she expostulated. The vehemence and sincerity with which she uttered this statement indicated that she had always regarded the prostitution as a hated offense against her. But it was totally impossible for some months to get from her any conscious awareness of that conviction.

Beneath the surface I knew Mercedes was profoundly helpless, apathetic, and chronically depressed. Such diagnostic statements don't help us much since anyone in her situation would have been similarly depressed. We have to see more of the inner dynamics of her life.

1. THE MISSING ANGER

When I asked her what she wanted from the therapy and from me, Mercedes could not respond for a while. She finally got out that she found herself often saying as a kind of prayer: "Let me have a child, let me be a good wife, let me enjoy sex, let me *feel* something."

For the second therapy session she brought in the following two dreams. Both were about her dog, Ruby, with whom, as she said, she often identified.

My dog, Ruby, was hurt. It must be a cut because I have one. I take him home but he runs away again into the subway. A man was there protecting a beagle. I asked, "Which way did Ruby run?" He said a big policeman shot him and they carried him off in an ambulance. I said, "It's my dog," but they didn't let me in to see him.

Ruby runs away again. I was yelling, running after him. I saved Ruby from a man. Because of this I owed the man some treat. He knew me because he had seen me doing my exercises. I invited him to dinner. He reaches over and touches me sexually. I try to kick him, but I get bumped in the back. I feel a push toward him every time I try to kick him. I turn around and see my mother pushing me toward him.

The dreams give a vivid picture of an extremely helpless woman. When, in the first dream, the dog is shot and carried away, the authorities ignore her cry that he is hers—a graphic picture of the members of the Establishment highhandedly discharging the "white man's burden." They show no respect whatever for Mercedes's feelings or her rights; they assume she simply has none. Such situations which she reflects and creates in the dream would themselves suffice to destroy any nascent individual sense of self-esteem if it were present in her. Anything she does in trying to get to her own wounded dog—or to save herself—is useless; this-is-the-way-the-world-is.

Since these dreams occurred almost at the beginning of therapy, we have to ask whether Mercedes is, in the second dream, also revealing her attitudes toward me, the therapist. All these strains could be read as referring to me—I shoot the dog (or *her*, since she is identified with it); I have no respect for her feelings; I am the man from whom she saves Ruby, the one to whom she "owes something" and who makes sexual passes at her. No wonder she hadn't leaped into therapy! She was completely unaware of these implications toward me (I noted them but judged it was too early in therapy to bring them out). And I am as sure as one can be that nothing happened in the first two sessions to account for this attitude. We must assume that she sees all relationships with men, especially white men, as a power struggle, in which they are the winners and she the powerless victim.

The I-am-only-a-servant attitude is carried further in the second dream: *because she saves Ruby from a man, she owes the man a "treat."* A strange "logic of injustice" is present in such persons who are forced to accept the fact that others have all the rights and they have none. It is the exact opposite of the assumption of one's worth as a person; she is indentured a priori; even saving herself is an act demanding she give some recompense to the man. The one form of giving, the one currency she has which is desired by men, is sex; this is the exploitation men demand as payment. Payment, in this case, is only for what ought to have been hers to start with. If she says no, if she gets what is hers, she is taking away something from the world.

But most important of all in this dream is the role of her mother. She pushes the girl toward the man. The dream says that the mother not only knows what is going on—knows about the prostitution—but actively abets it.

Shortly after Mercedes began therapy, she became pregnant by her husband. I then noted a tremendously interesting phenomenon. Every couple of weeks when she came in reporting that she had begun to bleed vaginally—which was in her judgment as well as medically a symptom predicting a miscarriage—she would also report a dream. This dream would be one in which her mother, and less frequently her father or others, were attacking and trying to kill her. The consistent simultaneity of this kind of dream and the bleeding as a harbinger of a miscarriage was what struck me.

At first I tried to draw out the anger I assumed the young woman must feel toward her assassins. She would sit there mildly agreeing with me but feeling nothing at all. It became clear that she was totally unable to muster any conscious rage toward her mother or stepfather or toward others who were out to kill her. This, again, contradicts all logic: you *ought* to feel rage when someone is out to kill you; that's what anger is for biologically— an emotional reaction to someone's destroying your power to be.

Taking my cue from the second dream, I hypothesized that some struggle with her mother was the reason behind the constant miscarriages, and that if she had a baby, she secretly felt her mother (or stepfather) would kill her. Having a baby was inviting death at their hands.

But we were faced with an immediate practical problem which would not wait: it often takes several months for a theory to become practically convincing and efficacious to the patient, no matter how correct it may be. We were confronted with the likelihood of a spontaneous abortion. Some rage had to be expressed, and I was the only other person in the room. So I decided, not wholly consciously, to express *my* rage in place of hers.

Each time she began vaginal bleeding and brought in such a dream, I would verbally counterattack those who were trying to kill her. Chiefly I attacked her mother with other figures thrown in from time to time. What did these blankety-blank people mean by trying to kill her for having a baby? That bitch, her mother, must have known about the prostitution all along and had been, as in the dream, pushing her into it. She was continually sacrificing Mercedes on the altar of homage to the stepfather, to keep him—or for whatever Godforsaken other exploitative reason. After all, Mercedes (I continued) had done her best, serving everybody, even submitting to sexual exploitation. And here these people still have the power to prohibit her from having the one thing she wants, a baby!

I was giving vent to the rage the girl had never dared express herself. I was allying myself with that faint autonomous element which we must assume is in every human being, although in Mercedes it was practically nonexistent to start with.

At first she continued to sit mute, somewhat surprised at my expressed anger. *But the bleeding would stop.* Each time she would have the warning of a miscarriage and such a dream, I would again leap to the attack, expressing the aggression she could not, or did not dare to, feel. Some of these dreams that occurred during the pregnancy were:

> My father was pounding me to interfere with the baby. He was furious at my having the baby. My husband did not come to help me.
>
> I was fighting a woman. I was being paralyzed. My voice was leaving me, and I was losing control of my emotions. My father would not leave me in peace. I was screaming to my mother and

father. . . . To my mother I screamed, "If you're going to help me, help me. If you are not, leave me alone."

After three or four months she herself began to feel her own aggression and expressed her own anger at the attackers in the dreams. It was as though she took over from me the project of anger; in this sense my anger was her first self-affirmation. She separately called up her parents—her mother, her real father, and her stepfather—and told them in no uncertain terms not to phone her or in any other way get in touch with her until after her baby was born. This act took me by surprise—I hadn't specifically expected it—but I was glad of it. I affirmed it as Mercedes's new-found ability to assert herself and demand her rights.

In the month before the baby was due there appeared some actual affirmation of giving birth. "Lynda Bird [the then president's daughter] is having a baby" was one dream, and "I took a job" was another. When a dream occurred at that point about the stepfather—"He got angry and got a knife"—she apparently had very little fear of him. "So what?" was all she said.

The baby was safely born at its appointed time, to the great joy of Mercedes and her husband. They picked out a name that, like "Prometheus," signifies a new beginning in the history of mankind. She and her husband were totally unconscious, so far as I could determine, of this significance. But I thought it fitting, indeed—a new race of man is born!

Several things about my anger need to be clarified. I was not assuming a role—I genuinely *felt* angry toward her mother and stepfather. The relationship in therapy can be likened to a field of magnetic force. This field has two persons in it, patient and therapist. Into this field is introduced a dream. Some rage was required against the destroyers in the dream. It is more therapeutic if the patient can muster the anger. But if she—as in this case—cannot, the therapist, also feeling the same anger, can express it. I also was not merely "training" Mercedes to establish "habit pat-

terns" by which she herself could become angry. No, we were
playing for keeps—to keep a fetus in her womb. Nor is this mere
"catharsis" or abreaction in the usual senses of those words. The
stakes were life itself—her baby's.

For what is this woman fighting? Why, in her dreams, this great
battle with fist and knife? The answer is both simple and profound; she is fighting for her right to exist, to exist as a person
with the autonomy and freedom that are inseparably bound up
with being a person. She is fighting for her right to *be*—if I may
use that verb in its full and powerful meaning—and to be, if necessary, against the whole universe, in Pascal's sense. These phrases
—the right to be, the struggle for one's own existence—are poor
ones, but they are the only ones we have.

The battle is pictured with knives and fists, which is the language of the streets on which Mercedes was brought up. She
knows that she is not permitted to assert her own being except
as she establishes herself through brute tooth-and-claw strength.
She later stated that she could not have fought her mother without the therapy—"I got my strength from you to stand against my
mother"—but obviously it was *her* strength when she got it, and
it was *she* who did the standing.

There is yet another point. Mercedes, different from the usual
patient in psychoanalysis, could assume her dreams were part of a
separate world (and this is what the analysts who had rejected her
found lacking in her). This is like the "magic world" of some patients. She could then simply go ahead as if she had no real anger.
All the while the rage and the anxiety connected with it were
exacting a serious price—her sterility. To *admit* this anger consciously would have been a threat with which she was unable to
cope; it would have meant admitting that her mother was her
sworn enemy. This mother actually *had* saved her when she was a
little girl—i.e., had been the provider for the family when her real
father had left. Hence she could not let herself admit any such
hostility; she could not lead the double life which is characteristic

of middle-class patients, operating under their double binds. Consequently what she got from me was not just the *permission* without condemnation to express her struggle to be; she got the prior *experience*, from someone in authority, of her own rights and her own being which (referring back to the first dream) she had previously lacked. My giving vent to my rage was my living out my belief that she was a person with her own rights. I didn't need to say it because she could see it from my actions.

2. THE RITES OF REBIRTH

But with the birth of her son, Mercedes's life-problem was only half solved. She took a leave from psychotherapy for six months after the birth because she could not (or did not wish to) get someone to take care of her baby while she came to the sessions. I agreed to this since I wanted to keep the therapy geared to her own wishes, directed as autonomously by her as possible. When she did return, I found her in obviously much better shape than when she had originally come. Her hatred of her mother continued—as we filled in the infinite details ("My mother tried to abort me before I was born"; "Her lips are hard, not soft, when she kisses me"; "She was late to every school play I was in, as well as my graduation"; "She goes around looking like a French whore"). But the hatred was not as overwhelming, it no longer caused symptoms, and she could handle it.

Mercedes, however, tended to build her whole life around her son, who was a beautiful, active, blue-eyed, red-haired boy. If he breathed irregularly, she was worried; if he awoke at night, she had to run to him and comfort him. She nursed him a long time at her breast with a perseverance that surprised even her pediatrician. She had trouble sleeping, partly because of her overconcern about her son. As a consequence of all this, she was weary most of the time.

She brought her son to my office one day when her sitter had not arrived. A boy of two at that time, he immediately took charge of the therapy, telling his mother to sit "here; no, there; no, in this other chair" (which she obediently did). He also gave me free directions from time to time. During this period in the therapy I had been hearing continually from her: "He is very intelligent in his nursery school"; "He is special"; "How lucky we are to have such a brilliant child"; and so on and so forth. Regardless of the fact that these comments were generally true, they indicated her subordination to her child, which was actually part of her original problem.

The crucial point is not that she praised the child, which every proud parent rightly does—and Mercedes had plenty of reason for doing so. But she did so as a substitute for her own assertion as a person; she gave him power as an evasion of assuming it herself. In her dreams during this part of the therapy, she and her child were the same person. She regarded herself as the boy's maid (a mistaken identity given to her by some of the other mothers at nursery school where she took her son). She did not like this phrase, but I used it repeatedly, to confront her with it. I pointed out that living through her son was a fine way to evade her own problems and would make him a first-rate candidate for the couch later on.

She heard this in somewhat the same way—though not nearly as pronounced—as she had heard my strictures against her mother. It was as though I were speaking a truth, but it was not yet real to her. Some *experience* seemed to be necessary for Mercedes.

It came when she went to the dentist. She had agreed to take gas, which she had been assured would not be unpleasant. Contrary to expectation, she felt horrible under the gas. She was convinced she was dying. As she felt this doom of death she kept repeating to herself: "Death is for the living, life is for the dying." She cried silently as she lay there. The point is that she did not dare tell the dentist of her terrible experience as she was going through it. She could make no protest, but simply had to endure her fate, do what the authorities expected of her. Finally, as she came out of the gas, she did tell the dentist, who was surprised that she had said nothing before.

For several days after this, the experience clung to her, filling her with sadness and grief. When she got to my office two days later, she was still crying.

Now for the first time with the foretaste of death—which it was to her—she could understand the preciousness of life. Also for the first time she could now experience the fact that she had as much right to live as any other human being.

From then on, a radical change occurred in her life as a whole and in her psychotherapy. The experience seemed to get her over the depression, which, though lightened greatly by the birth of her son, had plagued her continuously during her life. It now *did* make a difference whether she died or not; existence was no mere automatic set of years which one just endures. From now on she felt, as she put it, "simply happy." In the quarrels with her husband that occurred from time to time, she was not overwhelmed as she had been earlier. Some three months after the experience of "death in the dentist's chair," as she called it, she still, to her considerable surprise, found this confident mood still present in her. Even when she was sick with the flu, she would wake up in the morning and ask herself, "Do I feel bad?" and would be amazed to find out that, although she felt *sick*, she didn't feel *bad*.

This elemental experience, simple as it sounds, is one of great importance. What is the meaning of that cryptic sentence she kept repeating under gas: "Death is for the living, life for the dying"? One of the things it says to me is, death is *for* life, and life is for death. That is, you are reborn into life by dying. This would make it an experience in which she joins the race—an experience celebrated in different cultures by the rite of baptism— dying to be born again. It is also the myth and rite of resurrection

—dying to be raised again. Therapists see this myth of resurrection enacted, in varying degrees of intensity, every day of the week. It often comes as a prelude to experiencing the right to assert one's self.

This account indicates that, far from toning down aggression, it is of the very nature of psychotherapy to help people *assert* it. Most people who come for therapy are like Mercedes, though less pronounced—they have not too much aggression, but too little. We encourage their aggressiveness provisionally, confident in the hope that, once they have found their own right-to-be and affirm themselves, they will actually live *more* constructively interpersonally as well as intrapersonally. This, of course, means a different kind of aggression from that which is usually implied by the term.

3. VIOLENCE AS LIFE-DESTROYING AND LIFE-GIVING

But what needs to be said of the violence in Mercedes's existence? It was obviously present, and in abundance. Her dreams had so much violence in them that one had the feeling of sitting on a volcano. Most of her violence was in self-defense: she fought with fists and knives in her dreams simply to keep from being killed.

There are, however, several valuable points to be explored. One is the tendency in violence to erupt in all directions, to bypass all rational functions. In her fights at school or on the street she had become wild, not knowing what she was doing. Such letting go of all controls seemed to have worked well in these fights, as it did also in her occasional hysterical fights with her husband. It is helpful to examine Mercedes's experience in this regard since she is a highly intelligent person who, at the same time, was brought up in a primitive background.

Let us go back to the very first session of her therapy, when she told me of two dreams she had had the night before. I take these as both referring, at least in part, to the therapy she planned to commence on the morrow.

> I was asking Percy [her husband] or my brother for help. I didn't get it. My asking him should be enough. I awoke angry, and felt like hitting him.

> Ruby, our dog, was in the house, and had left feces all over the floor. I was cleaning it up. Maybe I was asking Percy for help.

She was aware that "the shit was mine" and of "what happened to me, what I did." But the dreams carry the message that she expected magic help from me: "My asking him should be enough."

This is a common defense of people overwhelmed by feelings of powerlessness. Some other force must have the power to change things since obviously these people don't; *their* actions don't really matter. To fill the vacuum left by their failure to act the powerless frequently rely on the practice of magic rites. Worried about her increasing weight, for example, Mercedes asked me to hypnotize her to cause her to eat less. I refused, saying it would take away her own responsibility; and why did she not learn to be her own hypnotist? The next session she told me that she had been enraged at me by my refusal. She recognized her reliance on magic.

This dependence on magic stretches back through the centuries of oppression of the blacks, colonial peoples, and minorities of whatever sort. It was assumed that the blacks could be made passive, docile, and helpless and could be kept this way by use of built-in threats and an occasional lynching. But in the false calm, we repressed the question we should have been asking: When an individual is rendered unable to stand up for himself socially or psychically, as in slavery, where does his power go? No one can accept complete impotence short of death. If he cannot assert himself overtly, he will do it covertly. Thus magic—a covert, occult force—is an absolute necessity for the powerless. The spread of magic and the reliance on the occult is one symptom of the widespread impotence in our transitional age.[1]

But magic is not the only symptom. Mercedes also fouls her own nest; her violence turns against herself. This is clearly stated in the second dream in which the dog—whom she recognizes as herself—leaves feces all over the floor. True, this can be an indication of hostility toward others (for which feces are often a primitive symbol), an aggressive revenge, an emptying of my refuse on your rug, your floor. But—and this "but" has within it a good deal of the tragedy of suppressed minorities—the feces are on *her* floor. The impulse to aggression, suppressed rage, is turned inward and comes out against herself. The impulse for revenge, the hostile surge, bypasses reason and finds its outlet in the muscles; it *is* irrational in this sense. It erupts against one's self if there is no one close against whom it can erupt; the direction and the aim of violence is secondary, only the eruption is important at that moment. This is the point at which suppressed tendencies for aggression are transformed into violence. Strictly speaking, the object of the violence is irrelevant.

This strange phenomenon, so patently self-destructive, is illustrated specifically in Mercedes. About ten months after her son's birth, she had the following dreams:

> I was being pursued by everyone, I had to kill them, hurt them, stop them in some way. Even my son was one of them in the room. I had to do something to everyone or they'd hurt me. I pinched my son, that was enough for him. But I had to punch everyone else. One at a time, so they wouldn't pounce on me. I awoke with an awful feeling that I was being torn in pieces.

> I was riding in a car with Percy and another man. A man was trying to get in the car. We were then in an office at a place where there was a nurse and a desk. I got under the desk, I chose a knife. The man was looking in, seeing me under the nurse's desk. I went for my knife, but it was gone. Then I got another knife. I now was fighting my son and my grandmother.

It didn't bother me; I was parrying their knives. Then it became a woman I was fighting, she was trying to hurt me.

She fights her son as well as her grandmother, the person whom she had taken care of in her childhood and for whom she had a genuine affection. This wild striking in all directions seems a paradigm for irrational violence. Here lies an important part of the explanation of the ghetto riots—the burning, looting, killing, which may turn out, paradoxically, to be against those closest and dearest to the rioters.

Now what do these people whom Mercedes fights have in common? *They are all persons to whom she has subordinated herself.* Whether for good reasons, as in the case of the grandmother and son, or bad, as ostensibly in the case of her mother, they represent people in whom she has submerged herself. In this respect they *should* be fought for the sake of her own autonomy. It is parallel to what Arnold L. Gesell calls the "counter-will," the child's self-assertion in opposition exactly to those upon whom he is most dependent. Thus the life-destroying violence becomes also life-giving violence. They are intertwined as the sources of the individual's self-reliance, responsibility, and freedom.

The "man looking in" may be me, the therapist; and why shouldn't she fight me also as she is asserting her own freedom? This is the unavoidably ambiguous state all persons in therapy are in; they must fight the therapist at some place along the line, although the therapist ostensibly is trying to help, and on deeper examination, precisely *for* the reason that he is trying to help. This occurs partly because in coming for help they have had to surrender temporarily some of the autonomy they do have; partly because of the humiliation of having to ask for help; and partly as a counterbalance to the excessive transference that turns the therapist into a god.

There is thus a self-affirmation precisely in self-destructive violence. Ultimately the affirmation is expressed in the person's demonstration of his right to die by his own hand if he chooses.

If, as is our tendency in this country, we condemn all violence out of hand and try to eradicate even the possibility of violence from a human being, we take away from him an element that is essential to his full humanity. For the self-respecting human being, violence is always an ultimate possibility—and it will be resorted to less if admitted than if suppressed. For the free man it remains in imagination an ultimate exit when all other avenues are denied by unbearable tyranny or dictatorship over the spirit as well as the body.

FIVE

THE MEANING OF
POWER

To be alive is power,
Existing in itself,
Without a further function,
Omnipotence enough.

> —Emily Dickinson

1. DEFINING POWER

Power is the ability to cause or prevent change. It has two dimensions. One is power as potentiality, or latent power. This is power that has not yet been fully developed; it is the ability to cause a change at some future time. We speak of this future change as *possibility*, a word which comes directly from the same root as power, namely *posse*, "to be able." The other dimension is power as actuality. It is to this aspect of power I shall be referring in this chapter.

Ancient Greek philosophers defined power as being—that is to say, there is no being without power. And since power is the ability to change, Heraclitus held that being is in continual flux. This definition has come down the mainstream and tributaries of philosophy through the ages to contemporary ontological thinkers like Paul Tillich, who describes power similarly as "the power of being." The philosophers of life, such as Nietzsche with his *will to power* and Bergson with his *élan vital*, emphasize the element of power in all living things.[1] Power is for them an expression of the life process.

The danger in the definitions of Nietzsche and Bergson is that they tempt us to identify power with the life process itself. This would lead us astray. There are many things in the life process—such as consciousness, desire, curiosity—which may be allied with power but are not to be identified with it. Power and love can be allied, but they also can be contrasted; the distinction between them must be kept clear. Power can be identified only with the original power of being itself, from which being gets its start.

Power was originally a sociological term, a category used chiefly to describe the actions of nations and armies. But as students of the problem have increasingly realized that power depends upon emotions, attitudes, and motives, they have turned to psychology for the needed clarification.[2] In psychology, power means the ability to affect, to influence, and to change other persons. Each person exists in an interpersonal web, analogous to magnetic fields of force; and each one propels, repels, connects, identifies with others. Thus such considerations as status, authority, and prestige are central to the problem of power. I have used the phrase "sense of significance" to refer to a person's conviction that he counts for something, that he has an effect on others, and that he can get recognition from his fellows.

What is the relationship between power and force? Certainly force, the lowest common denominator of power, has been widely identified with power in America; it is the automatic first association with power of most people in this country. This is the chief

reason power has been scorned and disparaged as a "dirty word."
John Dewey believed that coercive force is the middle ground
between power as energy and power as violence. "Not to depend
upon and utilize force is simply to be without a foothold in the
real world." [3]

There are some situations of power when force, or coercion, or
compulsion is an integral part of power. War is one of them. With
sick persons or children, compulsion or coercion has to be used in
proportion to the lack of capacity or knowledge of the other person. When my son was three years old, I kept a firm grip on his
hand as we walked across Broadway, a condition that was relaxed
as he grew and learned the intricacies of traffic enough to be able
safely to take on the responsibility of crossing himself.

But there are ultimate limits to the application of force. If a
species of animal uses its superior force to kill off all the other
animals in its vicinity, it obviously will not have them for food
when it needs them. This "balance of nature" is a delicate inter-
weaving of the force of various animals and plants in relation to
each other. When this balance is upset, we are faced with fearful
prospects, indeed—as we are learning to our sorrow in modern
ecology. Thus, to keep from self-destruction, power can be allied
with force only up to the point where it might destroy the identity
of the other. In a gun battle in the West, to destroy the identity
of the enemy is precisely the goal of the shooting. Hence I cite
this as an example of the self-destructive effect of power allied
with force. The one who is killed, obviously losing his being, is no
longer present to give what he can to the community, no longer
a person to whom to relate; and we are the poorer thereby.

Also the spontaneity of the other person cannot be destroyed
without a loss to the destroyer as well. This is the danger in
extreme forms of coercion and compulsion in brainwashing, conditioning, and hypnosis. If the person is transformed into something resembling a mechanism, he may still preserve some
spontaneity; but if he is transformed into a complete mechanism,

he ceases to be a person in the process. Power, therefore, ought to move with the affirmation of the spontaneity of the person it encounters; this will assure it most success in the long run. This is why I permitted Mercedes, an individual with practically no sense of her own power or spontaneity or choice to start with, to decide when she wished to come to her psychotherapy sessions and when she chose not to. It was a process not only of letting her use her own spontaneity but requiring her to use it.

While it is utopian to try to divorce power completely from force, compulsion, and coercion, it is cynical to identify all kinds of power with them.[4]

2. POWER AND THE INTELLECTUALS

There is, among intellectuals, a tendency to deny and renounce power. Some have done this under the rubric: "Intellectuals and power are incompatible." [5] Others have said: "Ought we to redefine [power] in a clear way, or ought we to banish it altogether? My initial reaction is that it should be banished altogether." [6] Indeed, outside Marxist circles, the subject has unfortunately been generally banished. There is a suspicion of the whole topic as though it were like Faust: whoever seeks power has already sold his soul to Mephistopheles.

Some intellectuals propose that they deal in *influence*, and that "influence is the opposite to power in that it restructures or alters preferences." These intellectuals believe that power is the "restructuring of action without altering preferences; you are made to do something irrespective of whether it is your preferred course of action." [7]

But is not this distinction between influence and power essentially false? If we take the university as the setting, we need only ask any graduate student whether his professors have power over him, and he will laugh at our naïveté. Of course the professors have power; the perpetual anxiety of some graduate students as to whether they will be passed or not is proof enough. The professors' power is even more effective because it is clothed in scholarly garb. It is the power of prestige, status, and the subtle coercion of others that follows from these. This is not due to the professors' conscious aims; it has more to do with the organization of the university and the teachers' unconscious motivations for being part of it. The more powerless the teacher feels himself to be, the more destructive, even though subtle and covert, will be his influence.

Influence is surely a form of power—intellectual power, but power all the same.[8] I agree that being coerced into doing something regardless of whether it is the preferred course of action is a form of power (albeit a kind we are all used to and accept a hundred times a day, from waiting for red lights to change to paying taxes). But the emphasis on "altering preferences" can actually be harmful in that it leads to the state that de Tocqueville described as characteristic of Americans—that we are bodily freer than Europeans, but intellectually more conformist and spiritually more in bondage.[9] Many academic examinations fall into this category, in which it is psychologically healthier for the student to realize that he is required to take the examination and he *doesn't* like it, and to study for it with that realization in mind. The damage to his integrity comes when he tries to persuade himself that he does like it. The idea of liking what you have to do is an illusion, and an unhealthy one at that. If we can like and choose a proportion of what we have to do, and do the rest because we are required to without trying to delude ourselves, we shall have more effectively preserved our autonomy and our humanity.

The denial of power in society on the part of the professor is an example of pseudoinnocence. The professor proposes an idea, which in turn has power. He ducks out by letting the idea be powerful, not him. It is as though he says: "I said it, but the 'it' is responsible for my action, not me." [10] No doubt this syndrome is related by both cause and effect to the general American tendency toward anti-intellectualism, the distrust of the intellectuals on the frontier. But one cannot purchase innocence so easily. Ideas unmated with reality produce few offspring, as Anthony Athos puts it.

When the intellectual realizes that he "has been increasingly pushed from the battlefield [of power] and put to flight," [11] the reason may be that he himself has defined himself out of the battle to begin with. It would clear the air if the intellectual were to admit that he also has power, although a different kind from that of the politician, the businessman, and the military leader. Furthermore, modern society clearly needs the intellectuals and their guidance; the corporate power needs to be shared with them as well as with the other disinherited groups in society. It is worthwhile to recall that in the first act of Beckett's *Waiting for Godot*, the intellectual in the person of Lucky appears with a rope around his neck, pulled in by the industrialist Pozzo, the man of power. But in the second act Pozzo struggles back in, now *blind*, led by Lucky, who, now dumb (no doubt an allegory meaning he talked too much before), cares for him and directs him. This is a graphic allegory of the role of the intellectual and the nutrient power that he can express in our day.

I have argued against the idea that there is an irreconcilable incompatibility between power and the intellectual. But there is a *creative* tension, which takes the form of the pull between power and consciousness. This is why men of intensive consciousness— like Nietzsche, Kierkegaard, Pascal—have preferred an ascetic life, in which there were at least periods of freedom from the paraphernalia of the world. It is the function of consciousness to be, as Socrates described himself, "a gadfly to the state." Consciousness can disturb the establishment of power. It leads to conflicts which can be turned into new integration. It is the function of consciousness to keep us alert, to keep our imaginations functioning, to keep us forever curious, forever ready to explore infinite possibilities. Whereas power requires decision and dispatch, consciousness requires a loosening of controls, a freedom to wander where the spirit listeth, an exploration of new forms of existence which may be far out on the frontiers of knowledge. The last form of power to be cited in the next section, integrative power, is an example of the allying of power with the consciousness.

3. KINDS OF POWER

A. *Exploitative* This is the simplest and, humanly speaking, most destructive kind of power. It is subjecting persons to whatever use they may have to the one who holds the power. Slavery is, of course, the obvious example—when one person has the power over the bodies and, indeed, over the whole organisms of many persons. Exploitative power identifies power with force. In pioneer America the use of bullets to transform others into lifeless hulks, as well as most other examples of physical force, fall into this category. In this sense the use of firearms, when employed at the whim of the person who happens to possess a gun, is a form of exploitative power.

In everyday life this kind of power is exercised by those who have been radically rejected, whose lives are so barren that they know no way of relating to other people except exploitation. It is even sometimes rationalized as the "masculine" way of dealing with women sexually. It is interesting that courtly love in the Middle Ages guarded against this kind of power—which would otherwise have been rampant in the society of knights and maidens—by the rule that force was never to be used in love.

Exploitative power always presupposes violence or the threat of violence. In this kind of power there is, strictly speaking, no choice or spontaneity at all on the part of the victims.

B. *Manipulative* This is power *over* another person. Manipulative power may have originally been invited by the person's own desperation or anxiety. Mercedes acceded to her stepfather's demand that she accept the prostitution because of her own hopelessness and inability to do anything else. After this initial agreement, there is very little spontaneity or choice left to the person (although Mercedes did refuse to have lesbian relationships).

The shift of exploitative to manipulative power is seen on our own frontier in the superseding of the gunman by the "con" man. In all of his dishonesty and misuse of Protestant ethics, as David Bazelon points out, the con man represents a less destructive power than the brute force of the gunman, if for no other reason than that he left his victim living.[12]

The proposal of operant conditioning, put forth by B. F. Skinner, is another example of manipulative power. Based on research with animals, it works gratifyingly with those who are already mentally limited, such as retarded children, some backward psychotics, prisoners, and with neurotics in limited spheres. And it certainly works with pigeons. These are groups in whom spontaneity has already been largely handicapped or rendered ineffective and for whom the principle of manipulative power is necessary. Recognizing that much of human life is manipulative, Skinner proposes that the manipulation be used for socially justifiable aims. No one, to my knowledge, would disagree with the above points.

The error lies, from the scientific viewpoint, in trying to apply a system developed from limited work with animals to human society and, indeed, to the whole realm of human experience. Everything must be made to fit this system of manipulation; and if it, like Dostoevsky novels, does not fit, it is summarily thrown out of the new Skinnerian world. "In the future no one will read them," remarks Skinner. But Skinner's arbitrary choice to use rats and pigeons to obtain his data necessarily rules out human freedom and dignity. If, like the behaviorist, you recognize the smile but not the smiler—that is, you omit the person performing the act—how can you expect to encompass a society of beings who smile and frown and weep and kill and love—indeed, beings who are *human*?

Skinner is himself a living illustration of the individual who does not consciously confront his own power needs. He calls them the "passion to control." For example, in his book *Walden Two*, Farris, the hero, speaks to his pigeons: "Behave, damn you! Behave as you ought!" But it does not take an intricate psychoanalysis to indicate that this is actually a strong power need under whatever name it may appear.

It is often pointed out that the Germans, in the years before 1933, were in such a state of economic hopelessness and anxiety about their future, that they succumbed to the manipulative power of Hitler in the hope of assuaging their anxiety. The danger similarly is, given the despair and anxiety of men and women living in this time of transition between historical periods, that people today will turn toward the utopian proposals of Skinner in the hope of escaping their anxiety.

The principle I propose with respect to manipulative anxiety is that although it is necessary in some situations, it should be used as sparingly as possible.

C. *Competitive* This third kind of power is power *against* another. In its negative form, it consists of one person going *up* not because of anything he does or any merit he has, but because his opponent goes *down*. There are many examples of this in industry and in universities, such as the appointing of a president or chairman when there is only one desired position and many applicants. This may also be the kind of power present in student rivalry due to the grading system, which promotes destructive personal influences directly counter to whatever impulses students have toward mutual caring and cooperation.

The chief criticism of this kind of power is its parochialism: it continuously shrinks—although not as drastically as manipulation —the area of human community in which one lives.

But at this point we note a very interesting shift from destructive to constructive power. For competitive power can give zest and vitality to human relations. I refer to the kind of rivalry that is stimulating and constructive. A football game in which one side immediately establishes its superiority is simply not interesting. We want our opponents to test our mettle; pure ease at winning is boring. David McClelland emphasizes that this kind of competition is much more present in the business world than most people assume; that the achievement (which I include in the realm of power) of businessmen lies in their own satisfaction in getting better results, more efficient activity, to which their competition pushes them.

It is worthwhile to remind ourselves that the great dramas of Aeschylus, such as the *Oresteia*, or Sophocles' Oedipus trilogy and many of the works of Euripides were produced in competitions. The implication is that it is not competition itself that is destructive but only the *kind* of competitive power.

The competition between nations, as Anthony Storr points out, in the race to the moon or to produce cheaper and better forms of technology (mousetraps), drains off a great deal of tension that would otherwise go into warfare. Konrad Lorenz also makes a great deal of this kind of competition in sports as a counteraction to the competitive power that might otherwise lead the nations to tear at each other's throats. Even if such assertions presuppose a too simplistic view of international aggression, they nevertheless do illustrate a positive form of competitive power. To have someone *against* you is not necessarily a bad thing; at least he is not *over* you or *under* you, and accepting his rivalry may bring out dormant capacities in you.

D. *Nutrient* This is power *for* the other. It is perhaps best illustrated by the normal parent's care for his or her children. It is a form of power not only because the child, in his younger years, needs our effort and attention, but all our lives we get pleasure out of exerting ourselves from time to time for the sake of the other. Obviously a good deal of this kind of power is necessary and valuable in relations with friends and loved ones. It is the power that is given by one's care for the other; we wish him well. At its best, teaching is a good example.

Statesmanship, again at its best, also shows an element of nutrient power. This is expressed in the projection on the political leader of parental images (the czar as "Little Father"; the "father image" given to the American president). Nutrient power comes out of a concern for the welfare of the group for which the statesman carries responsibility. It is the constructive aspect of political and diplomatic power.

E. *Integrative* This fifth kind is power *with* the other person. My power then *abets* my neighbor's power. A European friend of mine, when he was in this country working on his influential ideas and forming them into a book, would offer them for criticism; but the rest of us, rightly understanding how tender ideas can be when they are being born, would politely hold back any negative reaction. But our friend would regularly react with impatience, protesting: "I *want* you to criticize me." By this he meant that if we proposed an *antithesis* against his *thesis*, he would be forced to reform his thinking into a new and better *synthesis*. As John Stuart Mill, in his *Essay on Liberty*, says: "If opponents of all important truths do not exist, it is indispensable to imagine them and supply them with the strongest arguments which the most skilful devil's advocate can conjure up." An audience rarely realizes how valuable its questions are to a speaker after a lecture, for they stimulate and compel him to alter or defend his position with renewed insight.

I was tempted to call this kind of power "cooperative," but I realized it too often begins with the "victim" having to be coerced into the cooperation. Our narcissism is forever crying out against the wounds of those who would criticize us or point out our weak spots. We forget that the critic can be doing us a considerable favor. Certainly criticisms are often painful, and one has to brace one's self in the face of them. We can slide back into manipulative power (by forcefully silencing the critic) or competitive power (by making the critic look silly). Or we can even protect our thin skins by means of nutrient power (patronizing the critic by implying he is confused and needs our care). But if we do regress in these ways, we are losing an opportunity for new truth that the questioner, hostile or friendly as the case may be, may well be giving us. I recall my own experience in psychoanalysis. When my analyst would point out something about my character structure which I found painful, I would at first deny it out of hand. But later on, as I realized the truth of the insight, I would have to suffer the pain of changing my character structure according to this new truth. This confession is not as dramatic as it sounds, for everyone I have ever met also reacts in exactly this way in similar situations.

Integrative power, I have said, can lead to growth by Hegel's dialectic process of thesis, antithesis, and synthesis. All growth, even that of molecular structures, proceeds in this way: there is one body, then there is its anti-body, and growth proceeds by the repulsion or attraction of these two into a new body.

The Reverend Martin Luther King, Jr., illustrates integrative

power in his description of the effect of nonviolence on his opponents. He states that his method "has a way of disarming the
opponent. It exposes his moral defenses. It weakens his morale
and at the same time it works on his conscience. He just doesn't
know how to handle it." [13]

No one can deny that King is describing a kind of power. It depends for its success not only on the courage of the nonviolent
ones, but also upon the moral development and awareness of the
persons who are the recipients of the nonviolent power. The
same is true of Gandhi's militant nonviolence. While Gandhi and
his followers disciplined themselves to adhere rigidly to nonviolence, it is incontestable that they brought great psychological
and spiritual power to bear upon their British rulers. Pitted against
a whole empire, Gandhi moved it with eminent success by his
fasting in a way he never could have by military power.

As King says: "It works on [the] conscience." Nonviolent
power depends on memory, which in turn depends on the moral
development of the persons against whom this kind of power is
directed. The opponent has to live with himself, and Gandhi and
King put him in the position of having to remember that he has
injured them. Hence Maxwell Anderson, in his play *Winterset*,
based on, though written some years after, the Sacco-Vanzetti
trial, writes about the now aged judge who sentenced the two
men to death. This judge spends his senile years going from person to person trying to explain and justify his act. He cannot forget, and he cannot integrate his action with his self-image; and the
conflict this sets up preys upon him and contributes, if not
causes, his senile psychosis. Man is the curious being who is
afflicted with memory. If he cannot integrate his memories into
his self-image, he must pay for his failure by neurosis or psychosis;
and he tries, generally in vain, to shake himself loose from the
tormenting memories.

The authentic *innocence* of the nonviolent person is the source of his power. The genuine rather than pseudo quality of the innocence, at least in the examples I have given, is attested by the facts, first, that the nonviolence does not involve any blocking off of awareness. Second, it does not involve the renouncing of responsibility. Third, its purpose is not to gain something for the individual himself but for his community, be it the nation of India or a community of blacks.

Nonviolent power acts as a goad to rulers' ethics, a living rebuke to the smugness of their establishment. Members of the ruling class cannot turn blindly away from the nonviolent one, for he is obviously suffering and, by this, dramatizing the issue. Gandhi was a living antithesis set up against the thesis of the English; he forced them to move to a new synthesis in their own ethics. For the morally sensitive person, this synthesis—or integration—cannot be achieved by either simply rejecting the suffering one or by simply accepting his approach and joining his followers. The whole British empire creaked and groaned as it moved to find new ways of dealing with this little brown man who knew how to turn his suffering to constructive uses.

When it is authentic, nonviolence has a religious dimension, since by its very nature it transcends the human forms of power. It seems to be the fact, however, that for every authentic form of nonviolent power there are dozens of unauthentic attempts to claim the role.

These five different kinds of power are obviously all present in the same person at different times. Many a businessman who exercises manipulative or competitive power at work takes on nutrient power when he comes home to his family. The question—and it is a moral one—is the proportion of each kind of power in the total spectrum of the personality. No one can escape experiencing, in desire and in action, all five types of power, and only self-righteous rigidity leads one to claim that he is immune from any one of them. The goal for human development is to learn to use these different kinds of power in ways adequate to the given situation.

4. POWER AND LOVE

Love and power are traditionally cited as opposites of each other. The common argument goes as follows: the more power one shows, the less love; the more love, the less power. Love is seen as powerless and power as loveless. The more one develops his capacity for love, the less he is concerned about manipulation and other aspects of power. Power leads to domination and violence; love leads to equality and human well-being. This argument, which we have inherited from the Victorian period, is often, though not always, given as the foundation for the pacifist position. At times it is even cited as the basis for "moral law."

I believe that this argument is based on superficial reasoning and leads us into gross errors and endless trouble. Our failure comes from our seeing love as purely an emotion and our not seeing it as also ontological, a state of being.

In bringing up children, for example, the inherited argument is that the more a parent loves his child, the less he asserts himself or in other ways shows power. This was part of the structureless "permissiveness" that characterized many of the parent-child relationships of the past several decades. I do not wish to condemn permissiveness as a whole. Much of it was a reaction against Victorian authoritarianism and resulted in sound freedom and an increase of responsibility for youngsters. But this was chiefly in cases where the parent did not repress his power but let the child frankly see the structure by which he (the parent) lived. But the parent, on the other hand, who tries to continue showing love on the assumption that love is the renunciation of power will be manipulated by the child. Often the parent, now pushed to the wall, will try harder and feel guiltier because of his resentful attitude toward the child; and ultimately, in this vicious circle, he may blow up in rage and possible violence. These structureless families, which operate supposedly on love without power, lead to the development of rootless children, who later in life rebuke their parents for having never said "no" to them.

This endeavor to love with the renunciation of power is a product of the tendency toward pseudoinnocence. It underestimates the difficulty of loving, overlooks the fact that love is always, no matter how profound and lasting, afflicted by its moments of dishonesty. Such love is based upon our unawareness of our complicity, to paraphrase Arthur Miller, in the inescapable ambivalence of human life.

That power and love are interrelated is proved most of all by the fact that one must have power within oneself to be able to love in the first place. Thus Priscilla, until she had the power to assert her own "no" to those who sought to exploit her sexually, could not build a gratifying relationship. Until Mercedes had developed her self-esteem through such experiences as "death in the dentist's chair" she could not enter with any depth into a love relationship. A person must have something to give in order not to be completely taken over or absorbed as a nonentity.

The fallacy of this juxtaposition of love and power comes from our seeing love purely as an emotion and power solely as force of compulsion. We need to understand them both as ontological, as states of being or processes.

The relationship between power and love is shown in myth. Recall that Eros, god of love, is the offspring of Aphrodite and Ares, god of war or strife. In what better way could the ancient Greeks have told us that there is no love without aggression? But even more surprising is the name of another child which blessed this union, Harmonia. The word means that which is fitting, in proportion, in concord—and it seems paradoxical in the extreme. But is it not appropriate that harmony should be a dynamic proportion between strife and beauty?

The empirical relationship of power and love is illustrated in the closeness of the two in the problem of violence, the converse of power. Violence is most apt to occur between persons who are closely tied emotionally and, therefore, vulnerable to each other. According to a statistical study of homicides in Philadelphia, the majority of murders are committed against a member of the family. The most dangerous room, again judged in terms of the likelihood of murder occurring there, is the bedroom. "If you are a woman over 16," M. E. Wolfgang writes in this study, "your murderer will most likely be a husband, lover or relative. . . . When a man is killed, the killer is most likely to be his wife. . . . The bedroom is the most murderous room in the house." [14]

In marriage and in relations between couples we see a similar relationship between love and power. I have elsewhere written of the necessity of combining self-assertion (power) with tenderness (love) in the sex act.[15] Without tenderness, the caring and the sensitivity for the feelings and delight of the other is absent; and without self-assertion the capacity to put one's self fully into the act is missing. When love and power are seen as opposites, "love" tends to be the abject surrender of one partner and the subtle (or not so subtle) domination by the other. These are often the sado-masochistic marriages. When the aim is to be guided only by love, assertion and aggression are obviously ruled out as being too tainted with power. There results a clinging to one another, an absorption in each other. Missing are the firmness of assertion, the structure and the sense of dignity that guard the rights of each of the partners.

Such relationships may swing back and forth, from surrender as a form of love to violence as a form of power. Everyone is familiar with the news clippings telling how a devoted wife or husband of thirty years suddenly took a hatchet to his or her mate in a peculiarly bloody murder. This extreme example reveals the problem in a "love" that does not have within it a realistic assertion of power. There is statistical grounds for the common saying that marriage with someone who is undercontrolled—i.e., blows up from time to time—may make for turmoil and frequent fighting, but it does not make for murder. The docile, overcontrolled individual, the one who appears kind all the time, can be the one who releases his aggression in one big blowup. This accords with our thesis that violence occurs when a person cannot live out his needs for power in normal ways.

An interesting variation on the theme of power and love is seen in the film, *The Last Picture Show*. In this portrayal of a small town in Texas, the women have no overt power at all—no economic power, no political power. The only power they have is covert, connected with their sexuality. They are "condemned to innocence." They accept the pretense of their innocence, which takes the form of coyness and pretended modesty, and they trade on it. It is their "moral" position, and it turns out to be quite immoral. One girl who wants to lose her virginity to make herself more desirable takes her boyfriend to a motel, orders him to perform coitus. When he, understandably for the situation, is impotent, she heaps scorn upon him. But she tells the other girls waiting outside: "It was so wonderful, I can't describe it in words." It turns out that the women have power over the men at every turn; the men can only do their best to live up to the women's demands and expectations. All of the drive for these gyrations comes from the women who have been kept powerless and have only their pretense of innocence as their shield.

Another interesting aspect of the problem of power and love is the phenomenon of jealousy. I shall not go into the question of whether some element of jealousy, as a function of caring and valuing the other person, is normal and healthy beyond saying that

I believe it probably is. But what is generally called "jealousy" surely goes far beyond that normal care. It is a possessiveness which arises in direct proportion to the impotence of the individual. That is, the degree of threat he experiences at the loss of the other is the degree to which he feels jealous. He can do nothing; he has not power in himself to win the loved one back; and he experiences himself as left out completely in the cold. In such situations jealousy can become a form of violence.

One young man, near the beginning of his analysis, could not reach his sweetheart in London by phone and was seized with a fit of jealousy. He immediately took a plane to London, half "hoping" to find her in bed with another man. This young man was threatened greatly because his sense of powerlessness was so great. I put the word "hoping" in quotation marks to indicate that jealousy often arises from a special ambivalence in the relationship: the person loves but he also hates—that is, he would almost prefer it if she did force him, by making love to another, to break off the relationship.

Jealousy characterizes the relationship in which one seeks more power than love. It occurs when the person has not been able to build up enough self-esteem, enough sense of his own power, his own "right to live," if I may use Mercedes's phrase. Neurotic jealousy, strangely enough, may occur most strongly when the love is not very solid or well founded. It is a reflection of the person's feeling of inability to "win" the other back. This is power gone awry and can be very time-consuming and destructive. The jealous person seems to have a need to put all of his energy into the jealous fit, partly to "prove" a love that underneath he feels to be very problematic anyway.

The boundaries of power and love overlap each other. Love makes the person who loves want to be influenced and want to do what the loved one wishes. The intertwining of love and power is shown in relationships between lovers and between husband and wife in the concern for the dignity of the other, the preservation of his or her independent self. It is shown in child-rearing in the firm structure that the understanding adult gives to the child. Assertion, affirmation of the self, and even aggression at times are not only unavoidable but healthy in the developing love relationship.

Some readers may wish to call nutrient power and integrative power actually forms of love. I agree with their meaning, but I think it best to guard against power and love being swallowed up in each other. Hence I prefer to keep their separate meanings clear. But we can say that the lower forms of power—exploitative, manipulative—have a very minimum of love in them, while the higher forms—nutrient, integrative—have more. In other words, the higher up the scale we go, the more love we find.

Even in the religious realm, the belief that "God moves the world only by love" is a sentimentality. Persons who are of this opinion forget that the first word of the General Confession is "Almighty," and the Lord's prayer ends with "for Thine is the *power* and the glory forever." Often the Beatitudes are similarly misinterpreted—"Blessed are the meek, for they shall inherit the earth"—as well as the story of Jesus saying, when He is offered all power over the earth: "Get thee behind me, Satan." But we need to take into consideration that Christianity was born in a period in which the Roman army occupied the whole known world; and any kind of political power or lack of meekness would have meant that one would get himself quickly executed. Our problem is now different: we stand in a world dominated by giant technology, and men and women must be able to assert the power of their consciousness if they are to survive at all.

Social action—work for racial justice, international peace, helping of the poor, and so on—would not be possible without a combination of power and love.

No wonder Nietzsche proclaimed that the Christianity of his

day was a religion for weaklings, and that the time had come for a reassertion of the power and the aristocracy of the spirit. In his transvaluation of all values, Nietzsche asserts that joy does not come from submission and abnegation, but from assertion. "Joy is only a symptom of the feeling of attained power," he proclaimed. "The essence of joy is a plus-feeling of power." [16]

SIX

THE POWER TO BE

. . . For everyone who does not know
How to control his inmost self would feign control
His neighbor's will according to his own conceit.
          —Johann Wolfgang von Goethe,
                    from *Faust*, II

For the living person, power is not a theory but an ever-present reality which he must confront, use, enjoy, and struggle with a hundred times a day. Every person is born a bundle of potentialities. Very few of these have become formed into actual powers at birth; he cannot yet walk or talk or make a flying machine. But he can cry, as Harry Stack Sullivan has pointed out, and this cry is the potentiality that later develops into the complex system of communication in language.

No one can doubt the delight the normal infant gets at the maturing of these potentialities into powers as he is able to talk, to crawl, to walk, to run. All of us who have watched children running in the park, skipping and jumping as randomly as puppies, can appreciate the pleasure of sheer movement, of exercising muscles that demand to be used. The potentiality to explore, to see the world as a person of his age can, will increasingly become an actual power as his neuromuscular structure develops. Everyone who has observed his own development with wonder will be aware that there is both nature and nurture in every step of this actualization of his potentialities.

But these potentialities also bring anxiety. Kierkegaard, in his *Concept of Dread,* has pointed this out: Potentiality becomes actuality, but "the intervening variable is anxiety." The potentiality for sexual intercourse, which takes a decisive leap ahead at puberty, brings excitement and joy but also the anxiety associated with new relationships and new responsibilities.

Power pushes toward its fulfillment. It is neither good nor evil, ethically speaking; it only *is.* But it is not neutral. It requires in some way its own expression, although the forms of this expression vary greatly. There is an inescapable conflict between a man's or woman's individual powers and the culture to which he or she belongs; and there is bound to be a struggle of these powers against the culture that seeks to hold the individual within its bounds.

This constant struggle has a dialectical nature—as one pole changes, the other does too. To take our example of sex again: the genital potentialities mature into actual powers for intercourse in adolescence, and several years later the capacity to make a baby, long before our culture is ready to absorb such activities. This causes untold difficulties. The tendency of some people, then, is simply to call the sexual urge itself bad. But such mistaken logic prevents them from seeing the central issue and from admitting that although the difficulties of this conflict between individual and culture can be eased, there is no foolproof way of solving them. The dilemma is an eternal accompaniment to human existence. It can, when frankly confronted, lead to creative contributions such as art, music, the dance, and other constructive work.

1. ORIGINS OF POWER IN CHILDHOOD

The origins of power are also the origins of aggression. For aggression is one use—or misuse—of power. Clara Thompson states this well when she writes that aggression "springs from an innate tendency to grow and master life which seems to be characteristic of all living matter. Only when this life force is obstructed in its development do ingredients of anger, rage, or hate become connected with it." [1]

We noted in Chapter One that the word *power* comes from the root meaning "to be able." In this sense, it is interesting that Harry Stack Sullivan generally uses the terms "ability and power" together, and also speaks of nature and nurture together. "We seem to be born with something of this power motivation in us," he remarks. But this does not at all cast the die in favor of the "nature" side of the dichotomy in Sullivan's eyes any more than my own, for he speaks of this power motivation being formed in terms of security, status, and prestige. These characteristics are certainly social and are learned by the developing infant from and in his culture.

As one watches a child building with blocks and then knocking the construction down to build it again, one realizes that power and aggression have positive values. From there the child goes on to explore, to experiment, to master his world as best he can and as far as his level of development enables him. "At origin," writes Dr. D. W. Winnicott, "aggressiveness is almost synonymous with activity." [2] And Dr. Anthony Storr, referring to the Winnicott statement, goes on to say,

> If Freud had been right in supposing that our chief aim is blissful satiation, it would be hard to explain this exploratory behavior; but if we assume an Adlerian "Striving for Superiority", or else an equivalent to the appetitive behavior of animals seeking stimulation, the difficulty disappears. [3]

What we learn from psychotherapy is applicable to the growing child: if the authority present, either therapist or parent, condemns the activity before the child has established that beachhead of ability and power, the child will have difficulty establishing it later and will probably learn it with some admixture of hostile aggression. Thereafter he will tend to do the act in question with some anger and rebellion to compensate for the condemnation of the authority.

In origin the infant shows his power and aggressiveness always in conjunction with its opposite—i.e., with his need to be dependent and to be nourished. The whole process of growing up can be seen as beginning with the severing of the biological tie to the mother (when he is born from the womb, where everything was done for him automatically). After the cutting of the umbilical cord, he has to learn to form relationships on a psychological basis. Each venturing forth represents a use of his individual power and ability, and he then comes back to his mother.[4] The nutrient side of this development manifests itself in his need to be cared for and to be loved, and the aggressive side in his need to assert himself, to protest if necessary. The former is the "yes," the latter the "no." If his aggressiveness is blocked, as is often the case with suburban middle-class children, he will tend to remain forever dependent. Or if his need for love and care is unmet, he may well become destructively aggressive and spend his life wreaking revenge upon the world—as is sometimes the case with children brought up in the slums. Or if he has no boundaries, nothing against which to test his strength, no opposition in the firmness of parents, he may turn his aggression against himself in nail-biting and self-recrimination or senseless anger against anyone who happens to come along.

The child's mobility can be seen as a way of increasing the distance he can move from his mother. It is a practice of independence from her, a practice which increases through life regardless of where his actual mother is or whether she is alive or dead.

An unfortunate upbringing can and does turn the individual's powers to destructive ends. A female patient was periodically seized by uncontrollable anger against her husband and children, in which she would loose endless invectives and pound her husband in rage with her fists. It turned out that she had been the daughter of a prostitute, and that when she was a very small child she had often been used by her mother as a "conversation piece" to make contacts with different men in cafés. Then the mother would take the man to her room, while the child sat at the table for an hour or so alone. During her school years she lived with her grandparents and was generally ostracized by the people in the village because of her upbringing. She recalled going to the houses of women who gossiped about her and then defecating on their doorsteps as revenge. When other children had parties to which she was not invited, she would often go to the edge of the group and ask for some ice cream and cake. She had developed a sense of caring in feeding her rabbits and other animals at home, but this affection was a lonely one, and she had never overcome her nervousness in an intimate situation with her peers. It is entirely understandable that such an upbringing would lead to destructive rage and aggression in later human situations.

The normal development of an infant requires the love and care of the parent along with his own capacity to explore and increase his sense of mastery day by day. Storr has said: " 'Let me do it' is a recurrent entreaty in small children; and wise mothers encourage their children to do as much as possible for themselves, however tiresome it may be to wait patiently while the child takes minutes to tie a knot which the adult can tie in seconds." [5] Storr does not believe that reading *Grimm's Fairy-Tales* and playing cops and robbers and war games is harmful for children. The child has no difficulty separating fantasy from reality, and he needs to work out his aggressive tendencies in fantasy if they are not to be acted out in reality. Quoting Winnicott again, "If society is in danger, it is not because of man's aggressiveness but because of the repression of personal aggressiveness in individuals," Storr goes on to propose that parents who are anxious that their children not turn into warmongers may, by proscribing war games and the like, be cultivating just the opposite. They "are more likely to create the very type of personality which they are concerned to avoid." [6] For the child needs all the aggressive potential he can get to protect and assert his growing individuality.

2. THE LIFE OF OLIVER

Parts of the psychoanalysis of a young man will demonstrate what happens when an individual's power cannot be admitted consciously and openly. The power is not erased but comes out in a myriad of other, separate ways. These ways may be camouflaged power or they may be pseudopower.

Oliver, a Ph.D. student, good-looking, tall, appeared younger than his twenty-six years. He was the third and last child of an affluent Jewish family of which the oldest child, Oliver's brother, who was nine years his senior, had always been successful both socially and on the athletic field. Oliver's sister, who was seven years older, had been in some form of therapy most of her life, had been hospitalized after a schizophrenic breakdown, and had been mute for two years in the mental hospital where she now was. His father, the treasurer of a large chain of stores, was detached, successful at work, and hypochondriacal at home—kind at times, but completely unpredictable, wanting the children to be "sweet" to him and reacting to family fights by becoming sick and withdrawing.

Oliver's mother, who had been and still was a beauty, dominated the family constellation. She was flighty, subtle, inconsistent, intelligent, and in arguments would change her viewpoint with every sentence in order to put the other person on the defensive. She had "spoiled" Oliver—preparing special things he liked to eat, driving him to school so that he wouldn't have to take the subway like the other boys—and was more than glad when Oliver, who disliked school consistently and strongly, would feign illness in order to stay home with her. She was seductive toward him, actively opposing Oliver's ineffectual efforts later to date girls. The meal table was a constant battlefield of bickering, with one member of the family not speaking to another for weeks on end. This technique of "cutting the resented person dead" ("I would walk by my father as though he wasn't there," said Oliver) was resorted to particularly by Oliver and his sister, the weakest members of the family. Oliver's sister eventually enlarged the pattern to include the whole world by her muteness at the hospital.

Our opening question is: How was Oliver to achieve any power in such a family and such a world? Caught in a double bind, with a mother who would change her stance at the drop of a word, with a father who would withdraw with the threat of heart attack whenever the smoldering undercover warfare of the family burst out into the open, a pawn between his sister who was mentally disturbed and a "successful" brother who did come to protect Oliver at school but teased him mercilessly at home—what was Oliver to do? Should he try, now that he had grown to six feet and was good-looking, to assert himself on the social scale? But the girls at high school had always called him the "little shrimp" (which he had been), and this still bedogged him. The athletic field? He was a "stinker" there; and besides his brother had completely usurped that mode of recognition. Intellectually? For his entire life, until he got into college, he had hated school, didn't prepare his work. All of this in spite of the fact that he basically was highly imaginative and, as it later turned out, demonstrated a rich mind and active intelligence.

In his boyhood he presents the picture of the "little fellow," who had learned early to be "sweet" to others, never to blow up, and, like the little countries in Europe in the eighteenth century, to get some protection by making alliances with different important members of the family. This self-deprecation pattern went so far, he confessed, that he preferred to be *disliked* in high school (the other boys had for him a disparaging nickname, "Sappo") because that at least brought him some attention.

Where does his power go? When he was sixteen he had had two epileptic attacks and had been on a daily dose of dilantin since. These attacks are interesting for our purpose as a symptom of the seething caldron of emotions underneath the surface in Oliver. Whatever these attacks show physically, the psychological dimension is generally a massive rage. This rage builds up and finally explodes in the periodic seizure. The explosion is blotted out of consciousness, so the individual never has to be aware of, or has to be responsible for, what he does. But it turns out to be violence directed chiefly against *himself*—the person himself gets physically hurt, to a greater or lesser degree, as he falls at the time of the seizure. Furthermore he is, like Oliver, chronically crippled by having this Damocles' Sword hanging over his head, never knowing when it will fall. All the while Oliver denied this, saying: "I never get emotional or upset—I saw what it does to my sister so I vowed I'd never get that way."

Oliver's dreams early in the therapy were frequently of thieves breaking into the house, which was a kind of fortress for him. The only thing he could do was to play dead, the ultimate symbol of impotence and innocence:

> A group of thieves was in the house. Someone came downstairs—
> I curled up as though dead. He looked at me a long time. After
> a while I went outside. The thieves grabbed . . . me. Then a
> crowd of people were outside, where a woman began to chase
> me with a meat cleaver in her hand, and then a man took the
> cleaver and began to chase me.

"I remember moments of unhappiness," said Oliver, "never any joy in our family. I learned to roll with the punch in family fights, to go along, never to expect anything—you get hurt that way. Why struggle? It is painful, and I learned early never to believe in pain of any sort. . . . Nobody paid any attention to my feelings. I was always belittled." Later in the therapy, there came out a symbol which betrays his image of his own hidden power: "I was like Gulliver, all tied up with ropes by Lilliputians."

His only happy time over any period was the year he went to Israel. The Israeli-Arab war was beginning, and he covered it for an American newspaper. He looks back upon this period with fond memories; he loved the excitement, the enforced relationship with death in his walking along the Gaza strip among the bodies of fallen soldiers. For a brief period he felt himself to be of some significance.

He was twenty-four at this time, and he fell in love with a girl —the first time he had even been in love. The occasion, as distinguished from the cause, of his coming for psychoanalysis was his turmoil over whether to marry this girl or not. His family was aligned against her, but when I met her she seemed a sympathetic though somewhat hysterical person who, despite her impoverished upbringing, was someone to whom Oliver could talk and who gave him some recognition.

About three months after his psychotherapy started, he told me that he believed he could influence distant objects to change. He was shy and hesitant in telling me this, saying he knew it sounded irrational and adding that if I did not believe what he said he could not tell me. I replied that my task was not to argue the truth or falsehood of such ideas; but to find out what function they served for him; and obviously the ideas were significant for him. This apparently satisfied him, for he then began to reveal a whole system of belief in "retribution" at the hands of God and in harm being meted out to *others* as punishment for wrongs they had done.

When he awakens in the morning, he must think of his family or else they would get hurt. He must lift the sheets up two feet,

look at an exact spot on the wall, stand up exactly the right way
on the floor, go to the bathroom and urinate, all before he exchanged a word with anyone. He must take his clothes out, put
on his undershirt, sit down on the bed and put his left shoe on
first, then his trousers. If he makes a mistake in this ritual, he
must go back to bed and start the whole thing over. After that he
must say "good morning" to Mary (the maid) or to his brother.
At breakfast he has to eat in the same rigid order; he must drink
his orange juice, then eat his egg, then drink milk. And so on.

When he does something wrong in this system, his father will
have a heart attack or something will happen to his mother. Punishment and happiness, he believed, were portioned out by God.
Several years earlier he had been relatively happy when enrolled
in journalism school. As a "result" his grandmother died. Another time he mentioned that his grandmother had died because
he had placed the book *Huckleberry Finn* in a certain position on
his desk or because of the way he had placed his pennies on his
dresser. When I, testing the rigidity of the system, asked whether
his grandmother might not have died anyway, he replied, not at
that time or in some other way. If he does right, others will
benefit; if he does wrong, others, especially those in his own
family, will get sick or have accidents. He cannot have sexual intercourse in any complete sense, nor must he enjoy it very much.
Coitus interruptus had been the "right" way. When, about that
time, he did have complete intercourse, he waited in fear for several days for the retribution to fall. Surely enough, two days later
his mother was mugged and robbed in the train station in a
neighboring city.

What strikes us immediately in this complex system is the *tremendous power* it gives him. Any chance deed of his could decide
whether someone lived or died. He even had power over the
weather: "When it rains, the rain is sent by God to punish me."
He actually *controlled* the universe that way. "I have to control
everything about my life. I could not live if I did not control the

future." It is worthy of note that "control" was one of Oliver's favorite words, and he used it often.[7]

I contented myself at first by remarking that he must feel as if he were in a strait jacket with all those rigid compulsions, and didn't he find it a heavy weight upon him? He agreed that it was difficult, but he had no choice. Moreover, he had not been able to read *Faust* when in high school because of all the "demons" running around in it, and even *Mary Poppins* was prohibited when it became filled with devils. He could not say the word that goes before *Yankees* in the title of a contemporary play. As I supplied the word *Damn*, I remarked that saying such words must be a prime requisite of a modern fiction writer (Oliver's professional goal) and that this inhibition must bother him a great deal.

He did see the vast power that his system gave him, after I had pointed it out to him. He had lived as a child, he knew, in such emotional disorder that he had to have something solid. He was compensating for a boyhood that was completely powerless. "I would allow people to use me to build themselves up," he said; and one can be sure Oliver has to take revenge. The neurotic power (or magic) is in direct proportion to the early powerlessness. Such a person will not and *cannot* give up his "system" until he experiences some real power in the actual world. That Oliver had plenty of threats against which to protect himself is shown in several dreams that occurred during the weeks he was telling me about his retribution system. One was: "I was left in the house alone. A masked man and woman disguised as my mother and father broke into our house to attack me." He also often dreamed of the Mafia, and suddenly asked one day: "Is my mother this Mafia, the enemy?"

> Sometimes pain is the punishment or is an alleviating factor. I then can give up the compulsions. Generally the compulsion doesn't affect my life, but it leaves me very frightened. In some ways it is like voodoo. I keep thinking maybe I've done something I shouldn't. I don't want to be responsible for all those things happening.

What does this last sentence say? Not that Oliver doesn't want the controlling system to continue—it gives his life a tremendous sense of significance—but that he doesn't want to accept *responsibility* for the power. It is to be kept secret, not admitted openly; he is a controller of life and death for countless people related to him, and no one but he knows it. This way he can preserve his façade of innocence. This hypothesis accords with his statement that the compulsions had reached their height just before his Bar Mitzvah (the conventional rite of passage of the youth out of boyhood and into the responsible community of adults).

Despite our good relationship—I liked working with him and I knew he liked and valued working with me—he had a variety of techniques for belittling and demeaning me. "Your eyes were filled with tears," he remarked about a dream. "I want to ride you, but not to have you offended." This is a perfect paradigm for a system in which he could hurt others but remain perfectly innocent himself. These "upmanship" techniques must have been exactly the ones he had been subjected to all his life. He had learned them from the masters. At least the techniques must have been successful; he didn't go schizophrenic as had his sister.

But how humiliating it must have been for him to have to put himself in the position of needing and asking for help—thus he had to work out some covert system of secret control over me while he was doing so. He was, as he later said, a puppeteer, pulling wires, in reality or in fantasy, to direct me, his girl friend, his professors, and everyone around him. He was "weak," greatly needing me, trying to maneuver me into taking responsibility for the therapy, at the same time trying to direct both of us from some hidden position. He must, at all costs, not let his power come out into the open or let himself be *seen* as powerful; he must forever remain the innocent little boy. To make me *responsible but powerless*—this was the bind he tried to put me in. It must also be the bind he himself had been in all his life.

The pattern of God and retributions, I proposed, must have the effect of reversing the above pattern: it must be a way that he can be *powerful with no responsibility*. This young man had no confidence in the possibility of his changing; change must come from the outside. This conviction was necessary to keep the whole retribution system intact. He gets his power by being secretly allied with God. All power remains with God; God *requires* that he, Oliver, have no autonomous power to assert himself. If he once decided that he could make a fateful decision on his own, God himself would be challenged and the whole system would fall away like mist under the morning sun. Taking responsibility upon himself, asserting his own autonomy, was challenging God and committing the sin of hubris.

This pattern of overt innocence and covert power may be seen in Oliver's dream of the wolf in rabbit's skin (mentioned in Chapter Two), which seemed to be exactly the game he was playing, hiding his power—indeed, his ferocity—under a rabbit's skin.

In the middle of the analysis, there came a good deal of talk about killing. He would like to kill his father, mow down everyone on the subway with a machine gun; in dreams, he had men come into my office and shoot me. He described with relish the sadistic pleasure he had gotten as a child out of setting fire to grasshoppers and ants and watching them writhe as they burned. As he talked about his father and brother, he sounded like a latter-day Hannibal, proclaiming that he would never forget their cruelty and vowing to revenge himself. His associations during one hour were: "My penis is small . . . I'm always shorter than others [he then realizes this is no longer true] . . . violence . . . choking . . . I'm not puny any longer . . . taking over a city . . . *life has suddenly become important.*"

During the country-wide wave of student protests in May, 1970, after the invasion of Cambodia and the Kent State shootings, Oliver took part in the spontaneous protests and marches in New York, particularly on Wall Street. Since he was in psychoanalysis at the time, his words carry a special revelatory character that comes from his closeness to his own unconscious phenomena. I quote from an hour at that time:

> I had a spontaneous feeling that I was caught up in something above human desires to be achieved. . . .
>
> Business as usual was thrown out the window. . . .
>
> You forget your bodily needs and cares. . . . You channel everything through the group.
>
> The group was marvelous to see and marvelous to be part of— and I was part of it.

It is clear that he is caught up in an experience of elation or what I call "ecstasy" in a later chapter. He also is absorbed in his group and experiences the relief from individual moral responsibility which this gives him. It does not—strange to say, since responsibility is so difficult for him—preclude a strong feeling of responsibility for his group. After the attack of the hard-hats upon the student protesters, when he had been a couple of blocks from the melee, he moaned:

> Oh, damn it—I saw it coming—I saw the hard-hats waiting down that street, I could have shouted to the line: "Go down this other street!" but I didn't have the presence of mind. Damn it to hell!

An aura of joy was experienced by Oliver at the beginning of these protests. He appeared to me to be at his psychologically "healthiest" of any time I had known him—that is, at his most direct, most integrated, feeling things with his whole self and being able to say what he felt. The only other time in his life he had felt similarly integrated and authentic was during those weeks when he had been a reporter covering the Israeli-Arab war and had walked through battlefields with dead bodies around him. There is a quality of being at the boundary of life, *in extremis*, which is part of the self-transcendence in this elation.

But we also see in Oliver how very close despair is to violence. Two weeks later he went to Washington to take part in the larger

student protest march. He returned discouraged. He characterized the day's proceedings as having been "interesting but futile."
As he talked, he became increasingly despondent. He finally
mused: "When I was coming here this morning, I saw old ladies
going into the supermarket with their little bags to get groceries.
I would like to shoot them all." [8] This impulse toward violence is
verbalized because this young man is in the special situation of
analysis and has a more-open-than-usual relation to his unconscious proddings. But we can safely assume that the same kinds
of violent impulses are present, if not expressed, in many (if not
all) people when they are despairing.

He later saw the inadequacy of mere protests. They are negative, made always *against* something else, thus borrowing their
nature from what they are attacking. "Almost all my decisions are
negative ones—I get my anger up against my parents, Magda, and
you. Always I am strong, energetic; then, I become very active.
No guilt, then—no anxiety. Always *against* somebody else, or
what somebody else set up." He sees that a person is thus able to
avoid the more difficult task of responsibly working out the values
required by the future.

During this whole period, Oliver was making steady progress in
his practical life. He had moved out of his parents' apartment; he
had passed his doctoral exams; and his reliance on his system of
"retribution" had diminished greatly (and was now almost always
called "superstition"). He had been offered and had accepted a
teaching position which he genuinely liked, a literary magazine
he had started was flourishing, and his over-all relations with
women had become much less anxiety-ridden and more gratifying.
The problems at the moment seemed to focus on his relationship
with Magda.

She had continually pressed him to marry her. When he had
brought up the question, I remarked that since he obviously did
not want to, why marry now? Although they had some real attachment for each other they still had too many unclarified problems

to make any marriage workable. In saying these things, I was aware that I was taking from Oliver some of the responsibility for making the decision. But as he progressed in therapy, I pointed out that he could not forever rely on me as the "good" parent to make these decisions for him, and that sooner or later he would have to take these decisions upon himself.

While I was away for a week, Oliver abruptly married Magda. He was immediately overcome with the conviction that it was a mistake. The motives for the act were many: everything else in his life was going too well; he wanted to prove he was a man and could marry; he wanted to take revenge on me for going away and leaving him; and so on. Magda and he immediately intensified their tormenting and punishing of each other. Their attachment seemed to include a large amount of hatred, and they seemed bent on destroying each other. Oliver soon came to the resolution to wait till the exam period at the university for Magda was past and then get an annulment. This, despite the difficulties, he did.

But what is important is that this "trial marriage" gave us the chance to work on an important problem in Oliver's life which, so far, had barely been touched. This was his sister, then in the sanatorium. Magda and his schizophrenic sister liked each other and were similar in many respects—they were often identified in Oliver's mind. The punishment and torment which he received from and gave to Magda paralleled the sadomasochistic relationship he had had with his sister. This all came tumbling out now in a rush.

> I hated my sister yet I loved her. . . . She'd dote on me; she was my guardian, my closest friend. I learned my way of life from her . . . my interest in poetry, literature, the imagination. But I never could figure out what mood she'd be in. She tormented me, twisted my arm. . . . I went to bed hating her with a great violent hatred. I used to set her up for fights with my mother. . . . I was glad when she went to the sanatorium; it showed I'd won out over her. . . . If she went crazy, I figured I'd go the same way when I got to be her age.

His main feelings were guilt for the part he had played in her schizophrenia. He felt triumphant because of her difficulties; he felt he had helped destroy her (which he was now doing to Magda). He also felt the need for punishment, which would allay the guilt. He must suffer as much as she. All of these patterns were directly carried over into his relations with Magda. They had set up a relationship that remarkably duplicated the original situation with his sister. He got his orientation, his anchor in life, out of experiencing punishment and suffering at Magda's hands and by being sadistic to her in return. The clarification of this bind to his sister relieved him perceptibly and freed him of a great deal of his bind to Magda.

Oliver's life illustrates how power is bound to come out if all constructive ways are blocked, sadism being one alternative. More than that, it illustrates again the positive as well as negative aspects of rage. "Depression," he had remarked, "is like starting a small fire to stop a big forest fire. I got depressed to avoid my rage toward my sister. I wanted to kill her, yell at her, 'You ruined my life. Stay in the sanatorium!'" But he later saw the constructive use of rage. "Rage is the dynamic which makes me autonomous, independent of my parents. If I don't have my rage, I don't have my strength."

We recall that the rehabilitation of drug addicts depends on their "angry energy." And also that Mercedes's violence, which is an expression of rage, had both life-giving as well as life-denying aspects. Oliver is here making the same discovery in his own experience and own insights.

3. SELF-AFFIRMATION

Inherent in power-to-be is the need to affirm one's own being.[9] This, the second level in our spectrum, is the quiet, undramatic form of self-belief. It arises from an original feeling of worth imparted to the infant through the love of a parent or parents in the early months, and it shows itself later on in life as a sense of dignity. The word *dignity*, coming from the Latin *dignus*, "worthy," means a "feeling of intrinsic worth," an essential for every mentally healthy human being.

Many things may happen to this initial longing to be valued. In the instance of Priscilla we can picture her saying: "I'm worth something, but *nobody* in the world knows it." Mercedes, we can imagine, would have said: "I'm not worth anything, and I'm not supposed to be except when others can use me sexually." Oliver lived by the formula: "I'm not worth anything, but allied with God I am worth everything in the world."

The error many persons make, illustrated by Oliver, is that of bypassing self-affirmation and jumping straight from powerlessness into aggression and violence. When one has always been powerless, the heady feeling one gets when he first realizes he does have power seems to be intoxicating. It is as though he had to summon up adrenalin in order to experience the fact that he has "power to be," and once the adrenalin is present, he moves on the strength of it into aggressive behavior. Hence persons in therapy often go through periods of being what their friends and family call "excessively aggressive" just after they realize their own power to be. This aggression or violence can burn like a bonfire, but is generally no more than a temporary exercise. If self-affirmation, as a step in a person's development, is omitted or given short shrift, something of great value is lost. It is self-affirmation that gives the staying capacity and depth to one's power to be.

Many in our culture tend to deny self-affirmation on moral grounds. They have been taught that this urge is "selfish" or "egocentric" in the pejorative sense, and that the way to "love" others is to "hate" yourself. This is one of the most thoroughly anachronistic aspects of our deteriorated puritanism: Sullivan's thesis, that our attitudes toward others parallel our attitudes toward ourselves and that a basic love for ourselves is necessary if we are to love others, has now been proved beyond any doubt. The Biblical precept means what it says: Love your neighbor not as you hate yourself but as you love yourself. Therapeutically, it often helps to cast the patient's behavior into perspective by reminding him, "You wouldn't treat another person as badly as you treat yourself."

The confidence that one has worth is normally picked up first from the attitudes of a mother or mother-surrogate toward the infant, and is then cultivated in the family by loyalty to the infant. As the child grows this initial feeling is reinforced by persons outside the family in their appreciation for him and his potentialities. Later, the more mature human being seems to keep within his memories, to refer to in difficult times, the images of those people who have believed in him. When I was in college I found the experience of having some adult believing in me crucially important; and at times thereafter in my life when I was faced with fateful decisions, I found myself casting about to fasten upon one of these persons. It was not that he or she would, in my memory, tell me what to do. It was rather that at such a time it was important for my own psychological security to find somebody who believed in me. This "belief" included his or her liking me, although it was not chiefly that; it included his confidence in my abilities and other qualities which the reader can experience through his own treasuring of such persons in memory better than through my attempt at enumeration.

Part of the aim of psychotherapy is to help the individual in the steady, often long-term building up of his own self-affirmation. With Oliver this came in the form of the day-to-day affirmations of himself, less dramatic (so that they rarely get into our notes, and then into case histories) and often hesitantly made, in every session. His dreams began to show a small amount of awareness of his own power: "I was climbing a ladder in which the rungs were weak, but I kept it working by holding the sides together." Again: "I tamed some horses." Or: "I wish I could do such and such." Or: "I think I can accomplish it." I would always make sure he knew I had heard such statements by responding in some way. Perhaps at the time I did not believe he could do the thing he wished (if I would fake it he would in some way sense it), but I would affirm him by saying: "I too hope that someday you can do it" or "I don't see why you can't do it eventually."

One way of avoiding this less dramatic but necessary step is shown in Oliver's approach to one of his dreams. That morning he had come in saying three times in three sentences: "It's hard." Talking in a weak voice he related the following:

> I was with my brother in a rowboat on the Hudson—then we, or rather I, lost the oars. We were then swimming upstream. I said to my brother: "Why don't you rest on my shoulders?" He put his hands on my shoulders and I began to sink. I cried out, thinking I would drown, and he got off. We landed. Then he wanted to keep swimming. I said: "No, the river is polluted." He acted as though it didn't matter, and he swam down from the George Washington Bridge. I asked about the dirt in the river, and he said: "No, there wasn't much, just a little around the shore." My father was waiting for him.

When Oliver talked of this dream he spoke of the water as representing the mother figure and the vagina; he was afraid of pollution; he would get a terrible disease; and he brought God and punishment into the discussion. I kept asking: Where are the indications in the dream of all these cosmic, grandiose things? The dream seemed to be a realistic representation of his problems. Sure, he *is* swimming upstream, and he *does* have some real problems to be met; but why the esoteric references all the time? Does he have some special reason for this tragic pose, as when he came into the office moaning? At this point Oliver relaxed perceptibly. He averred it made life interesting never to see things as they really are; it kept everything superficial, "so grandiose I just grope around. It's never a problem—it's God's cosmic action."

Whatever the esoteric meaning of the dream, the purpose of his dreaming seemed eminently practical. He put his brother into it, the most down-to-earth member of the family, who had at least worked out a modus vivendi in relating to the mother. Why not take the chances his brother took? The fact that he dreamed it at all shows he was considering the idea. It is, of course, easier to preserve his innocence by shifting the discussion to cosmic, grandiose levels; but I believe he should be kept to the concrete, realistic considerations first.

The fact that a human being can be self-conscious vastly increases his need for self-affirmation. We can know we affirm ourselves; or we can experience the lack of self-affirmation and feel shame. In man, nature and being are not identical. But for my kitten, romping around the room, nature and being *are* identical —it becomes a cat regardless of what it does about it. A cat does not bear the burden of self-consciousness or of *knowing* that it knows; and while it escapes the guilt of this experience, it is also bereft of its glory. In the oak tree nature and being are also identical: the acorn grows into an oak if the physical conditions are right; and it is not burdened with thinking about it or even knowing it.

Consciousness is the intervening variable between nature and being. It vastly enlarges the human being's dimensions; it makes possible in him a sense of awareness, responsibility, and a margin of freedom proportionate to this responsibility. The reflective nature of human consciousness accounts for the fact that studies of animal behavior cast only peripheral light on human aggression. The human being can be infinitely more cruel and can destroy for the sadistic pleasure of it—a "privilege" that is denied animals. All of this follows from the fact that in the human being nature and being are not identical.

Thus man becomes a self only as he participates in his development and throws his weight behind this or that tendency, no matter how limited this choice may be. The self never develops automatically; man becomes a self only to the extent that he can know it, affirm it, assert it. This is why Nietzsche continually proclaims the need for commitment and dedication. And this is why man is infinitely more educable than animals and the rest of nature; being less instinctually guided, he can, through his own awareness, influence to some extent his own evolution. Therein lies the collective shame and bewilderment of being a man, and therein also lies the greatness of being one.

4. SELF-ASSERTION

An incident taken from the life of Mercedes will illustrate the transition from self-affirmation to the next level in our spectrum, self-assertion.

Mercedes had to cash a check at the store to pay for her groceries:

> I went to the manager's office to ask him to O.K. the check for me. A woman called him, so he closed the door. I stood by the door a few minutes, then knocked. He opened and said: "We have no money to give out today. . . . I don't have time now, I'll do it later." Then I went around the store getting my groceries. I saw two white ladies go up to him and he O.K.'d their checks. I went back to him but he said: "No, no, I can't now," and sent me to another man who, it turned out, didn't have authority to O.K. checks.
>
> All that night I couldn't sleep. The next day I went back and said to him: "You hurt me yesterday." He apologized and O.K.'d my check all right.

When I thought about this incident after the session, I had the feeling that it was somehow incomplete. At her next session I asked her again about the incident. She turned to me, looking embarrassed and continued with a half-smile:

> I didn't tell you all yesterday. The first time I went up to him I was wearing curlers and looked frozzy. The next day I fixed myself up. I put a face on. My breasts are larger now since I'm nursing, I let my coat hang partly open. When I came up to him

he said: "Can I do anything for you?" Then I explained about yesterday and how I had not wanted any money, just to pay for groceries. He said he had turned me down because the two white ladies had wanted cash. He put his hand on my shoulder and called me "dear," said he was sorry he had hurt me.

As I laughed, Mercedes said she hadn't told me that because she was ashamed of the incident.

I entirely agree with those who protest that Mercedes is using her sex as a vehicle for her self-assertion. I do not agree, however, with those who say it is merely an extension of her earlier pattern of prostitution. It is now a consciously used strategy, not one to which she is forced to accede by her situation. We are discussing here the *fact* of self-assertion, not the means.

When self-affirmation no longer works—which Mercedes, in this incident, realized as she lay awake that night—the individual gathers his or her powers together to pit against the opposition.

A curious aspect of self-assertion is that human beings often *seek out* opposition in order to practice assertion. This, again, indicates that self-assertion is not pathological but a constructive expression of the power to be. One can observe this relatively early in children, in the second to fourth years. They will "test the limits," see how far they have to go to invite the opposition of parents, cross the parents for the sake of crossing them, say "no" for the sake of saying "no."

Dr. Charlotte Buhler has pointed out that when the environment has introduced the moral issue—for instance, a four-year-old's assertion is bad because it is in opposition to his mother's demands —the child may concern himself with the question of "good" and "bad" in ways quite different from what the mother expects. Thus Peter, four, was "overheard speaking loudly to himself and asking, 'Is he a good boy? Or is he a bad boy?' To which followed a stubborn declaration brought forth with glee, 'No, bad boy is he.' " [10]

In this seeking out of opposition, the child will often refuse to do something he is told, standing in the middle of the floor with just a suggestion of a smile on his face as though he somehow knows that this is all a game anyway. The sensible parent accepts this behavior not as a reason for increasing the guilt feeling of the child nor as a pretext for giving in—which would only mean that the child has to try harder to find some other issue in which to get bona fide opposition. For what he wants is to try out his "psychological muscles." It is a normal and necessary aspect of growing—a will to self-assertion is "practiced" by the child. Folklore is full of references to the child going out "to learn to shiver and to shake," as the German nursery rhyme puts it.

Unless there is an actual encounter or the potentiality for an actual encounter, as Paul Tillich brings out, an individual's power of being remains hidden. The power to be becomes evident in the continual struggles of being against nonbeing, in Tillich's words, Tillich seeing nonbeing as all aspects that negate and destroy being. These include conformism, which destroys uniqueness and originality; hostility, which shrinks courage, generosity, and capacity to understand the other; destructiveness; and, eventually, death itself. We have being to the extent that we can absorb nonbeing into ourselves. "A life process is the more powerful, the more non-being it can include in its self-affirmation, without being destroyed by it." [11] The aim is not to overlook or repress expressions of nonbeing, but to confront them directly, accept them as necessity, endeavor to absorb them—all of which reduces their destructive power. Out of this struggle comes creativity.

Being is manifested only in the process of actualizing its power; otherwise how could we even be aware of it, let alone know its ramifications? Power becomes actualized in those situations in which opposition is overcome.

Nietzsche saw this aspect of the will and gave us a way of gauging it: "I estimate the *power of a will* according to how much resistance, pain, and torture it endures and knows how to transform to its own advantage." [12] "Every smallest step in the field of free thinking, and of the personally formed life, has ever been fought for at the cost of spiritual and physical tortures. . . . Nothing has been bought more dearly than that little bit of human reason and freedom which is now the basis for our pride." [13] He believed that this is *necessarily* so—ease and affluence are the enemies and corrode and undermine the development of the authentic self. Life is a pitting of the self against difficulties; we hear Nietzsche saying time and again: "Life consists of self-overcoming." He scorned the Darwinian concept of a struggle for existence, contending rather that "all living creatures, far from tending to preserve their existence, strive to enhance themselves, to grow, and to generate more life." In doing this they *risk* their existence. He writes in *Thus Spake Zarathustra:* "'This secret Life itself confided to me: 'See, it said, I am that *which must ever overcome itself.* Indeed, you call it will to generation or drive to an end, to something higher, farther, more manifold: but all this is one.'"

This is why power cannot, strictly speaking, be given to another, for then the recipient still owes it to the giver. It must in some sense be assumed, taken, asserted. For unless it can be held *against* opposition, it is not power and will never be experienced as real on the part of the recipient.

SEVEN

AGGRESSION

Item: the *New York Times*:

> A man walked into a tobacco store in Brooklyn at
> 9:00 at night. The store was owned and run by an
> elderly couple who had survived a concentration
> camp in Germany before escaping to this country.
> The man asked for money and the elderly couple
> answered that they had practically none in the store.
> He shot them in cold blood and walked out.

Item: Piet Mondrian in a letter to James Johnson Sweeney of
the Solomon R. Guggenheim Museum:

> My style of painting is this: First I had to annihilate
> the form by reducing it to lines, color and circles.
> . . . Then I had to destroy the color. . . . Then I
> had to tear out the circles to leave only the planes
> and lines. . . . My art consists of the purest possible
> line and proportion.
>
> Yours, sincerely,
> Mondrian

We would all agree that the first example above is one of wanton
aggression and violence, and we would find ourselves talking
about psychopathology. But if we were to ask, in a context other

than this one, whether the second is also an example of aggression, many people would look surprised and answer certainly not. But look at the words "annihilate," "destroy," "tear out"—these are surely aggressive. Appearing to outsiders as a quiet, unassuming man, Piet Mondrian was, in his art, engaged in strong aggression against traditional forms. There is considerable power in hoary academic traditions, reflected in our early education and art schools and galleries; and Mondrian was energetically committed to breaking and restructuring them.

It is true that the first item describes acts committed against persons and the second against impersonal plastic forms. But we cannot define aggression on a sheer personal basis. The so-called impersonal enemies—such as cancer or totalitarianism—are not at all powerless. Shall we make our criterion of aggression how much influence the aggressive power has? If so, then we find that the forms of art for and against which Mondrian was battling are at the very center of our psychic life and will influence people on deeper levels for centuries to come.

Aggression has many more facets than is customarily recognized.

1. THE MEANING OF AGGRESSION

In contrast to self-assertion, which may be simply a holding fast —"Here I stand; you can come this far and no farther"—aggression is a moving out, a thrust toward the person or thing seen as the adversary. Its aim is to cause a shift in power for the interests of one's self or what one is devoted to. Aggression is the action that moves into another's territory to accomplish a restructuring of power. This fourth level in our spectrum occurs because of the individual's or group's conviction that the restructuring cannot come by self-affirmation or self-assertion.

Perhaps the aggressor wants land and resources, as nations do when they annex the other's territory in war. Or perhaps the aggressor has an intellectual stake in the change, as Mondrian did in his new art forms. Or perhaps the aggression grows out of a hatred of injustice, like that of Frantz Fanon in calling the blacks of Africa to rebel; or has a spiritual aim, like that of the abolitionists. Whatever the aim and motive may be, and without reference at the moment to when it is justified and when it is not, aggression itself consists of the endeavor to seize some of the power, prestige, or status of the other for one's self or for the ideas to which one is devoted.

Aggression emerges on the spectrum at that point where overt *conflict* also emerges. Although conflict may be faintly detected in self-affirmation and may be even slightly more noticeable in self-assertion, on those levels it is typically directed *inward*. An example is Mercedes' lying awake at night smarting over the store manager's rejection of her. There is a conflict *within* me, for another example, when I get my nerve up to assert myself before a large audience to ask a question of the speaker; the conflict may then be invisible to the outside world. But in aggression there is no question about the *overt* conflict. There occurs a pitting of interest against interest, and the aggressive act is an endeavor to come to some resolution in this conflict.

A Pandora's box of moral maladies is opened if, following the habit in America, we condemn aggression as evil as soon as it shows its head. To that kind of thinking, the power of the status quo is automatically beneficent and God-given, whether it be the state troopers going in to slaughter at Attica or the police quelling a Chicano riot; just as automatically the rebel is seen as evil. Thus we have the tendency to label one act as aggressive and, therefore, to be condemned when performed by those *out* of power, and to label the exact same act as good when performed by those *in* power (or vice versa).

The reason aggression terrifies people so much is that it involves the potentiality of force. The force in aggression can take away our lives in the physical, intellectual, or spiritual sense. Physical force is understood well enough. Intellectual aggression may have the same compelling quality, as in abrasive argument—especially *argumentum ad hominem*. Or the coercion may be spiritual, as in the threat of ostracism or excommunication. That this last can be a great threat is shown by the phenomenon known as "voodoo death." A condemned person who is "cut dead" in primitive society, as a punishment, say, for breaking one of the taboos, falls to the ground; his pulse becomes thready; he pants and breathes hard; and in a few hours he dies.[1] Even in advanced societies "cutting one dead" is an aggressive act that is both psychological and spiritual and produces potent results.

The Janus-faced nature of aggression can be seen in that word's Latin root *aggredi*, which means "to go forward, to approach." Primarily, this means "to approach someone for counsel or advice." Second, it means "to move against" or "to move with intent to hurt." In other words, aggression in origin is pure conjuncture, a reaching out, a making contact either for friendly affirmation of yourself and another or for hostile purposes the way a bear hug is part of a pugilist's technique. The opposite of aggression is not loving peace or consideration or friendship, but isolation, the state of no contact at all. This is actually the state of the person— the understanding of whom may be obtained by looking within one's self and not necessarily observing in a mental hospital—who can brook no rebuke of what he does or thinks; soon he can accept no correction; and, finally, no comment at all. He becomes totally isolated from other persons.

As so often happens in psychotherapy, when the patient expresses some negation—"I feel you are attacking me. I can't stand that . . ."—or when the therapist says: "What you're saying makes me angry; let's see why," both together can explore what sensitive spot was hit. When these aspects of aggression are worked through, there is not only a clearing of the air but both arrive at a new and deeper understanding of the other and, generally—since we love people for their faults as well as their virtues—a greater affection for the other too.

The constructive forms of aggression include cutting through barriers to initiate a relationship; confronting another without intent to hurt but with intent to penetrate into his consciousness; warding off powers that threaten one's integrity; actualizing one's own self and one's own ideas in hostile environments; overcoming the barriers to healing.

Love-making and fighting are very similar neurophysiologically in human beings. Anthony Storr points out that lovers' quarrels often end up in sexual intercourse.[2] There is a strange relationship between the fighter and the lover: the knight rescuing the maiden from the dragon and making love to her are part of the same fable. In fighting there is a vivid intimacy, a closeness that partakes of both hate and love, an intimacy held off by hatred but an intimacy nevertheless, and it can blossom into affection or love.

The negative side of aggression is what is normally referred to in our society and thus does not require much definition here. It consists essentially of contact with another with intent to injure or give pain, taking power from the other for one's self-protection or simply to increase one's own power.

Why has the positive side of aggression been so consistently repressed and the negative side so emphasized? One obvious reason is that we have been terrified of aggression, and we assume—delusion though it is—that we can better control it if we center all our attention on its destructive aspects as though that's all there is. This identification of a word with only its negative meaning (such as *fuck* and *devil*) is one of the oldest misuses of the daimonic. In so doing we proscribe the whole area by labeling it "off limits," so that anyone who talks about the "devil" is already under his power.

Another reason we tend to emphasize only the negative side of aggression is that it carries with it anxiety and guilt. We think we can better avoid that anxiety and guilt if we call Prometheus a fanciful legend and posit ourselves as saved from anxiety and guilt by the "second Adam," Christ. When this is done dogmatically, as it is by many fundamentalists, it does give the individual a certain amount of control. But the system of control is shaky at best. Its value is grossly outweighed by the harm it does in truncating consciousness and blocking off sensitivity and understanding of others.

The truth is that practically everything we do is a mixture of positive and negative forms of aggression. Before I give a lecture, I find myself getting in the mood of "If anyone goes to sleep, my voice and ideas will be so importunate that I'll wake him up" (which is positive aggression). Sometimes I defiantly feel: "If anyone tries to interrupt me by heckling, I'll shut him up by making him look silly" (which is negative aggression).

2. VARIETIES OF AGGRESSION

The word *aggression* crops up in our day-to-day speech in an endless variety of ways. We speak of an "aggressive business deal," used as a compliment and meaning a deal that risks a lot to make a lot more money. On the stock market it is the aggressive broker and aggressive way of handling stocks that usually pay off. "We follow an aggressive policy" is generally welcomed in the business world as an indication that these fellows are on their toes and plan to get some place. It is good to have an aggressive lawyer pleading your case because he knows how to put your legal opponent at a disadvantage. In the business world the positive use of aggression is widely accepted.

Most aggression is indirect, masked, taking the form of subtle put-downs of the other person. This shows itself in psychotherapy under the guise of civil, friendly cooperation. A patient will say he has to be "honest" and will then let loose with a stream of fault-findings, covering everything from the therapist's way of working to his family and his office. When the therapist says something that doesn't strike the patient as true, the latter finds one negation not enough, but has to say, "No, no, no, no," as though he is surprised that anyone could suggest such a stupid thing. These techniques of upmanship go on in daily conversation between people of all sorts, especially between married couples. They take the form of an interminable superiority-inferiority struggle, in ways generally not picked up by the "victim" but obvious to everyone else. This indirect kind of aggression is almost always destructive, and I can see no good in it whatever.

There is another kind of aggression—that *within* the self or, as it is generally experienced by the person, *against* the self. I sit down early in the morning to work on this book. Up till now I have been relaxed, relatively happy, even a bit placid. But as I sit here thinking of the subject of aggression, I summon up my rambling thoughts, I open my mind to whatever insights may come, I contemplate the topic. I summon the rebellious parts of myself; inwardly I look for a "fight," aware that creative power and vision come out of such a struggle. I summon the daimonic—so far as it can be summoned. If I were describing it mythologically, I would say that a swarm of dwarfs, elves, and trolls become embroiled in my mind and refuse to do my bidding. The melee that results until some clear ideas and insights emerge is actually my own self, tearing down conventional ideas and ways of seeing in order to grasp anew man's life and problems. It is the daimonic in full force.

All art must be aggressive in some sense. Artists are not necessarily belligerent people as a group; they are generally the ones who fight their most important battles within themselves and on canvases, typewriters, or some other medium of art. No one can look at Hans Hofmann's paintings, with their bright colors clashing and half the edges free to form their own boundaries or mixing with other colors, without being aware that he is seeing in action this very daimonic, this plastic aggression before his eyes. Robert Motherwell and Franz Kline, as they seek to paint the tension and restlessness of our time, splash a black form across a canvas and leave it hanging in air with the rough edges, as though some great object was bodily torn apart right there on the canvas. The power in conflicting forms is, in these paintings, strained to the breaking point. But how can we, today, create in any authentic sense without such straining and, indeed, without such aggression? Norman Mailer's passion is boxing, and Ernest Hemingway not only climbed into the ring whenever he could but described getting ready to write a novel as being similar to getting in shape for a fight. Both of these writers have had a need to assert their power; and out of this need also springs, at least in part, their ability as writers.

3. THE PSYCHOLOGY OF AGGRESSION

At first, in his writings, Freud ignored the problem of aggression. Neither this term nor the term *sadism* appears in the index to his seminal work, *The Interpretation of Dreams*, published in 1900. Aggression is first mentioned in 1905 as a derivative of Freud's libido theory; it is part of the sexual development of the individual and takes the forms of oral aggression, anal aggression, and oedipal aggression. About this time Adler, then a member of the "inner circle" in Vienna, began emphasizing aggression as a primary urge in the human personality. This may partially account for Freud's resistance to accepting the concept as an independent urge in human life.

In any case, Freud's second theory, appearing in the middle of the second decade, is an ego theory. "The ego hates, abhors and pursues with intent to destroy all objects which are the source of pain." [3] The first World War forced Freud into a deeper confrontation with destructiveness: men by the millions kill their fellow men; nations commit suicide. Out of his pondering there came the strange psychophilosophical theory of the *death instinct*, formulated and published by Freud in 1920 when he was sixty-four years old, to deal directly with the reality of man's vast cruelty toward himself and others. Though most psychoanalysts find the theory unacceptable, it does have the merit of confronting the theme of aggression on its most basic level. It also emphasizes the fact that aggression is primarily against one's self—I am the one who ultimately dies—and it must be turned against others and external objects to avoid this self-destruction. The death instinct is a metaphor which is by no means the whole truth, but it is an important part of the truth that cannot be neglected. One implication in Freudian theory is that depression is often the "return of the repressed," namely the indirect expression of unconfronted aggressive tendencies. We saw this in Oliver's statement, "I get depressed to avoid my rage toward my sister."

Freud's theories of aggression leave us unsatisfied. Anna Freud's statement is credible, that if Freud had lived, he would have radically revised his concept of aggression. [4]

Taking off from Freud's second theory, a group of talented young men in the graduate school at Yale published a famous monograph on *Frustration and Aggression* in 1937. Their theory, which started a great train of researches both pro and con, holds that aggression is always the result of frustration, and wherever there is frustration there will be aggression. The theoretical flaw is that it tacitly assumes, like practically all American theories, that all aggression is negative, and implies that when we some day construct a society without frustrations in it, there will be no aggression. But most important of all, the theory fails to take seriously the cruel realities of life, such as in Negro ghettos or in slavery. How can aggression in the prisons, where men are fighting for their lives as human beings, be encompassed in the term *frustration?*

To Alfred Adler goes the credit of first insisting that aggression, which he originally called "will to power," was fundamental in human life. A small man, Adler was fond of saying half-jocularly that all small people, like Napoleon, develop a compensatory striving for power. Adler believed that civilization itself arises out of man's need to increase his power vis-à-vis nature. He grew up in the poor section of Vienna and was a committed socialist all his life. This may have much to do with the simplistic perfectionism that mars his later writings, shown particularly in his changing the phrase "will to power" to "striving for superiority" and then to "striving for perfection." Adler left out the tragic view of life which, to my mind, is inextricably related to the theory of power.

Konrad Lonrenz's study of aggression is essentially biological and has both the excellence and the failings of most biological approaches.[5] It is read by many as a rationale of war and of all acts of aggression, regardless of the fact that Lorenz does not mean this. The critical issue is that human beings are different from animals. Man creates symbols and bases his culture upon them; the flag and patriotism are examples, as are status, religion, and language. The capacity to create and deal with symbols, actually a superb achievement, also accounts for the fact that we are the cruelest species on the planet. We kill not out of necessity but out of allegiance to such symbols as the flag and fatherland; we kill on principle. Thus our aggression occurs on a different level from that of animals, and not much can be learned from animals about this distinctively human form of aggression.

4. DESTRUCTIVE AGGRESSION

Since we generally think of aggression as being destructive, I shall not need to illustrate this beyond a brief personal example. I was engaged to speak at a conference of the junior executives of the American Telephone and Telegraph Corporation. This conference was part of a six-week training session held on the campus of a New England college and, I assumed, an expression of the humanistic interest of AT&T. I had spoken at such conferences before with gratifying results.

But I found, to my surprise and some bewilderment, that my talk was confronted with strange, invisible barriers. I have always been convinced of the truth of Walt Whitman's statement that the "audience makes the speech." This audience seemed alert and fresh but, try as I would, I just could not communicate my main ideas. At a recess I discovered that, for this part of their training, these young executives (being judged for possible promotion to the few top positions in the corporation) were being trained to be "aggressive," and that AT&T had retained a couple of professors from the college to grade the men on how efficiently they could "shoot holes" in the arguments presented. What I was really facing was not an audience that wanted to learn or even a group present for the pleasure of intellectual stimulation. Its aim was entirely different; the audience was listening not to what I said, but for the errors, the weaknesses in the argument. This was, in short, a sophisticated form of listening geared toward "putting down" the speaker. The aggression had a weighty competitive reward, namely promotion to high office.

This is an example of noncommunication. Such an attitude will successfully inhibit any speaker; you cannot bring forth your ideas unless you feel that they will at least be *heard*. This does not mean that they will be agreed with; but it does mean that they will be listened to for their own intrinsic merit. If I had known about the purpose of this audience at the outset I could have simply changed the whole theme of my talk to aggression and its purposes and effect; then we would at least have been communicating.

5. CONSTRUCTIVE AGGRESSION

The following example of constructive aggression is taken from a noble and inspiring chapter in American history which also has striking parallels to the present-day situation—the abolitionist movement in the decades just before the Civil War. I shall discuss four men who were prominent in the movement: Wendell Phillips, William Lloyd Garrison, James Gillespie Birney, and Theodore D. Weld.[6] No serious person would doubt that the ultimate effect of the abolitionist movement was constructive. It is even possible that if it had been more successful, the Civil War, with its inconceivable suffering, might have been averted.

These men fit our definition of aggression very well. They were actively moving into the territory of others (slaves were personal property and sanctified thereby) to accomplish a restructuring of power. Their activities were characterized by great conflict, both inward and outward, the latter including continual threats on their lives and limbs.

In their early lives, these four seemed like very unlikely candidates for their later profound aggression in the cause of anti-slavery. Wendell Phillips had led the typical life of a Boston Brahmin of his time, taking a law degree at Harvard; William Lloyd Garrison was attracted first to writing and politics; when one first hears of Theodore Weld, it is as a lecturer on the art of improving one's memory; James Birney was twice suspended from Princeton for drinking, although he was readmitted and graduated with honors, and eventually became a planter and lived like a young southern aristocrat, drinking and gambling in excess. What characteristics in these men determined the fact that their aggression was to be constructive rather than destructive (like John Brown's, for example)?

When we look back into their childhood, each had been consistently *loved* by his parents. I believe that this is crucial to the understanding of the constructive nature of aggression. When a person has not been loved or has been loved inconsistently or by a mother or father who was himself radically insecure, there develops in his later aggression a penchant for revenge on the world, a need to destroy the world for others in as much as it was not good for him.

Each had—and we must assume that this begins early in infancy —a deep *compassion* for others, which took the later, particular form of compassion for slaves and the persecuted. Garrison and Weld were attracted to the movement by empathy for the blacks. Birney wrote: "It is hard to tell what one's duty is toward the poor creatures; but I have made up my mind to one thing, I will not allow any of them to be treated brutally." [7] Phillips was first attracted to the abolitionist movement by the mob's murder of fellow abolitionist Elijah P. Lovejoy, and later joined the movement when he saw the mob threaten Garrison's life. Thereafter, his motivation differed slightly from the others in that he was continually outraged that in his beloved Boston there should be such a disregard of civil liberties.

The *physical courage* of these four, made necessary by their being under constant threat of mob violence, bears deeper scrutiny. For the kind of aggression in which they moved, they had to have a capacity for *risk*, for existing *in extremis*. All four had had an abundant amount of energy as children, which had taken the forms of vigorous play and of fighting with their peers. But their courage seemed more a triumph over anxiety (as, in the last analysis, courage may always be) rather than something with which they were born. Garrison tells, in a letter to a friend, of his "knees shaking in anticipation" of a lecture he had to give to the Congregational Societies of Boston, and a newspaper account of the day tells of his voice being so faint that the audience could scarcely hear him. But he recovered and gave a strong plea for the emancipation of the slaves. "Although Garrison suffered least of the four abolitionists and indeed appeared to enjoy combat, it would be a mistake to overlook the fear he experienced on numerous occasions when his life was in jeopardy from angry mobs." [8]

The *social courage* required here is even more impressive. Birney wrote that the pain of alienation from those "with whom we [went] up from Sabbath to Sabbath to the house of God—many of our near . . . relations estranged from us, and the whole community . . . looking upon you as an enemy to its peace, is no small trial." [9] In 1834 he wrote to Weld: "I have not one helper —not one from whom I can draw sympathy on this topic!" Again and again, he faced censure and threats of violence from mobs, while he believed

> that if ever there was a time, it is now come when our republic with her cause of universal freedom is in a strait, where everything that ought to be periled by the patriot should be freely hazarded for her relief. . . . [Men must] themselves die freeman [rather] than slaves, or our Country, glorious as has been her hope, is gone forever.[10]

The opposition they received served to strengthen them in their commitment. Garrison responded to it with increasing aggression and closer identification with the Negro. He wrote with eloquence:

> I am aware, that many object to the severity of my language; but is there not cause for severity? I will be as harsh as truth, and as uncompromising as justice. On this subject, I do not wish to think, or speak or write, with moderation. No, no! Tell a man whose house is on fire, to give a moderate alarm; tell him to moderately rescue his wife from the hands of a ravisher; tell the mother to gradually extricate her babe from the fire into which he has fallen; but urge me not to use moderation in a cause like the present! I am in earnest. I will not equivocate—I will not excuse—I will not retreat a single inch—AND I WILL

BE HEARD. The apathy of the people is enough to make every statue leap from its pedestal, and to hasten the resurrection of the dead.[11]

No sensitive person can go through such prolonged aggressive activity without serious doubts from time to time about the rightness of his position. Birney's period of doubt and indecision touches us particularly for it hinges on a typically contemporaneous worry. He was continuously afraid that his decisions would be influenced too much by feeling, trying as he was to convince by reason others as well as himself: "When I remember how calmly and dispassionately my mind has proceeded from truth to truth connected with this subject [i.e., slavery] to another still higher, I feel satisfied that my conclusions are not the fruits of enthusiasm." [12] He later despaired that the South could ever be reached by reason. Despite failing health he came to New York to serve as secretary of the American Anti-Slavery Society. Interestingly enough, he, who had depended on reason, despaired of gradualism before he died in 1857: "When or how it [slavery] will expire I must say I see not." [13]

Constructive aggression causes suffering as well as inner conflict. The suffering that dedication to such a cause entails was responsible for the commitment of greater and greater numbers to it. Prominent Bostonians were incensed when the mob threatened the life of Garrison. Dr. Henry Ingersoll Bowditch, a prominent physician, wrote: "Then it has come to this, that a man cannot speak on slavery within sight of Faneuil Hall." When Bowditch volunteered to help a member of the city government, Samuel Eliot, standing nearby, to suppress the rioters, Eliot, "rather intimated that the authorities, while not wishing for a mob, rather sympathized with its object . . . to forcibly suppress the abolitionists. I was completely disgusted and I vowed from my heart as I left him with utter loathing, 'I am an abolitionist from this very moment.' " [14]

The role of the forces of law and order presents a dismal picture in this period, as in our own. It reveals a truth that we know but, for our own peace of mind, try to forget. Not only did members of the government covertly instigate violence by sympathizing with it, as in the incident quoted above, but there was also an incident the like of which could be multiplied a thousand-fold: the good people of Boston watched, ashamed and helpless, as a former slave was taken by force to be shipped back to slavery *while their own militia guarded the capture.* Indeed, many who had regarded the abolitionists as hotheads and spokesmen for the lunatic fringe had second thoughts when they observed incidents like this.

The aggression of the abolitionists succeeded in its central aim —to combat the apathy that always emerges in a time of anxiety and guilt. The anxiety was caused by the social upheaval of that historical period; the guilt for holding slaves was felt even among the southerners themselves. But the abolitionists would not permit escape into apathy. They continued to jar the populace and permitted no man's conscience to sleep.

These four men had a powerful grievance—the inhuman character of slavery. They also had a powerful aim at stake—the possibility of correcting injustice. While destructive aggression sometimes contains only the first, both of these must be present in constructive aggression. In contrast to affirmation and assertion, aggression occurred because the opposition was so entrenched and apathy and inertia were so strong that greater force was necessary for stirring up effective action. It is the nature of any society to protect the status quo, and aggression, from time to time, moves into violence not only because of the blind rage of mobs but also because of the action of police and militia on the side of "law and order."

It is inspiring to watch how each of these men gathered his individual strength, not present to start with, and transcended himself with his own effort in bringing the power of his oratory and his example to bear upon the opposition. In this self-transcendence there must often have been the experience of ecstasy, which we describe in the next chapter.

EIGHT

ECSTASY AND VIOLENCE

At the heart of our violence, in act or in feeling, lies
the wish to show ourselves men with a will. [But]
the complexity of society makes the man lose heart.
Nothing he does any longer seems a skill to be proud
of in a world where someone else always hits the
headlines. This is a plausible picture, in despair of
which men cheerfully join any private army which
will offer them the ambivalent identity of a uniform: the right to salute and be saluted.
                                    —Jacob Bronowski,
                             from *The Face of Violence*

One of the reasons we have made so little progress in our mitigating
of violence is that we have determinedly overlooked the elements
in it that are attractive, alluring, and fascinating. Our minds tend
to castrate the topic in the very act of understanding it. When a
congressman delivers a tirade against violence, he seems to forget
entirely that as a child *he* ran after fire engines, *he* was fascinated

by pictures of bullfights, and *he* also shared the strange combination of allure and horror which leads people to crowd around accidents.

We deny with our minds the "secret love of violence," which is present in all of us in some form, at the same time as we perform violent acts with our bodies. By repressing the awareness of the *fact* of violence, we can thus secretly give ourselves over to the enjoyment of it. This seems to be a necessary human defense against the deeper emotional implications we would have to face if we were to admit the reality of this "secret love." At the outset of every war, for example, we hastily transform our enemy into the image of the daimonic; and then, since it is the devil we are fighting, we can shift onto a war footing without asking ourselves all the troublesome psychological and spiritual questions that the war arouses. We no longer have to face the realization that those we are killing are persons like ourselves.

I shall lump these alluring and fascinating elements together under the term "ecstasy." The word may seem strange, partly because in common parlance it is pegged at a high level of intensity: we go into ecstasy over a great painting or we become ecstatic upon winning a million dollars in the lottery. But the historical meaning leaves the question of intensity of emotion entirely open. Coming from the Greek 'εκστασις, ecstasy means etymologically "to stand outside one's self," to be "beside one's self," or to be "out of one's self." The experience that takes one "beyond one's self," beyond conventional ego boundaries, and gives one a new and enlarged awareness of the self—such as Hindu or Buddhist meditation—is legitimately called ecstatic, although its intensity may not be quantitatively great. Aesthetic experiences or moments in love are commonly spoken of as ecstatic. The experience of being of worth, of knowing that other people change because of your influence, also gives you the feeling of being "beyond yourself"—in other words, a kind of ecstasy of low intensity.

Hence I have used, for these experiences of lesser intensity, the phrase "sense of significance."

That violence is often associated with ecstatic experiences is seen in our using the same phrases for both. We say a person is "beside himself" with rage; he is "possessed" by power. There also occurs a self-transcendence in violence which is like the self-transcendence in ecstatic experiences. The total absorption, furthermore, that is present in violence is also present in ecstasy. In our day of anti-intellectualism, when there is a reaction against all things "sicklied o'er with the pale cast of thought," the absorption of the self in violence is especially attractive.

In what ways does violence yield for us this experience of ecstasy, this sense of significance? Jerry Rubin gives us our first example. In his typically flamboyant style he tells of stopping a troop train in Oakland:

> Cops tried to arrest those who had jumped on [the train]. As they moved to grab people, we split in all directions—only three or four were caught.
>
> We ran, yipping and whooping, away from the tracks and through the streets, like a bunch of crazy mother-fuckers.
>
> We were victorious warriors.
>
> We were ecstatic.
>
> We had stopped the troop train.
>
> WE STOPPED THE WAR MACHINE DEAD IN ITS TRACKS.[1]

Whatever one's impression of Jerry Rubin, this is surely an experience of the ecstasy of violence.

A less dramatic example, but one containing some of the ingredients of ecstasy in their embryonic form, comes from my own experience in graduate school. Several young Negroes in California had been accused of rape and had been lynched by a mob without a semblance of a trial. A clergyman in New York had, in a sermon, commended the lynching. As a result a group of us decided to picket the church the following Sunday morning. The incident would not be worth relating except for the fact of the excitement, even joy, that went hand in hand with our anxiety on this occasion. Painting the signs the night before, organizing the march, feeling the solidarity with the others—comrades who would walk beside me in this cause, the rightness of which we had no doubt—all of these activities had an element of ecstasy. I recall walking home late at night after these preparations and finding, when I was alone, that questions and doubts came into my mind as to the effectiveness of our proposed course. But no! My comrades and I had decided, and I must not let them down. We expected some opposition in the form of mounted police (which actually occurred); we hoped it wouldn't be too violent but great enough to make an impression on the news media. We also secretly hoped for opposition because that would give an added cohesion to our group and would even add to our ecstasy.

An extreme emphasis on individual responsibility can become an egocentric manipulation of others, a compulsion that defeats genuine morality and yields only a counterfeit sense of significance. Most Americans are oppressed by the sense of individual responsibility, not only for general humanitarian reasons (as described by Dostoevsky) but for reasons specific to our own nation. An American receives very little aid from his culture in carrying this responsibility. Americans have no sacraments like penance, no rituals like confession (except in psychoanalysis for the few) to help free them from the burden of the past. The whole weight rests on the shoulders of the individual, and we have already seen that he feels powerless. Perhaps this accounts for the moralistic and picayune forms that responsibility tends to take: in the past it centered on not smoking and not drinking, and now it centers on not stepping on insects and not throwing away anything made of plastic. In any case a person cannot carry the burden of responsibility for his own moral salvation without a corresponding depth of culture to give him structure. Otherwise he will end up feeling isolated, lonely, and separated from others.

This emerging sense of ecstasy in a successful rebellion accounts for some important changes in the character of the rebellion itself. The typical rebellion normally begins with highly moral aims—the students at Berkeley, for example, proclaimed their opposition to the unhuman facelessness of the modern factory-university. But with the state of ecstasy which accompanies the initial success, the psychological character and meaning of the rebellion change. A new *élan* is added. For many, the goal of the rebellion now becomes the ecstasy itself rather than the original conditions. The rebellion has become the high point in the lives of many of the rebels, and they seem dimly aware that they'll never have that much sense of significance again.

This often leads to an elaboration and multiplying of the original conditions that the administration, be it of a university or a prison, is asked to meet. The rebels are saying, in this action, that the conditions originally set are no longer the main reason for the rebellion. Hence, at Brandeis, the university president remained in his office during the week of the black sit-in to negotiate with the rebels, and each day the blacks sent over a different bargaining committee with different conditions. It is as though they were saying by this action: "Can't you see that this rebellion means much more to us than the specific conditions?"

This also accounts for the curious presentation of the condition of amnesty, which obviously cannot be granted without complete capitulation on the part of the administration. I interpret this as saying: "All along what we wanted was this experience of ecstasy, this sense of our own significance." The ecstasy may reach such a pitch that it approaches Malcolm X's concept of "revolutionary suicide."

The value of the group contrasted with the individual must also be mentioned. The group is constituted around issues that are, to the participant, of life-and-death importance. The question about any group is: What is its psychic center—to what is it devoted?

1. VIOLENCE IN LITERATURE

Simply citing the violence in TV westerns and in paperback mystery-thrillers would make our task too easy.[2] We must ask instead the more difficult question: What is the function of violence in the classics, the literature that, through the ages, has been the guide to man's psychological and spiritual development?

First, let us consider an aspect of Melville's *Billy Budd, Foretopman*. When Billy is brought before Captain Vere and Master-at-Arms Claggart to answer the accusation by the latter that he plans a mutiny, he is so dumbfounded by the injustice of the charges that he cannot speak. Seized by sudden rage in his verbal impotence, Billy stares at Claggart for a taut, silent moment. Then all of his rage goes into his right arm, and he strikes the master-at-arms, who falls dead.

When this act of sheer violence occurs on the stage or screen, *a sigh of relief goes through the audience*. We feel that the violence fits the situation. It is aesthetically called for; nothing less would have sufficed. Violence makes complete the otherwise incomplete aesthetic Gestalt. At that point there is for the audience the experience of the ecstasy of violence in aesthetic terms.

But if "violence is evil," why is it so essential to this novella as well as to many other classics of literature? There must be something about some violence that meets a need in human beings, something that cannot be wholly "bad." This something must be in *Grimm's Fairy-Tales*, in Shakespeare's plays, and in the dramas by Aeschylus and Sophocles. It must be a reality in life which, on the level of unconscious experience, demands its own recognition. What is it?

Death is a violent act for all of us; we are forcibly separated from this life. This fact is not in the slightest gainsaid by modern drugs and whether or not a man dies in a hospital bed, doped into a zombie state with morphine. Death is always present to us as a possibility. It is this possibility which gives meaning to life and to love.[3] No matter how much we may fondly hope that we can set our own manner and time of death, the dread of the horror of death is present in our imaginations. For it is not the fact itself, but the meaning of it that is important.

Death is not the only violence—or violation—we must all suffer. Life is full of other violent acts. Our very birth, the necessary struggles between parent and child, the heart-rending separations from someone we love—all these are experiences in which physical and psychological violence inevitably occurs. No life is free from violent episodes as it runs its course.

The aesthetic ecstasy of the violence in great literature *brings man face to face with his own mortality*. This is one of its services to us. After seeing a tragedy on the stage or reading one, we often find ourselves wanting to walk by ourselves and think about it. We experience what Aristotle called the catharsis of pity and terror, and we long to savor it. It not only brings us closer to our own center but also makes us more appreciative, paradoxically, of our fellow men. It helps us to see that we, ephemeral creatures all, are born and struggle and live for a season and then, like the grass, wither away; and our "raging against the passing of the light" will then have, if not more practical an effect, at least more meaning.

This is why a deeper level of experience is called forth in tragedy—say in Shakespeare or Eugene O'Neill—than in comedy. The Greeks solved this problem by having the violence—of which there was plenty in the tragedies of Oedipus, Medea, and others—take place off stage. In Shakespeare and Melville, on the other hand, the violence occurs on stage; but there it is demanded by the aesthetic meaning of the drama. This is the difference between drama and melodrama (as in contemporaneous TV programs, which capitalize on the violence as such).

The question we must ask is: Is the violence in a movie or drama inserted for shock value, horror, and titillation, or is it an integral part of the tragedy? In *Macbeth, Hamlet,* and *Antigone,* the violence is *required* for the aesthetic wholeness of the drama. In tragedy we not only experience our own mortality but we also transcend it; the values that matter stand out more clearly. We do not experience the sheer wanton destructiveness which occurs when we see East Pakistanis bayoneted to death on TV, which is only a gruesome evil which we would have given anything to have been able to prevent.

Although death always wins empirically in literature as in life, man wins spiritually by virtue of his acts of forming experience into aspects of culture like art, science, and religion.

2.   ECSTASY IN WAR

Immediately after the hanging of Billy Budd, in the cinema version of Melville's novella, the sailors on this British man-of-war suddenly see a French warship coming around the promontory several miles to port. They all cheer.

Why the *cheer?* These men know that they are going into battle, into the grime and cruelty and death that war represents, yet they cheer. True, a minor part of the cause can be seen as an outlet for the pent-up emotions that have been engendered silently and oppressively as the sailors experienced the hanging of their favorite comrade. But there is a more basic reason. We turn, then, to another area, the most difficult of all with which to come to terms, that of the violence in war.

On the rational level practically everyone rejects and abhors war. When I was in college before World War II, I recall how taken aback I was when a professor of English literature remarked that he was fairly sure there would be more wars. This teacher was a soft-spoken, sensitive, unwarlike type, if ever such existed; but I silently looked at him as though he were a pariah. How could a man *entertain* such a thought? Wasn't it clear that we must refrain from thinking of or believing in war—and certainly from predicting it—if we were ever to attain peace? Several other hundred thousand fellow collegians and I, who were pacifists, were under the illusion that if we only believed in peace strongly enough, we could that much more insure international peace. We had no idea of how close our attitude came to superstition—do not *think* of the devil or he will already be in your midst.[4]

We were so engrossed in blotting war out of everybody's mind that we completely ignored the points in William James's provocative essay "The Moral Equivalent of War." Written because of his detestation of our "squalid war with Spain," William James delivered this as a lecture in 1907. It still presents the central problem penetratingly, even if its answers are no longer cogent. "In my remarks, pacifist though I am," says James, "I will refuse to speak of the bestial side of the war-regime (already done justice by many writers). . . ." He cautions then against the belief that describing the horrors of war will act as a deterrent:

> Showing war's irrationality and horror is of no effect. . . . *The horrors make the fascination.* . . . When [it is a] question of getting the extremest and supremest out of human nature, talk of expense sounds ignominious. . . . Pacifists ought to enter more deeply into the aesthetical and ethical point of view of their opponents.[5]

Now for all our opposition to war, we cannot escape the obvious fact that we have been notoriously unsuccessful in our efforts to curtail it.[6] I believe our lack of success is due, at least in part, to our having ignored the central phenomenon: *"the horrors make the fascination."* In this century—which began arrogantly as a "century of peace"—we have seen the steady change from a state of relative tranquility to that of revolutions and violence. At this moment we find half a dozen wars going on around the globe, including that most disgraceful one of all, Vietnam; we witness the fact that America has changed from a volunteer army to a peace-time draft, and has shifted from fighting declared wars to fighting undeclared wars. Why have we, who are opposed to war, been so ineffectual? Is it not time to inquire whether there is something wrong in our approach to this ultimate form of aggression and violence? I propose that we ask directly: What is the allure, the fascination, the attraction of war? [7]

I choose as my chief source of data J. Glenn Gray's *The Warriors*,[8] a diary of the author's four years as a soldier in World War II. Three of these years were spent in an armored division in Europe, and one as an agent of the European theater of operations. Ten years after the armistice Gray returned to Europe as a Fulbright scholar to make an extensive study of war and the personal motivations of people he had known in it.

Now there is not the slightest doubt that Gray—who is now professor of philosophy at a western college—is as strongly opposed as anyone to war as a way of settling international disputes, and no one can tell him more than he already knows about its horrors. But he is also trying to do something that is, in my judgment, more important, namely *to discover and describe the subconscious fascination this ultimate form of violence has for mankind.*

"Beyond doubt there are many who simply endure war, hating every moment," Gray writes, "and few wish to admit a taste for war. Yet many men both love and hate combat. They know why they hate it; it is harder to know and be articulate about why they love it." [9]

Despite the horror, the unutterable weariness, the grime, the hatred, many soldiers found the war the one lyric moment in their lives.

> Many veterans who are honest with themselves will admit, I believe, that the experience of communal effort in battle even under the altered conditions of modern war, has been a high point in their lives . . . which they would not want to have missed. . . . For anyone who has not experienced it himself, the feeling is hard to comprehend, and for the participant, hard to explain to anyone else.[10]

And again:

> Millions of men in our day—like millions before us—have learned to live in war's strange element and have discovered in it a powerful fascination. . . . The emotional environment of war has always been compelling; it has drawn most men under its spell. . . . Reflection and calm reasoning are alien to it.[11]

> When the signs of peace were visible, I wrote [in this diary] with some regret, "The purgative force of danger which makes men coarser but perhaps more human will soon be lost and the first months of peace will make some of us yearn for the old days of conflict" [12]

What are the sources of war's allure? One is the attraction of the *extreme* situation—that is, the *risking all* in battle.[13] This is the same element, although to a different degree, that Oliver cited when he said the protest march caught him up "beyond human desires." A second is the strengthening effect of being part of a tremendous organization, which relieves a person of individual responsibility and guilt. The declaration of war is thus important as a moral statement, as a moral justification, and enables the soldier to give over his moral responsibility to his outfit. This point is generally cited in criticism of the war machine; and no one can have the slightest doubt that war does erode individual responsibility and the autonomy of conscience. Mylai and the Calley case prove this in a horrible way. But what is generally overlooked is that man has a desire to avoid freedom as well as to seek it; that freedom and choice are also a burden—as Dostoevsky and countless others have known throughout history; and that to give one's conscience over to the group, as one does in wartime, is also a source of great comfort. This is why the great determinisms of history—such as Calvinism and Marxism—have also demonstrated great power not only to form people into ranks but to inspire in them a degree of active devotion that other movements may not find available.

Closely related to this is the feeling of comradeship in the ranks—that I am accepted not because of any individual merit on my part, but because I am a fellow in the ranks. I can trust my fellow soldier to cover my retreat or my attack because of the role given to me. My merit is the role, and the limits the role places on me give me a species of freedom.

The breaking down of this capacity to feel as if one were part of the larger whole is the explanation of cowardice among soldiers Indeed, physical courage in whatever scene—judging from my experience in psychotherapy—seems to hinge on whether the individual can feel he is fighting for others as well as himself, assuming a bond with his fellows, which means he will come to their aid as they will to his. The source of this physical courage appears to lie originally in the relationship between the infant and its mother, specifically his trust in his solidarity with her and, consequently, with the world. Physical cowardice, on the other hand, even in avoiding physical fights as a child, seems to come from an early rejection, an early feeling that the mother will not support her child and may even turn against him in his fight; so that henceforth every effort the youngster makes, he makes on his own. Such a person finds it inconceivable that others would support him and that he is also fighting for them, and it takes a conscious decision for him to take up their part. This latter type of person may have great *moral* courage, which he has developed as a loner; but what he lacks is physical courage or courage in the group.

There is in the ecstasy of violence, furthermore, the lust for destruction. The reader will recall Oliver's comment: "All my life I've wanted to smash a computer." There seems to be a delight in destruction in man, the atavistic urge to break things and to kill. This is increased in neurotics and others in despair; but it is an increase of a trait that is there anyway, and centuries of the veneer of civilization cannot hide it.

Anyone who has watched men on the battlefield at work with artillery, or looked into the eyes of veteran killers fresh from slaughter, or studied the descriptions of bombardiers' feelings while smashing their targets, finds it hard to escape the conclusion that there is a delight in destruction. . . . This evil appears to surpass mere human evil, and to demand explanation in cosmological and religious terms. In this sense, human beings can be devilish in a way animals can never be.[14]

In this lust for destruction, the soldier's ego temporarily deserts him, and he is absorbed in what he experiences. It is "a deprivation of self for a union with objects that were hitherto foreign." This is technical language for what is referred to in the mystic experience of ecstasy: the ego is "dissolved," and the mystic experiences a union with the "Whole," be it called light or truth or God. Through violence we overcome self-centeredness.

All of these are elements in the ecstasy of violence. There is a joy in violence that takes the individual out of himself and pushes him toward something deeper and more powerful than he has previously experienced. The individual "I" passes insensibly into a "we"; "my" becomes "our." I give myself to it, let myself go; as I feel my old self slipping away, lo and behold, a new consciousness, a higher degree of awareness, becomes present, a new self, more extensive than the first.

Now when we consider contemporary man—insignificant, lonely, more isolated as mass communication becomes vaster, his ears and sensitivities dulled by ever-present transistor radios and by thousands of words hurled at him by TV and newspapers, aware of his identity only to the extent that he has lost it, yearning for community but feeling awkward and helpless as he finds it—when we consider this modern man, who will be surprised that he yearns for ecstasy even of the kind that violence and war may bring?

Consider this man in society—living year after year in the anonymous anxiety that something might "happen"; aware of "enemy" countries that he can destroy in his imagination, a fantasy to which he resorts when he is fed up with his day-to-day life; existing with a dread that he feels somehow ought to be translated into action but hanging in abeyance, lured on by "secret" promises of ecstasy and violence, feeling that continuing the vague dread is worse than giving in to the allure, fascination, and attraction of action—is it any wonder that this man goes along with a declaration of war in apparent sheeplike fashion?

For the first time in my life I can now, for example, understand the American Legion. That organization has always been, for me, a negative conscience—whatever it was for, I was against, and whatever I was for, it was against. This worked quite well as a *pro tempore* device when I didn't have time to figure out on which side justice was. But I never could understand the motives of the legionnaires or other veterans' organizations in their saber-rattling and their stretching the hunting-under-every-bed-for-Communists to absurd lengths. Now, however, I see that these groups had originally been, by and large, young men who had held insignificant jobs pouring gasoline into Buicks, Fords, and Chevrolets when they were called to war. In France they became heroes, the pride of the women; flowers were strewn in their paths, every honor thrust upon them. They were *significant*, possibly for the first time in their lives. Returning to this country, some could find only the same jobs pouring gasoline into Buicks, Chevrolets, and Fords, and those who found better jobs may have experienced a similar despair in the empty life of peacetime. No wonder they band together, out of their ennui, to recreate the *closest experience to that of the war*, such as the "search and destroy" anti-Communist missions. They hark back in their yearning to find something that will give their lives a significance it intrinsically lacks.

3. THE SEARCH FOR RECOGNITION

When Glenn Gray went back to Europe in 1955 to interview his comrades-in-arms and his friends in the resistance of fifteen years ago, a French woman, living in her comfortable bourgeois home with her husband and son, confessed earnestly: "My life is so unutterably boring nowadays! . . . Anything is better than to have nothing at all happen day after day. You know that I do not love war or want it to return. But at least it made me feel alive, as I have not felt alive before or since." [15] Relating the experience of listening to a German comrade-in-arms, Gray continues:

> Overweight, and with an expensive cigar in his mouth, he spoke of our earlier days together at the close of the war when he was shivering and hungry and harried with anxieties about keeping his wife and children from too great want. "Sometimes I think that those were happier times for us than these." . . . And there was something like despair in his eyes. . . . Neither one of these people was longing for the old days in sentimental nostalgia; they were confessing their disillusionment with a sterile present. *Peace exposed a void in them that war's excitement had enabled them to keep covered up.*[16]

This void is that from which the ecstasy of violence is an escape. Some of the sterility is due to the inescapable conditions of civilized existence that remove much of the risk and challenge from life—risk and challenge that seem to be more important for many, if not most, people than our much touted affluence. Violence puts the risk and challenge back, whatever we may think about its destructiveness; and no longer is life empty.

We are going to have upheavals of violence for as long as experiences of significance are denied people. Everyone has a need for some sense of significance; and if we can't make that possible, or even probable, in our society, then it will be obtained in destructive ways. The challenge before us is to find ways that people can achieve significance and recognition so that destructive violence will not be necessary.

NINE

THE ANATOMY OF VIOLENCE

Violence and suffering are critical in a democratic
society, in heightening antipathy for violations of
democratic values and in heightening sympathy for
the victims of such violations.

—Silvan Tomkins,
from "The Constructive Role
of Violence and Suffering"

Violence is like the sudden chemical change that occurs when,
following a relatively placid period, water breaks into a boil. If
we do not see the burner underneath that has been heating the
water, we mistake the violence for a discrete happenstance. We
fail to see that the violence is an entirely understandable outcome
of personalities fighting against odds in a repressive culture that
does not help them. Violence often follows quiet periods, like
that of the "silent generation" of students of the fifties. Only

later were we to see, to our sorrow, how explosive were the forces
underlying this apathy.

1. THE PSYCHONEUROLOGICAL ASPECTS OF VIOLENCE

In its typical and simple form, violence is an eruption of pent-up
passion. When a person (or group of people) has been denied
over a period of time what he feels are his legitimate rights, when
he is continuously burdened with feelings of impotence which
corrode any remaining self-esteem, violence is the predictable end
result. Violence is an explosion of the drive to destroy that which
is interpreted as the barrier to one's self-esteem, movement, and
growth. This desire to destroy may so completely take over the
person that any object that gets in the way is destroyed. Hence the
person strikes out blindly, often destroying those for whom he
cares and even himself in the process.

Violence is largely a physical event. But this physical event occurs in a psychological context. Either because of the period of
unseen build-up or the suddenness of the stimulus, the impulse
to strike out comes so fast we are unable to think, and we control
it only with effort. If someone suddenly gives me a hard shove
on the subway, I "see red" and have an immediate urge to punch
him in return. But I know, when I calm down, that if I make a
practice of punching men on the subway, my early doom is
assured. A football player may control his urges to wreak violence
by reminding himself that he will have a chance to express his
power in the next play; but for the rest of us, bystanders in most
activities in our civilized life with muscular expressions prohibited
us, the control and direction of our violent urges are much more
difficult.

Aggression and violence are rightly linked in the public mind—
one speaks of aggression *and* violence. Aggression is to violence,

remarks Gerald Chrzanowski, as anxiety is to panic. When aggression builds up in us, it feels, at a certain point, as though a switch has been thrown, and we become violent. The aggression is object-related—that is, we know at whom and what we are angry.[1] But in violence, the object-relation disintegrates, and we swing wildly, hitting whoever is within range. One's mind becomes foggy, and perception of the enemy becomes unclear; one loses awareness of the environment and wants only to act out this inner compulsion to do violence, come what may. Man, Kurt Goldstein reminds us, is the creature who can think in abstraction and who can transcend the concrete situation. The violent man's capacity to abstract has disintegrated, and this accounts for his crazy behavior.

The suddenness with which most violent episodes erupt suggests some questions. In violence, is there a direct connection between the input stimuli and the output muscles (i.e., the muscles that suddenly tend to strike back)? And is this connection subcortical, which would be related to the fact that it happens so quickly that the person doesn't think until after the episode has passed? Such discussions of the pathways by which the excitation travels are only analogies to the experience itself, but as analogies they may be useful in our understanding the process. Specifically, they may help us see why a person is possessed *by* violence rather than possessing *it*.

Ever since Walter B. Cannon's classical work in the Harvard physiology laboratory,[2] it has been generally agreed that there are three responses of the organism to threat: *fight*, *flight*, and *delayed response*. Cannon demonstrated, for example, that when somebody suddenly shoves me roughly on the subway, adrenalin is poured into my bloodstream, my blood pressure rises to give my muscles more strength, my heartbeat becomes more rapid—all of which prepares me to fight the offending person or to flee out of range.[3] The "flight" is what occurs in anxiety and fear; the "fight" in aggression and violence. With these physiological changes, the experience of violence gives great energy to the person. He feels a kind of transcendent power that he did not realize he had; and he may, like Mercedes, fight much more effectively in this mood. This fact can act like a drug, tempting the person to give himself over again and again to violence.

The third possibility is that I can delay my response. This is what most people actually do. The lower down the scale of education and status a person is, the more apt he is to react directly; the higher on the scale, the more apt he is to delay reaction until he has had a chance to think and assess the prospects of fighting or fleeing. The capacity for delayed response is a gift—or burden—of civilization: we wait to absorb the event into consciousness and then decide what is the best response. This gives us culture, but it also gives us neurosis. The typical neurotic may spend his whole life trying to fight with new acquaintances the old battles that never got worked out in his childhood.

But is it not true that on the crowded subway I am in a "readiness" to respond hostilely? I am much more apt to have a counterurge of the violent type in that situation than, say, when someone jostles me on a dance floor. So there must be some symbolic scanning process going on. How I *interpret* the situation will determine my readiness to strike back in hostility, making it *causa belli*, or to simply smile and accept an apology, if one is offered. Interpretation takes in unconscious as well as conscious factors: I give a certain meaning to it; I *see* the world as being hostile or friendly. Here enters the *symbol*, the means we have as human beings of uniting conscious and unconscious, historical and present, individual and group. This is why Sullivan and others have said that the organic processes are *subsumed under the symbolic process*.[4] It is the symbolic process that determines the individual's intentionality.

How a person sees and interprets the world about him is thus crucial to his violence. This is what gives the readiness to fight to a black man quietly sitting in his car who becomes enraged when a policeman asks him for his identification. This also under-lies the "machismo" of a policeman who is driven by his own power needs to humiliate a black. Whether the interpretation is pathological or merely imagined, illusory or downright false, it does not change the situation: it is *his* interpretation that will be decisive as to how he reacts. The paranoid shoots other persons because he believes they exercise a magic power and will kill him; thus he's shooting in self-defense. Calling this "paranoid" does not help unless we are able thereby to get behind the symbolic interpretation and see the world, at least temporarily, as the mur-derer sees it.

Even in international relations symbolic interpretation of the movements of other nations is crucial to the understanding of violence and war. Violence has its roots in impotence, we have said. This is true in individuals and in ethnic groups. But in na-tions violence comes from the *threat* of impotence. Nations seem to find it necessary to protect themselves on a periphery farther out; they must be aware, precariously balanced as they are on the seesaw of armaments, of whether another country is building up power to gain an advantage over them. If a nation becomes gen-uinely impotent, it is no longer a nation.

Senator J. William Fulbright has pointed out how important our interpretation of the behavior of other nations is.[5] Ever since Yalta, American administrations have interpreted Russia's be-havior—e.g., the Cuban missile episode and the USSR's reaction to the U-2 flight—as motivated by Russian aggression toward the United States. These events, Fulbright indicates, could as well have been interpreted as motivated by fear on the part of Russia. More specifically, he proposes that the bellicose posture of these events were sops thrown to the Russian generals, who needed to be placated by Khrushchev if the latter were to succeed in his hope of establishing more amicable relations with the United States. Interpreting Russia's moves as aggressive, we opposed them with a vehemence that helped the counterparty in Russia, the army, to depose Khrushchev and institute a less friendly government. Nations, in their misreading of the motives of other nations, can do what the paranoid patient does: they can work against their own interests because of their projection of hostility and aggression.

2. VARIETIES OF VIOLENCE

There are at least five recognizable kinds of violence. There is, first, *simple violence*. Mercedes's dreams of violence, in which she wards off knives and guns, is of this type. This is characteristic of many student rebellions, and carries with it the muscular freedom, the surging up of pent-up energy, and the freedom from the restrictions of individual conscience and responsibility of which we have spoken. It is the general protest against being placed continuously in an impotent situation, and it typically carries highly moral demands.

But very little violence stays at this first level. There is, second, *calculated violence*. Many, if not most, of the student rebellions were surrounded by calculated violence. The rebellion of French students in Paris was taken over by professional revolutionaries on the second or third day, and the leadership, which began with moral demands, changed as the leaders exploited the profound frustration of the students and their energy.

The third type I call *fomented violence*. This is the work of a Himmler or of the rabble-rousers of the extreme right or left in any country. It is a stimulation of the impotence and frustration felt by the people at large for the purposes of the speaker. Modern history is full of illustrations of how treating people like beasts leads them to become beasts in the process.

Fourth, there is *absentee violence* (or instrumental violence). Obviously all of us who live in society partake to some extent of the violence of that society, although most of us do it from our own vantage point of moral elevation and hide behind a zombie-like unawareness of conscience. The war in Vietnam could not continue except that our taxes are voted for it; in this sense we all are part of the war effort, whether we are for or against the war itself.

There is a fifth category of violence, different from those above, which occurs when the party in power, threatened with encroachment on its power, strikes out with violence to stave off these threats. This we may call *violence from above*. Its motive is generally to protect or re-establish the status quo. The police are taken out of their rightful role as apprehenders and are made punishers. Such violence is said by students of the field, such as Hans Toch, to be regularly more destructive than other violence—partly because the police have the clubs and guns, and partly because they have a large reservoir of inner individual resentment on which they can draw in their rage. The age-old assumption, especially in the American dream, is that government is instituted for the protection of the weak and poor against exploitation, as well as for the strong and rich. The policeman on the corner, who is everyone's friend and will direct you when you are lost, is the ideal model, as is the law-loving sheriff bringing order to the West. But in this fifth kind of violence, this is all thrown aside. And the violence becomes the more destructive precisely because it is a perversion of previous protectiveness. Government itself is then reduced to battling on the level of combatants.

3. DESTRUCTIVE VIOLENCE

Violence is a uniting of the self in action. Jean-Paul Sartre writes that violence is creating the self. It is an organizing of one's powers to prove one's power, to establish the worth of the self.

It is a risking all, a committing all, an asserting all. But it unites the different elements in the self, *omitting* rationality. This is why I have said above that the uniting of the self is done on a level that bypasses reason. Whatever its motive or its consequences may be within the violent person, its result is generally destructive to the others in the situation.

The physical element which bulks so large in violence is a symbol of *the totality of one's involvement.* When violence erupts I can no longer sit idly by on the sidelines. Movement seizes my body, which I am called upon to risk as an expression of my total commitment. No desire or time to think is left once the violence breaks out; we are in a nonrational world. This can be subrational, as it generally is in the riots in the ghettos; or it can be superrational, as it assumedly was with Joan of Arc. Reason no longer has even a pretense of command.

In the movie *If,* the conventional dullness of life at a British boys' boarding school is portrayed with stark realism. The burden of routine, the loneliness, the artificial moralistic rules soon develop into sadism and homosexuality. In the face of the severe beatings they receive, the boys begin to form a bond of camaraderie. Then the leading boys discover a cache of machine guns and ammunition under the cathedral. The movie ends with a surrealistic scene in which the boys take their guns to a position on top of the church and mow down guests, dressed in all their British pomp, who have come to commencement exercises. The movie is a presentation of the steps of violence from separation to loneliness to camaraderie to sadism to violence.

The availability of guns has a curious and macabre relation to violence. This form of technology not only vastly increases the range and the effectiveness of violence but also has a strong effect —generally dulling—on the consciousness of those who use them. One day when I was on a farm in a fairly remote section of New Hampshire, I noticed under an apple tree a stray dog which seemed to be diseased. Having been alone for some time, during which time one's imagination often comes up with weird ideas, I decided the dog had rabies. Although I couldn't get to it in the tangle of branches, our own dog, to which our whole family was deeply attached, could and did. She went sniffing around the "rabid" one, and, being a chow, she would not come back to me no matter how much I called. I went in the house and got the Luger pistol that my son used on the farm for target practice, inserted a clip in it, and came out to shoot the rabid dog. Now the point of this story is that my having in my hand a pistol with which to shoot some living thing changed me into an entirely different person psychologically. I could deal out death to anyone since I was possessed by this instrument of death; I had become an irrational man of hostility. The gun had me rather than my having it: I had become *its* instrument.

Seized with dislike for this person I had become, I took the gun back to the house and put it away; and the incident was resolved in a quite different way.

We understand only vaguely the effect that technology can have on the consciousness of a person, but it is clear that the possession of guns can radically change personality. Glenn Gray remarks that, as an officer in the army, he did not feel dressed when he went out without his pistol strapped to his belt; not being in the army, I felt myself to be a misdirected robot, without conscious control over my actions, when I had my finger on the trigger with the intent to kill.

An extreme form of such an effect on personality can be seen in the career of Charles Fairweather, the teen-ager who went on a rampage in Nebraska and murdered eleven people before he was caught. "I love guns," he had said as a boy. "They give me a feeling of power like nothing else." His story follows along common lines: as a queer-looking child with bowlegs and thick glasses he was mocked regularly when he first went to school. He developed early in life the symbolic interpretation of the world as a place of mockery, and his cry for recognition became that much the stronger for never having any answer. He then discovered that he could get recognition by letting loose his temper and flailing away at the school bullies in fights, which he managed to win by the sheer vehemence of his violence. His father described him as "always one of the quiet ones," illustrative again that the docile-appearing person may be precisely the violent-prone one. Despite his poor eyesight, he became a remarkable marksman with a gun.

Upon getting out of high school he managed to find a girl friend and a job as assistant on a garbage truck. When the scant recognition that these afforded him was wiped away—he lost his job and his girl friend's mother threw him out—he got three guns and shot his girl friend's mother and stepfather, living for several days in their house with their bodies wrapped up in paper and stowed in the chicken yard. Forcing the girl to go with him, he then went on the path of violence made familiar by Dillinger and Bonnie and Clyde.

The important element in this bloody story is his early symbolic interpretation that the world is a place of derision. His ultimate violence achieved a double response: it answered his cry for recognition and it also mocked the world in revenge. (Again, we see the macabre logic in such outbursts of violence.) From his complete lack of feeling when he was later questioned about the persons he had murdered, we cannot conclude that he was always so unfeeling, so typically schizoid. It is obvious that the person on a binge of violence must *become* unfeeling and detached, like a soldier mowing down the enemy with a machine gun, or else he could never do what he feels he has to do.

We are haunted above all by his childhood obligato: "I love guns. They give me a feeling of power." The symbol of the gun as a phallus and its relation to sex is well known. Both are long and slim, both eject a substance that can radically change the person into whom it is directed. Hence the gun has become, especially with simple people, a symbol par excellence of masculine power. The line delivered by Mae West on greeting her boy friend remains the classic expression of this: "Is that a gun in your pocket or are you just glad to see me?"

But the cultural aspect of guns is also convincing, as Stanley Kunitz remarks. We hunted with guns to eat; we hunted with guns to make the land safe for our houses; we hunted with guns to live in our pioneer period, from which we in America are removed only by a little over a century. In all these ways the gun was valuable, a laudable symbol of power; and handling it well was also laudable. Many a person feels when he possesses a gun that he has a power that was unfairly taken away from him. And what a power it is! He can now make this big explosion and hurl that projectile to kill things much larger than himself. Consciousness is surrendered willingly. In the film *Patton*, the general's running out and emptying his pistol into the air at German airplanes bombing his Algerian base is a childish gesture, an anachronistic hang-over from a boy playing with guns; but it is nevertheless a convincing expression of violence.

4. CONSTRUCTIVE VIOLENCE

Psychologically speaking, there are an infinite number of situations in which people live at subhuman levels, and they find that some violence is life-giving. The overly shy person; the suspicious one who cannot let himself make relationships; the one unable to love deeply or to give to another; the coward who insulates himself from experiences that would enrich him—the list becomes endless. These are all individuals in whom some admixture of violence may help to correct a deficiency. But it requires a burst of effort that goes beyond rationality, a risking of one's self, a committing all, to give the person a sense of fulfillment. When a woman who has been docile all her life finally loses her temper and breaks out in a tirade, we find ourselves smiling and silently cheering; at least she is no longer apathetic. A friend of mine told me recently that his two sons had come home from college and had stepped into a situation where there was a lot of tension because of the illness of two relatives. After a couple of days one of the sons had torn up his hat in rage, and the other son had broken two ash trays against the wall. My friend remarked: "It was a good violence." A burst of anger seems to clear up the psychological relationship, making for greater honesty. Hence most people feel better after having gotten angry.

We have said that violence unites the self on a level below the human one. Now it so happens that many people (in fact most people) do live this way—that is without consciousness in any degree and without personal dignity. Frantz Fanon writes about such people in Africa. They spend their lives as only partially formed human beings, as do millions in Central America, South America, India, and China, and millions living on a substandard in this affluent country. For these people, violence may raise the level of psychological and spiritual existence. Just as it unites the self that has attained consciousness on a level *below* the human one, it may *raise* undeveloped persons to a human level. This may take the form of political rebellions, which cause groups to break out of their apathy and succeed in wrenching social reforms from the dominant party. There are few, if any, instances where a dominant group has given up its power willingly and freely; power has a way of burrowing in to stay.

I mention Fanon here because, as a black psychiatrist and as a participant in the Algerian rebellion, he describes the prototype of constructive violence. Born in Martinique and trained in Paris, Fanon went to Algeria during the revolution; he later contracted cancer of which he died in his late thirties. His book *The*

Wretched of the Earth made him the theorist not only for the Algerian revolution but for all the blacks in Africa. The colonial powers, his thesis runs, make a distinction between human beings, the white man being above the semibeast who is black. Government then becomes the institution that preserves the status quo, for the maintenance of which the natives must be kept continually subdued. Fanon's book is a passionate affirmation of the dignity of the natives, their potential consciousness, and their future freedom. He believes this will not come to pass without violence. These are people who have suffered centuries of exploitation and have endured the apathy this causes; and to become alive psychologically and spiritually, some violence is necessary.

But the violence is not of the natives' choosing, even though it is generally made to look that way. The colonial powers took an active role in setting natives against each other and, as a result, consolidating their own interests. This was often called by such platitudinous phrases as "the white man's burden"; but the important point is that government was for the sake of the foreign country rather than for that of the native people, be they black or brown or yellow.

Violence is the only way for the blacks not only to throw off the yoke of the colonial powers but also to develop some unity among themselves. Fanon believes that the underdeveloped nations, after having been exploited for so long, are on a different level than the colonial powers; violence is a stage in the development of the blacks toward nationalism. It is the way to integrity, self-esteem, and awareness of their own powers. When Fanon's books were reviewed by a pacifist Quaker, the reviewer remarked that wherever Fanon uses the word violence, one could read nonviolence and the meaning would be the same. In other words, Fanon is talking of human dignity, the birth and growth of consciousness, integrity of relationships.

Fanon tells us of the Algerian blacks he treated as a psychiatrist. There was one who fought with the resistance at night and drove a taxi during the day. His wife was taken by French soldiers, raped successively, and then beaten for the purpose of wringing out of her information about him. Such a man *has* to have a depression (for which Fanon treated him) and *has* to be a rebel to have any self-respect at all.

Fanon argues for going *beyond rationality* as the white man has known it. The dignity of the blacks will spring not merely from their brains but from their total organism and their collective unconscious, which is an expression of their organism. They are climbing toward a new order, toward new forms, and these are part of a new rationality. The old order and old forms will be destroyed in the process, but no sane person would argue that the forms of colonial society, based upon inhuman sexual, social, and economic exploitation of the blacks, with its "yes, sah" and its kowtowing, ought not to be broken. What follows it can scarcely be more unjust; let us hope it will be more just. In his introduction to *The Wretched of the Earth*, Sartre writes: ". . . in the period of their helplessness their mad impulse to murder is an expression of their collective unconscious. . . . Violence is suppressed rage," which, as we have said, is often turned against themselves. In arguing that the violence be turned back against its causes, the representatives of the colonial powers, Sartre and Fanon sound cynical. But looking at the situation from the long-term perspective of justice one is convinced that their stand is realistic, however disturbing it may be for the affluent nations.

Fanon writes,

> We ought to uplift the people; we must develop their brains, fill them with ideas, change them and make them into human beings. . . .
>
> . . . The living expression of the nation is the moving consciousness of the whole of the people; it is the coherent, enlightened action of men and women. . . . [We] ought first to give back their dignity to all citizens. . . .[6]

The violence Fanon recommends does not consist of sticking needles in dolls or pounding on pillows but is aimed at the real evils of social oppression. In his rage the black man not only gives himself vicariously for his brother black but affirms himself as well, even if in the process he sacrifices his own life.

PART III

TEN

INNOCENCE AND MURDER

> Murder rarely fits the stereotype of an unsuspecting,
> helpless, passive victim stalked by a cold, calculating
> killer. Most homicides are preceded by angry quar-
> rels in which the victim plays an active part in
> bringing about his own death.
>
> —Elton B. McNeil,
> from "Violence Today"

Can innocence, once it becomes involved in action, escape murder? This troublesome question confronts us with renewed sharp-
ness after the events of the past years, especially the shootings in
Kent State, Jacksonville, and Augusta. But it is a question that
has troubled man ever since the dawn of consciousness and the
forming, in our forefathers' minds, of the myth of the Garden of
Eden. Albert Camus pondered the problem and recorded his
thoughts in *The Rebel*. Melville was obsessed with the issue and
wrote his last work, *Billy Budd*, in an endeavor to resolve the
knotty question.

Does the victim, for example, have anything to do with *making* himself the victim? The question takes us into the very heart of the meaning of innocence. Does the virgin herself, beyond flirting, constitute the challenge to the man to end her virginity? Is not innocence curiously bound up with murder in the ritual of sacrifice in practically all cultures? What is the meaning of the phenomenon to be found in the dim beginnings of human history and coming down to this very hour of sacrificing *virgins* and *youths* to the Cretan Minotaur or to the Moloch of modern warfare?

When we push the question of innocence and murder to the furthest reaches of human consciousness, we may find it to be one of those perdurable problems that we cannot answer satisfactorily via intellect alone but must, in Rilke's advice to the young poet, "*Live* the questions now. Perhaps you will then . . . live along some distant day into the answer." [1] But in our endeavor to think it through, we can expect new light to be thrown on the mainsprings of violence. Most important of all, an analysis of the problem of innocence and murder foreshadows the emergence of a new ethics for the coming age.

In one of his descriptions of Billy Budd, Melville speaks of a "generous young heart's virgin" experience. Innocence is generosity, especially in children, who can still believe and trust since they have yet to experience that betrayal which leads to cynicism. Innocence has to do with the "heart" in that it is a feeling state, a way of perceiving life rather than a calculation. It is "virgin" in that it is *before* the awakening to the vast possibilities in life for sensuality, tenderness, exploitation, and betrayal. The lack of sexual experience has historically been taken for the symbol of innocence, although it should be remembered that it is a symbol and not the content.

Innocence is, in addition, a condition of powerlessness. One of our problems, as we discuss innocence, will be to establish the extent to which this powerlessness is capitalized on by the innocent person. The question is: How far is innocence *used* as a strategy of living?

1. THE TRAGIC DAY AT KENT STATE

As we start our discussion with the shootings at Kent State in 1970, we immediately see a demonstration of part of our thesis. This lies in the fact that two of the four students killed were not involved in the protest at all. One was dressed in his ROTC uniform and was going across the campus to take a test in war tactics, and another was on her way to a music class. The moral of this is clear: *there are no bystanders anymore.* This implies something about the solidarity of human beings—the fact that we are all part of the tragic event. Without a surrender of one's own consciousness, no one today can draw his own moral skirts about him and claim an immunity from these events. Television and mass communication are only symptoms of a basic participation in the events of importance to the human race. "To breathe is to judge," Camus reminds us.[2] We can be confident that we shall find that this awareness of our own involvement is not at all the excuse for masochistic breast-beating or quietist withdrawal from the struggles. It can lead us rather to a new sharpening of our own ethical sensitivity and a discovery, though it be only partial, of the basis on which a lasting and effective struggle for racial integration or a relief from the compulsive hold of warfare may be founded.

As representative of these four students and their innocence, I shall choose one of them, Allison Krause, who was reported to have dropped a flower the day before the shooting into the barrel of one of the guardsmen's rifles, saying: "Flowers are better than bullets." She is pictured in a poem by Russian poet Yevgeny Yevtushenko, which, despite its tendency toward sentimentality, reveals some important points:

Nineteen-year-old Allison Krause,
You were killed because
You loved flowers. . . .

Bullets,
  Pushing out the flower . . .
Let all the apple trees of the world,
  Not in white—
    But in mourning be clothed.

So far we see only the event as it occurred that day: four victims of murder, the whole event summed up in the ironic and
cruel trajectory of stray bullets. But Yevtushenko knows that in
this simple innocence he has only touched the surface. In the suc-
ceeding lines we see the complexity of innocence and of evil:

But a Vietnam girl—the same age as Allison—
Taking in her hand a gun,
Is an armed flower
  The wrath of the people . . .[3]

I take both the phrase "armed flower" and "thorny flower of
protest," a phrase that appears later on in the poem, as referring
to the dimension of experience added to the original purity of
innocence. We now have wrath as the basic motivation.

Yevtushenko is now talking about a different kind of innocence
—an "armed flower" no longer the product of childlike powerlessness but of the power of wrath. The Vietnamese girl knows that
the flower grows on a thorny bush and has to be handled with
care. She has an innocence that does not avoid evil but confronts
it, an innocence predicated on the assumption that human history is an endless dialectic between good and evil and that there
is, in the depths of the human soul as well as in human history,
no such thing as pure evil or pure good. Yevtushenko's juxtaposition of "flower" and "armed" reminds us of the phrase used by
Jesus in the Gospel according to Saint Mark with which He ad-

jured His disciples as He sent them out into the world: "Be ye wise as serpents but harmless as doves." This is, again, a curious juxtaposition of innocence and experience, which, it was hoped, would become the foundation for effective social action in the work of these disciples.

2. THE GUARDSMEN

Let us now consider the innocence of one of the "enemy," a typical young member of the Ohio National Guard, roughly the same age as Allison. I am helped in this by a letter I received from a college girl whose brother was exactly in that position. I shall quote from this letter:

> My younger brother Michael was afraid to answer the telephone in those days for fear it would be his National Guard Headquarters calling him for riot duty on one of the nearby campuses. He had joined the National Guard to avoid being drafted into the regular army and sent to Vietnam. Michael says that the rest of his group were as afraid of a phone call as he. He was not at all sure the student protestors were wrong, and even if they were, the presence of the National Guard was no answer.
>
> If my brother had been called for riot duty, and if some irresponsible officer had provided him with a loaded gun, and if the confrontation had become strained, he may have shot a student. . . . I think that both Allison Krause and the Guardsman who shot her were playing roles that didn't belong to either of them.

Let's assume, with my correspondent, that Michael is mobilized and arrives on the Kent State campus. He picks up the fact that the students at Kent State had woefully neglected any real communication with the townspeople—indeed, had gone out of their way to irritate them. On Saturday nights, according to a dispatch in the *New York Times*, students would sit on the downtown sidewalk, making the townspeople walk around them to the accompaniment of obscenities, totally unaware, although it is hard to believe, of the degree of hatred this was engendering in the people of the town of Kent. Over a period of two days Michael sees one building burnt down, he gets only three hours sleep the night before, the students yell obscene jokes at him and pelt him with rocks as he is marched with his battalion through the taunting crowds.

Shall we condemn Michael, our hypothetical young guardsman, as murderer? If we do that—because he was the one who squeezed the trigger—and fold up our briefcases and go home, we are preventing ourselves from understanding a large segment of reality, and we are capitulating exactly at the point where we should press on the hardest. Michael's sister, my correspondent, goes on to point out where she thinks the culprit is:

> I think the country has evolved into a kind of massive unreality and fear. . . . It is a kind of out-of-touchness which robs people of most of their alternatives except survival.

There is no denying that this massive "unreality and fear" exists. In our day we tend to live out the state of mind that Camus predicted in his early novel, *The Stranger*, in which Meursault, the anti-hero, exists in a general state of semiconsciousness. He makes love to a girl as though both were half-asleep, and he finally shoots an Arab in the sun on the desert in a condition of semiawareness that leaves us, as no doubt it left him, wondering whether he had really shot the Arab or not. He is tried for murder. His crime is actually the *murder of himself*.

What my correspondent calls this "massive unreality" and "out-of-touchness" makes every man a stranger to other men as well as to himself. And the fact that it is the sickness of contemporary man, who surrenders his consciousness in the face of the continual assaults on his senses, like surf in a perpetually stormy ocean, does not make our problem any easier.

But you and I also make up this country which has become so filled with "massive unreality and fear." When we think of the "country" or the "society" as at fault, we tend to posit the country as an anonymous "it" which does things to us, the people in it. It is then, in part, a convenient peg on which to hang our own projections. Thus we evade the issue on its deeper levels. I am not discounting the importance of social psychology, the study of the way groups take on roles and use them for their various purposes of security. I am also aware of the effect of electrotechnics on the individual, of the mass impersonality of technology, and of the experience each of us undergoes as the sport of innumerable pressures operating on us in "a world we never made."

But our society, our country, has this power because we as individuals capitulate to it; we give over our own power, as I have tried to point out earlier, and we then are offended because we are powerless. To that extent, we victimize ourselves. Our survival depends on whether human consciousness can be asserted, and with sufficient strength, to stand against the stultifying pressures of technological progress. If the country has evolved into a state of "massive unreality and fear," it must be you and I who experience this unreality and fear.

And so we must push on in our endeavor to understand the psychological uses of innocence and murder.

3. BILLY BUDD'S TRAGIC FLAW

Melville's Billy Budd is pictured, like Allison Krause and her fellow students, as the personification of innocence. Called the "Handsome Sailor," he is a saintly young man who happened, during a war with France, to be taken from his ship, the *Rights of Man,* and impressed into service on the man-of-war, *Indomitable.* He has a sunny disposition, is very strong, and always seems to be the center of any group on shipboard. Apparently he is loved by everyone. Melville calls him "virginal," and frequently compares him to an "angel." An old Danish sailor on the ship calls him

"Baby Budd." Like the flower children, Billy totters at the edge of being too good to be true.

In Billy, Melville is obviously seeking to preserve the innocence of a child (which will become our problem presently) carried over into adulthood, when it should normally be absorbed into something new. He writes: "Yet a child's utter innocence is but its blank ignorance, and the innocence more or less wanes as intelligence waxes. But in Billy Budd intelligence, such as it was, had advanced, while yet his simple-mindedness remained for the most part unaffected." Like the flower children of our own day, this kind of character has been set up for some ultimate tragedy.

Billy has only one obvious flaw, which none of us would call tragic but only human: he stutters when his emotions are strongly aroused.

Did I say everyone loved him? Not quite. Claggart, the ship's master-at-arms, is caught in his own ambivalence about Billy. On one hand he is attracted by Billy's beauty and spontaneous grace, and on the other he hates him for the very purity and innocence he represents. Claggart is, according to Melville, "the only man on the ship who is intellectually capable of adequately appreciating the moral phenomenon presented in Billy Budd." But at the same time Claggart despairs of ever sharing it and is filled with a cynical disdain for it—"To be nothing more than innocent!" [4]

It is important to see that this attitude toward innocence is different only in degree from the attitude most of us maintain. Innocence expects something from us, demands something, draws out our tendencies for care and sustenance; and many a man or woman hates these tendencies in himself, and hates more whatever causes him to act on them. When we are confronted by authentic childlike innocence, we are touched by it and want to protect the child, but we hope he will grow to the age when he can protect himself. But when this innocence is present in adults —as in some nonviolent or pacifist persons, or flower children, or commune-dwellers—we are attracted by it, our consciences are pricked, but we are also bothered by our own sympathies being drawn out in spite of ourselves, and we vaguely feel that we are being exploited. These innocents are a thorn in the flesh of the world; they threaten to annihilate "law and order," the police and the authority of government. The symbolic action of Allison Krause, the day before she was killed, dropping a flower down the barrel of the guardsman's gun defies all of the accepted beliefs about the power of guns. Thus innocence threatens to upset the world as we know it.

Authentic innocence is a kind of goodness, and this also throws many people into a state of ambivalence. The citizens of ancient Athens, one remembers, voted out of office a candidate known as "Aristides the Good" because they were tired of hearing him always referred to as "the Good." Goodness makes demands on us, and the naïve belief that people simply love the good is one of our earliest illusions, though it takes a Dostoevsky adequately to clear up that misconception.

Claggart cannot stand such pure innocence in his world. The development of his ambivalence is pictured as envy and antipathy that feed upon themselves. About Billy he seems to smile, but is this smile really a grimace? Melville writes that Claggart was a man "in whom the mania of an evil nature, not engendered by vicious training or corrupting books or licentious living," was "born with him and innate, in short 'depravity according to nature.' " [5] Again he describes Claggart as a man "apprehending the good, but powerless to be it; a nature like Claggart's surcharged with energy as such natures almost invariably are, what recourse is left but to recoil upon itself. . . ." Melville is here describing the daimonic—a force that grips people beyond even their own needs for survival, that makes them, as Goethe puts it, challenge the whole universe to combat; and thus feeding on itself, sooner or later it comes to a tragic end as it seeks to overthrow nature itself.

On the simplest level, Melville's story proceeds with an amazing clarity. On a dark, hot night when Billy is sleeping on deck, one of the crew approaches him and asks his help in planning a mutiny. Billy indignantly spurns the whole idea. But, like all good-natured persons who hate to hurt other's feelings, he did not come out with a radical "no" and would not have ever considered informing on a fellow shipmate.

Billy is then denounced by Claggart before the captain as having planned the mutiny, and is called in to defend himself. As Claggart repeats his accusations, Billy is so flabbergasted at the injustice that he stammers and cannot say a word. The captain cries: "Defend yourself, man"; and then, seeing the sailor's impediment of speech, he adds: "Take your time, my boy." But this fatherly concern makes Billy's speaking block all the worse. In his impotent rage, all Billy's passion goes into the blow that kills Claggart.

There is no choice, Captain Vere knows, under the laws in effect on a warship in wartime, but that Billy must be hanged. The chaplain, who comes to see him before the hanging, finds that Billy takes his imminent death "as a child hears it," and kissing the sailor on the cheek, concludes that "innocence was even a better thing than religion wherewith to go to Judgment." Billy is hanged on the main yard at dawn the next morning. But just before he is raised, with the sullen crew piped out to watch the hanging, he shouts: "God bless Captain Vere!" And catching some of Billy's spirit, the crew repeats the cry. This is a demonstration of Billy's purity of heart and lack of malice or revenge.

What is the parallel between Billy Budd on one side and the four Kent State students on the other? The one radical difference is that Billy throws the punch that kills Claggart while at Kent State the students are the ones who are killed. But we cannot let our judgment or our ethics hinge upon a split-second use of muscles, for that would make us entirely dependent upon the individual's self-control. We would then end up with a legalism without ethical content. This is the error of all rigid dogmatism, whether it is religiously or computer directed, and our primary purpose is to avoid such rigidity.

Billy Budd and the students have several important features in common. Both are the *personification of essential innocence.* Both experienced completely unexpected ends. Neither Billy nor the students were aware of the evil of the world; they did not permit themselves nor want to see the cruelty and inhumanity of earth's inhabitants. Also both fit the "vicarious suffering" pattern of the crucifixion of Christ—Billy Budd by Melville's intent and the students by virtue of the symbol they have become for countless people. Melville's summary sentence about his hero would have emphatically fit the students as well: Billy Budd's "agony proceeded from a generous young heart's virgin experience of the diabolical incarnate and effective in some men."

As we push our understanding of the story to deeper levels, we discover exceedingly important things about innocence. Why did Billy not *sense* Claggart's enmity toward him? Not that he wasn't warned. Dansker, the old sailor who occupies the role of prophet in the book like Tiresias in Oedipus (and the psychoanalyst in modern culture), tells him time and again that Claggart is "down on him." But when Billy rejoins: "But he never passes me without a pleasant word," Dansker points out that this is also a symptom of Claggart's evil designs. Billy has no sense of "suspicion" or "distrust." We must regard the lack of these qualities, which are essential to understanding our contemporary world as well as the internal world of the daimonic, as tragic flaws in Billy's character, of which his stuttering is only an outward, physical symptom.

Melville says in so many words: *"Innocence was his blinder."* This is a remarkable sentence, especially since it is preceded by the statement that if Billy had been "conscious of having done or said anything to provoke the ill will of the official, it would have been different with him, and *his sight might have been purged if not sharpened."* There must have been some need in Billy *not*

to see. Indeed, Billy capitalizes on being liked: he remembers remarks Claggart has made to him such as: "Handsome is as Handsome [does]," and he thinks, as he is brought to the captain's
office to be queried, that "the captain looks kindly on me," and
he "may be appointed to a new and better post on the ship." In
short, the preservation of his innocence has become for Billy—
although entirely unconsciously—a useful strategy by which he
lives.

But note also that "his sight might have been purged if not
sharpened" had he been conscious of anything said or done to
provoke the officials. He does, indeed, fail to *see* or to *know* because of his blinder. This is part of Melville's curious thought
that *spirituality is opposed to innocence.* They are not only *not*
the same thing, but they work *against* each other. Billy is pictured
throughout as having very little spiritual quality (the "spiritual
sphere wholly obscure to Billy's thought"). Billy's "essential innocence" is defined as "an eruption of heretical thought hard to
suppress." Later, when he dies, his innocence is felt by the
chaplain to be "a better thing than religion" (and Melville writes
this just before his own death). Billy Budd is "spiritualized now
through late experiences so poignantly profound."

All of this adds up to the fact that Billy is innocent but not
spiritual. For the latter requires and is based upon experience—it
tempers the self, deepens consciousness and awareness, purges
and sharpens our sight, as Melville says—whereas innocence acts
as a blinder and tends to keep us from growing, from new awareness, from identifying with the sufferings of mankind as well as
its joys (both being foreign to the innocent person).

These are two potential poles of experience: to remain innocent, blocking out what does not appeal to you, striving to preserve the Garden of Eden state; or to strive toward spirituality
and move to the "deeper music of humanity," in Wordsworth's
phrase.

Does a victim have something to do with *making* himself the victim? What does the interdependence of human beings mean —the fact that we are all bound in a web, which includes unconscious as well as conscious factors, that spreads out from ourselves and our parents and children like rings from a wave to include ultimately whole oceans of humanity? Can Billy Budd be excused from responsibility for sensing the effect of his actions—indeed, the effect of his very beauty and innocence—on others around him, including Claggart? What about the blithe existence built on one's own convictions and one's own integrity alone, unaware of the outreaching waves from one to others? Is this not a kind of unreal purity—a mortal life fashioned as though one is not a mortal—which can no longer, in our interdependent world, be accepted, let alone praised as righteous? Because the likelihood is that this kind of innocence has as its purpose to cover up something; it is the innocence of the child when the person is no longer a child. Having the capacity to experience the world, one has at the same time the responsibility for not closing one's sensibilities to that experience.

4. VIRGINS AND DRAGONS

What is the source of the great emphasis through human history and prehistory on the sacrifice of *virgins* and *youths*? Why do we always sacrifice the innocent? Is it not that Sphinxes and dragons are projections of our own aggression and violence? [6] The citizens of the early city-states had a difficult time—as does modern man —in controlling their internal tendencies toward aggression and violence. They could do it only by projecting their internal dragons *outward* on the mythical beast in the cave outside the city. It is a fascinating endeavor of our forefathers to put out their "animal," "dark," "wild," "subterranean" tendencies into the forests which surrounded their cities.

Year after year, the Sphinx who hovered outside the gates at

Thebes took her ransom of human flesh to eat. "There is a symbol in her act, though she has only one act, murder," writes Bronowski.[7] The spell could be broken only by guessing—a very human act in its rationality and its intuition—the answer to a riddle, which turned out to be simply "man." This has, indeed, always been a riddle to us, although it ought to be stated slightly differently: Why is it that "man" requires this sacrifice of human flesh, this need to crush and destroy and eat his fellow citizens? "Man feeds on others" goes the song in the *Threepenny Opera*—a truth which demands that it be faced each time our society disintegrates, exposing the bare bones of human existence to us. Is there some element within us that demands this cannibalism for the sake of our own manhood? The idea is too cruel to contemplate, but contemplate it we must.

But what is even more illuminating is that the man (Oedipus) who guesses the Sphinx' riddle is he *who takes the Sphinx back to its rightful place within himself*. Oedipus, the man who dares to become *conscious* of the fact that man—in fantasy at least, which is where the meaning of the act counts—sleeps with his mother and kills his father, who sees himself in true perspective, who understands that he has within himself both good *and* evil, who understands the Sphinx within. Oedipus, the man who pursues the questions of his own identity with decisiveness and rage but never gives up: "I must know who I am and where I am from." Oedipus, the one who forces himself to *see* it all; and then in an act that dramatizes the eternal conflict, cuts out his *eyes*, the very organs of sight, the symbol of becoming conscious, of understanding human life and the world. Oedipus, the man who then at Colonnus must ponder the problems of guilt and responsibility. For the drama of his life says that the only way to deal with the Sphinx is to take her back to her true home within our own psyche, and to face her there—which is to confront guilt and responsibility. The choice is clear: we must pay our human sacrifice to the Sphinx outside the city gates, or we must accept guilt and responsibility as realities within ourselves. He who cannot accept his guilt with responsibility will find himself projecting his guilt on the Sphinx outside the city.

The dragon is a similar symbol; society tries to rid itself of its own evil by projecting it on the figure of the dragon in the forest. And it deals with it by delivering to the dragon the annual tribute of virgins and youths. The dragon is not an alien nature; he has allies within the city itself and, indeed, within the individual person himself. "If St. George was indeed a Christian saint, then the dragon he fought was a more ancient ritual of human sacrifice, and was himself man-made." [8] Saint George seems to have existed chiefly in the northern regions of Europe where the forests are thick, ominous, and provocative of delightful and scary fantasies. Part of the rapture of walking in the woods is the inspiration it gives us to live out our own poetic and erotic fantasies. It is not by accident that the stories and paintings of a knight rescuing a helpless maiden from a dragon occur out in the forest—we are tempted to wonder what the maiden was doing out there in the first place, but then we recall that she got there on the lovely fantasy wings of a powerful projection. It was largely an erotic projection, and one that both maiden and knight shared.

To return to our question at the beginning of this section: Why is the human tribute so often taken in the form of virgins and youths? The seven virgins and youths sent annually from Athens to satisfy the Minotaur in Crete is but one of countless examples. Why do we always sacrifice the *innocents*? They obviously have a special attraction for the human-flesh-eating creature; it loves the tender, the helpless, and the powerless rather than the experienced. We know that this is true in the fantasies of all of us—the innocent and powerless, the inexperienced, have a special attraction. Is it that we can *give* them the experience, thus augmenting our own self-esteem? We never hear of the dragon devouring an eighty-year-old man or woman. But it is the youths and virgins that are required to satisfy the taste of the dragon.

We can best try to answer this from the viewpoint of our contemporary situation. Let no one think for an instant that we, in our vaunted modern civilization, have gone "beyond the primitive human sacrifice." We do it as well, only not in sevens but by the tens of thousands. And the name of the god to whom we sacrifice them is Moloch. More than fifty thousand of our youths have been sacrificed in Vietnam, and if we add the Vietnamese, as we surely must, the sacrifice goes into the millions. It is fantastic how the modern form of the age-old dragon is re-enacted in an event like Vietnam, with the scorched-earth policy, flame-throwing tanks, the fire and smoke laying waste to huge sections of land, the defoliation of the country, and, indeed, the mass murder of the Vietnamese people. Our modern Moloch is greedy. Which means we have much inner aggression and violence to project. We do it with protests and internal conflicts, resignation and apathy, but we still continue to do it.

It is difficult to formulate why we sacrifice particularly virgins and youths to this Moloch, perhaps because our thinking gets so mixed up with a so-called military necessity which is really irrelevant to our problem—i.e., that we draft the young because they can be taught much easier to fly a plane or to use a gun. But that sounds like a rationalization. The parallel to the old ritual of sacrifice is too close to ignore.

It is obvious that the establishment is *envious* of youth, envious of the innocent, whose lives are ahead of them. This is exacerbated, particularly in America, by the worship of youth; it is always better to be young. The older people, those who have lost their innocence long since, declare wars that these virginal youths are required to fight; and we go through the complex ritual of uniforms and bands and songs and disseminating an enormous amount of propaganda which is largely a projection of our own aggression and violence on the Japanese or the North Vietnamese.

The established people, who represent established ways, are also *afraid* of the youth. This is particularly obvious in our own day and society. *Envy* and *fear*—these are two motives for the sacrifice, and while they do not go very deep, they may help us for the moment.

Curiously, but understandably, there seems to be inherent in human life *an urge to get over innocence*. Is this related, in some curious way, to the urge to get beyond the age when we can be so easily sacrificed? The normal child wants to grow up, to experience what is about him, to become a man of the world; and although he possesses natural guards against too precipitous experiences, he looks forward to the age when he will be sufficiently self-reliant to let down these guards. There is a tendency for normal innocence to get lost. The flirtatiousness shown by girls just entering into their teens, most of it quite unconscious, is also part of the drama in the age-old urge to get over innocence. The temptation of Adam and Eve, symbolized by eating the apple and thus gaining "the knowledge of good and evil," was a headlong drive to experience and be experienced, to leave innocence behind, to make it something of the past.

It is not by accident that sexual experience is taken as the symbol for the loss of innocence, the attainment of "experience." The headlong push to get rid of virginity at an early age can well backfire into a *loss* of experience rather than a gain. The experience itself is not very momentous (some of my female patients tell of saying to the man who has deflowered them: "Is that all?"). The girl/woman and boy/man can be released into a whole new dimension of experience which, if they are ready to leave their innocence behind, can present them with infinitely more possibilities for awareness and tenderness than life had before.

In rebellions on campuses, one can often observe the curious need—generally unconscious—on the part of the student to get himself caught and in this way to overcome his innocence. A friend of mine who was a junior at one of the eastern universities took part in protests that at first seemed to be rather aimless. The students then hit upon ROTC; in their protest against that they soon won their point. They then took over an academic building. When the police arrived, my friend, apparently his need for self-preservation in conflict with his need to protest, leapt from a back window and escaped. He then joined a group that had as its issue the hiring of the same number of blacks in college halls and cafeteria as existed in the town. The students insisted that it be done forthwith and "captured" the dean in his office to hold him prisoner until it should be accomplished. The predictable result occurred: my friend and his cohorts were arrested by the police and were promptly dismissed from the university for the rest of the year. One of the best students in the university, my friend found himself thrown out of his class and with plenty of leisure on his hands.

What did he do? He went up into New England and took the next few weeks to meditate. One had the feeling that this was the purpose of it all: he had wanted to be caught. He was calling for a structureless world to give him some structure; a young man with a steady stream of successes behind him, son of a famous father, never anything against which he could test his strength, nothing yet that would stand in his path and require him to try his mettle. In such students, this is a cry for experience equivalent to their previous innocence. Young people have already lost their innocence in one sense: concentration camps and atom bombs have rendered their world structureless, but they are without the equivalent experience to go with it. They cry for experience to match their precociously lost innocence.

"The dragon and the Sphinx are within you." If that is where the dragon and the Sphinx are really located, we must first become aware of them. Our error is not in our myth-making; this is a healthy, necessary function of the human imagination, a help toward mental health; our denial of it on the basis of rationalistic doctrines only makes the evil in ourselves and our world harder to get at. No, the dragon and the Sphinx are not in themselves the problem. The problem is only whether you project them or confront and integrate them. To admit them in ourselves means admitting that evil and good dwell within the same man, and that potentialities for evil increase in proportion to our capacity for good. The good we seek is an increased sensitivity, a sharpened awareness, a heightened consciousness of both good and evil.

Pollux, one of the characters in Bronowski's play *The Face of Violence*, says near the end of the drama: "Violence has the face of the fallen angels." But what are fallen angels except human beings; and what are human beings except fallen angels? Surely enough, in the next speech at the very end of the play, Castara answers: "Forgive the man his violence . . . for violence has a human face." [9]

ELEVEN

THE HUMANITY
OF THE REBEL

The love of violence is, to me, the ancient and symbolic gesture of man against the constraints of society. Vicious men can exploit the impulse, but it is a disaster to treat the impulse as vicious. For no society is strong which does not acknowledge the protesting man; and no man is human who does not draw strength from the natural animal. Violence is the sphinx by the fireside, and she has a human face.
—Jacob Bronowski,
from *The Face of Violence*

In Truffaut's film *The Wild Child*, we see a re-enactment of an actual event that took place in the eighteenth century but which has special poignancy for us here. A doctor tries to teach a savage boy who was found in the forest living as an animal to see if he can be brought back to the human condition. The affectionate Victor, as Truffaut has named the boy, learns to speak and to count in rudimentary fashion. But these small successes and failures only add up to ambiguity. In a moment of discouragement, Truffaut as the doctor resolves to stake all on one unambiguous test to find out whether Victor is human—will the boy fight back when he is unjustly punished?

Knowing that Victor accepts punishment—being shut in a closet —when he has made a mistake, Truffaut tries to shut him in the closet when he has correctly done the task he was assigned. Victor puts up a great fight. With a glad sign of recognition the doctor states that there is present in the boy the central element which constitutes the human being.

What is this element? It is the capacity to sense injustice and take a stand against it in the form of I-will-be-destroyed-rather-than-submit. It is a rudimentary anger, a capacity to muster all one's power and assert it against what one experiences as un-fair.[1] However it may be confounded or covered up or counter-feited, this elemental capacity to fight against injustice remains the distinguishing characteristic of human beings. It is, in short, the capacity to rebel.

In the present day, when multitudes of people are caught in anxiety and helplessness, they tend psychologically to freeze up and to cast out of the city walls whoever would disturb their pre-tended peace. Ironically, it is during just those periods of transi-tion when they most need the replenishing that the rebel can give them that people have the greatest block in listening to him.

But in casting out the rebel, we cut our own lifeline. For the rebel function is necessary as the life-blood of culture, as the very roots of civilization.

First I must make the important distinction between the rebel and the revolutionary. One is in ineradicable opposition to the other. The revolutionary seeks an external political change, "the overthrow or renunciation of one government or ruler and the sub-stitution of another." The origin of the term is the world *revolve*, literally meaning a turnover, as the revolution of a wheel. When the conditions under a given government are insufferable some groups may seek to break down that government in the convic-tion that any new form cannot but be better. Many revolutions, however, simply substitute one kind of government for another, the second no better than the first—which leaves the individual citizen, who has had to endure the inevitable anarchy between the two, worse off then before. Revolution may do more harm than good.

The rebel, on the other hand, is "one who opposes authority or restraint: one who breaks with established custom or tradition." [2] His distinguishing characteristic is his perpetual restlessness. He seeks above all an internal change, a change in the attitudes, emotions, and outlook of the people to whom he is devoted. He often seems to be temperamentally unable to accept success and the ease it brings; he kicks against the pricks, and when one frontier is conquered, he soon becomes ill-at-ease and pushes on to the new frontier. He is drawn to the unquiet minds and spirits, for he shares their everlasting inability to accept stultifying control.[3] He may, as Socrates did, refer to himself as the gadfly for the state—the one who keeps the state from settling down into a complacency, which is the first step toward decadence. No matter how much the rebel gives the appearance of being egocentric or of being on an "ego trip," this is a delusion; inwardly the authentic rebel is anything but brash.

True to the meaning of the rebel as one who renounces authority, he seeks primarily not the substitution of one political system for another. He may favor such political change, but it is not his chief goal. He rebels for the sake of a vision of life and society which he is convinced is critically important for himself and his fellows. Every act of rebellion tacitly presupposes some value. Whereas the revolutionary tends to collect power around himself, the rebel does not seek power as an end and has little facility for using it; he tends to share his power. Like the resistance fighters in France during the last world war, the rebel fights not only for the relief of his fellow men but also for his personal integrity. For him these are but two sides of the same coin.

The slave who kills his master is an example of the revolutionary. He can then only take his master's place and be killed in turn by later revolutionaries. But the rebel is the one who realizes that the master is as much imprisoned, if not as painfully, as he is by the institution of slavery; he rebels against that system which permits slaves and masters. His rebellion, if successful, saves the master also from the indignity of owning slaves.[4]

1. CIVILIZATION NEEDS THE REBEL

The humanity of the rebel lies in the fact that civilization rises from his deeds. The function of the rebel is to shake the fixated mores and the rigid order of civilization; and this shaking, though painful, is necessary if the society is to be saved from boredom and apathy. Obviously I do not refer to everyone who calls himself a rebel, but only to the authentic rebel. Civilization gets its first flower from the rebel.

Civilization begins with a rebellion. Prometheus, one of the Titans, steals fire from the gods on Mount Olympus and brings it as a gift to man, marking the birth of human culture. For this rebellion Zeus sentences him to be chained to Mount Caucasus where vultures consume his liver during the day and at night it grows back only to be again eaten away the next day. This is a tale of the agony of the creative individual, whose nightly rest only resuscitates him so that he can endure his agonies the next day.

But note also that Prometheus is released from his sufferings only when an immortal renounces his immortality in Prometheus' favor. This Chiron does. What a vivid affirmation of human life, one of the essential characteristics of which is that each one of us will some day die! It is saying: "I willingly give up immortality to affirm humanity; I am willing to die in order to affirm human civilization." As Heidegger says time and again, it is death which humanizes us. And the fact that we die is intimately bound up with our rebellion and our creating civilization. This is a truth which can be known in its full force only by the rebel.

A similar rebellion and a similar acceptance of mortality are central in another account of the beginning of civilization, that of the story of Adam and Eve. The essence of their deed is rebellion—with prompting from that daimonic element in nature, the snake.

The remarkable parallel in the stories of Prometheus and Adam is that the gods are pictured as the enemies of man; they seek to keep man perpetually subordinated. Yahweh is worried lest Adam and Eve, having eaten of the tree of the knowledge of good and evil, will also eat of the tree of eternal life. Again, the fact of man's mortality is brought in as a necessary prerequisite for creativity and civilization. True, we yearn for immortality, we struggle to form symbols of it, and we smart under the necessity of dying. Dylan Thomas's poem says; "Do not go gentle into that good night," "Rage, rage against the dying of the light." [5] But if we did not know that we will die we would create no more than did the gods, lolling away their endless days on Mount Olympus, a boring succession of tomorrow and tomorrow relieved only by occasional sexual affairs with mortals.

Consciousness itself, which includes anxiety, guilt, and a sense of responsibility, is born when Adam and Eve are ejected from Eden. And all this happens in an act of rebellion. This is not foreign to psychology: there is no meaningful "yes" unless the individual could also have said "no." Consciousness requires the exercise of the individual's counterwill; it is called forth, inspired, and developed by the conflicts that occur in every individual's life which force him to wonder and to call on power he did not know he possessed.

Consider also the tale of Orestes. This is a representation of man assuming responsibility for his own life, likewise a prerequisite of civilization. It is similar to the story of Prometheus and that of Adam and Eve in the sense that it depicts the taking of a giant step forward in the humanization of man; and the fact that Orestes identifies with his father should not be allowed to obscure the fact that the myth emphasizes even more profoundly that an individual's existence must start with a rebellion against his mother, to whom he is tied at birth by the umbilical cord. After Orestes' murder of his mother, and his cutting himself loose from Mycenae, he endures persecution by the Erinyes, who drive him to virtual insanity. Likewise many persons in psychotherapy struggle, on the brink of psychosis, toward autonomy. The stages of the dramas are Orestes' act, his guilt and atonement, his assuming responsibility for his deed, and his ultimate forgiveness in the *Eumenides*, the final play of Aeschylus' trilogy, by a court composed of *men*, not gods. It is a portrayal of the importance of rebellion for the capacity to assume responsibility for one's own and one's fellow's lives.

We also note the startling regularity through history with which society martyrs the rebel in one generation and worships him in the next. Socrates, Jesus, William Blake, Buddha, Krishna—the list is as endless as it is rich. If we look more closely at the first two, we shall see how the rebel typically challenges the citizenry with his vision. Jesus' dictum was: "It was said unto you of old, . . . but *I* say unto you . . ." Although Socrates refused to evade the law, he challenged it: "Men of Athens, I shall obey God rather than you, and so long as I live I shall never cease from the teaching of philosophy." Both are introductions to frank espousal of rebellious teachings; they are challenges to the structure and stability of the society. Society can tolerate only a certain amount of threat to its mores, laws, and established ways. But if civilization has only its own mores and no input to fertilize its growth— that is, has *only* its established ways—it stagnates in passivity and apathy. The adaptation that has been worked out is to martyr the rebel during the time in which he lives and then, when he is dead and there is no chance for him to alter his message (it is now *established*), disinter him, apotheosize him, and finally worship him.

If the gods are occupied with keeping man subordinate, why don't we simply say: "Away with them!" Then we could, as rationalists through the ages have tried to do, simply accept Jesus and Socrates as the sensitive human beings they were. But that is to misunderstand the function of the gods. Gods are, culturally speaking, symbols of our ideal yearnings and visions. (*Symbol* encompasses diverse strands of reality and participates in the reality itself.) God is the symbol of the power human beings yearn for but do not have. We are always enlarging our insights and visions. To simply deny the god function in human life is to impoverish our lives, specifically our ideals and our visions. But as we enlarge and purify our insights (say about justice) and our visions (say of a better world), we also enlarge our symbols of the gods. This is why one reads in the Old Testament of the curious phenomenon of Abraham arguing with God not to destroy Sodom and Gomorrah, saying: "Far be that from Thee! Shall not the Judge of all the earth do right?" (Genesis 18:25). He *takes God to task for not living up to his own principles.* Time and again in the Old Testament a figure will *rebel* against God in terms of his new vision of what God *ought* to be and stand for.

This curious phenomenon—source of much gymnastics among theologians—makes no sense when we define God as the all-perfect, purely ineffable. But it makes entire sense when we see God, as I believe the higher religions have always seen Him, as the confluence of the Ground of Being (the *given* aspect of life) and man's own capacity for spiritual insight (the *autonomous* aspect of the individual man). The highest function of rebellion is rebellion in the name of the "God above God." That is the title of the last section of Paul Tillich's *Courage to Be,* itself an excellent example of my point.

2. REBEL AND SOCIETY: A DIALECTIC

The rebel insists that his identity be respected; he fights to preserve his intellectual and spiritual integrity against the suppressive demands of his society. He must range himself against the group which represents to him conformism, adjustment, and the death of his own originality and voice. Continuously through human history and through the life-span of each one of us, there goes on this dialectical process between individual and society, person and group, man and community. When either pole of the dialectic is neglected, impoverishment of the personality sets in. Every man has from time to time impulses to shock his society, fantasies of outraging his neighbors. Paradoxically enough, his own continued mental vitality depends on this. Also, paradoxically, the community itself, even though it condemns the outrage, gets its health, vitality and new growth *from* the outrage. This shows once again that human beings do not grow in one-dimensional fashion toward something "better and better," but rather by a dynamic process, a thesis and antithesis; they grow "down" at the same time as they "grow up," deeper while they grow higher.

The Garden of Eden myth portrays the rebellion as being against God. And, indeed, it is against authority, against the status quo, against whatever clings to the values of the past rather than looks to the future. What is omitted from the rhetoric in this rebellion is that the outcome is not either/or, but a dialectical interplay: we need authority *as* we rebel against it. We rebel against the culture with the very language and knowledge that we learned from the culture; we revolt against our parents while loving them at the same time.

The rebel also needs his society. His language, his concepts, his way of relating to others all come from that culture which he now opposes. He rises from the society, criticizes it, and aligns himself with those who are trying to reform it; and all the while he is a member of the very culture he opposes. If one thinks of civilization as ungrateful in killing its prophets, one also sees the absurdity of the whole question of gratitude or ingratitude in the behavior of the rebel. This is why I call the relationship *dialectic*. It is a dynamic interrelationship in which each pole exists by virtue of the other pole—as one changes, the other does likewise.

Jacob Bronowski states this well:

Men therefore have a right to fear that society may unman them. Yet no man has made the best of his gifts without the setting [up] of a helpful society, such as the Greek or the Italian city states. Always the animal drive for self, the jungle of nature, waits to disrupt his city. And yet that force, anti-social as it is, is not all alien or all bad. The mind that drives it is full of human wishes. The Greeks remembered that every mind, good as well as bad, takes strength from our animal body.[6]

It is the nature of society to suppress the individual person. Pointing this out, Hannah Adrendt expresses surprise that people so often talk as though the group *ought* to behave differently. Contemporary writers all the way from Reich to Fromm speak indignantly of society, venting their irritation with such words as "bureaucratic," "juggernaut," "supertechnocratic," implying all the while that it is society's fault that we are what we are. On one hand, this arises from a utopianism—the expectation that when we develop a society which trains us rightly, we'll all be in fine shape. On the other hand, it is like a child wheedling his parents because they aren't taller or in some other way different from what they are. All of which society cannot be expected to be. For society, on one side, is *us*. The rebel is a split personality in that he realizes his society nursed him, met his needs, gave him security to develop his potentialities; yet he smarts under its constraints and finds it stifling.

The rebel is continually struggling to make the society into a community. "I rebel—therefore *we* exist," as Camus puts it.[7] In our particular day, the rebel fights the mechanizing bureaucratic trends not because these in themselves are evil, but because they are the paramount modern channels for the dehumanizing of man, the stultifying loss of integrity, and the indignity of man. He fights affluence for a similar reason, for he knows that "an abundance of wealth may erode power, and riches are particularly dangerous for the . . . well-being of republics." [8]

The rebel also may be found in the colorful, albeit sometimes tattered, clothes of the dropout. The young person, rightly sensing the threat to his values and to his life in the Vietnam war, pollution, and the dehumanization which seems to accompany our vast technological progress, drops out of society for a period. His action is a protest against the rigidity of society, but it is also a time in which he can find himself. It is similar to the withdrawal of Buddha to the mountain and that of Jesus to the wilderness to find inner integrity before beginning their ministries. It is also similar to that period of wandering taken by the students of the Middle Ages as an integral part of their education.

True, the dropout can never completely deny his culture, never entirely sever his umbilical cord. He takes it with him to the mountain or the dessert in his language, his way of thinking, and even as an object against which to protest. But in his withdrawal he can get a new perspective, a new awareness of himself which may stand him in very good stead later on. I have had the impression in talking with hippies that for some of them the year or so they "dropped out" protected them from psychosis. It gave them some breathing time in the burdensome sequence of nursery, elementary school, high school, college, graduate school— during which many of them find themselves in genuine danger of suffocation. Often the dropping out serves a purpose similar to psychoanalysis. No one would argue that the dropout has not selected a more satisfactory way of working things out, not to say less expensive for all concerned, than a stint in a mental hospital. It is entirely possible that he comes back from his seemingly lighthearted wanderings with a new seriousness in his relationships to himself and his society.

We find in our psychology textbooks a plenitude of experiments in which the subject "obeys" instructions to the extent of hurting, even "killing," the "victim" of his actions, whom he sees writhing in pain through the glass in the next room. Obviously these are rigged experiments.[9] One might well conclude that human beings can be conditioned into any form of Nazilike obedience or antlike organization of colonies. But we must not forget at the same moment that there are individuals who from time to time pull themselves out of this mass, rebels who take the risk upon themselves and oppose the group even to the extent of going to prison if necessary. The Berrigan brothers and Bonhoffer come to mind. Daniel Ellsberg's decision to make the Pentagon Papers available to the people was the one tangible step he felt he could take to shorten the meaningless killing in Vietnam.

What makes an individual step forth from the conditioned mass as a rebel? Many partial answers are given in Ellsberg's case: his empathy for the suffering of the Vietnamese, expecially of the helpless children he saw on his trip to Vietnam; his frustration at being unable to get the effective attention of McNamara and others in a position to take steps to stop the war; indeed, his own style, his flamboyance, and his long struggle for psychological integrity. But whatever motives one assigns to the action, the truth remains that Ellsberg *did* step out. He did perform the act against the forces of "law and order." In propagating the truth, he occupied a position of which Prometheus is the prototype. Ellsberg is the typical modern hero in that in our age of super-technology, conformism, and apathy, he stands forth as using mass communication and modern technology in the service of his rebellion.

There is no escape from living through this dialectical conflict of individual and society. The only choice is whether one will live it through constructively and with zest and dignity or waste his energy and substance protesting against a universe which is not organized according to his liking. No matter how much society is changed—and much of it cries to high heaven for change—there still will exist the fundamental dialectical situation of individuation against the conformist, leveling tendencies of the society.

Some societies have recognized and made allowance for the destructive, protesting, anarchic needs of the citizens. Dionysian revels, carnivals, riotous saturnalia of all sorts give testimony to

these answers. The ancient Greeks had a spate of them: from the
Eleusinian mysteries to the Corybantic dances on the mountain
top (some of which were exclusively for women) to the simpler
use of the fruit of the god Bacchus to help ideas flow in the alco-
holic banquet of the friends of Socrates and Plato in the *Sym-
posium*. This was what Dionysus stood for: dancing, joy, anarchic
pranks, release from inhibitions, times when all authority was
mocked and the daimonic tendencies had full sway. How else
can your society have a healthy Apollonian aspect if you do not
have the contrary Dionysian release to give vitality to the form
and order? It is difficult for us in America, where the ancient
festival of carnival has survived only in such feeble gestures as
Mardi gras in New Orleans, to realize how health-giving these
carnival periods were, not only for ancient countries but for
modern ones as well. The masked ball, where personal responsibility is bracketed for the evening, possesses an anonymity which
may be subpersonal but also may be transpersonal as well. Most
of Europe, especially in Catholic countries, bursts out in celebra-
tion and last flings before settling down to the arduous deprivation of Lent.

We need our ways of mocking authority. We have our Hallo-
ween and our April Fools' Day. But we need ways of channeling
our secret dreams of outraging our neighbors and scandalizing the
town fathers—in short, of symbolically expressing our dreams of
revenge on a society that thwarts and confines us. An interesting
example of this is the scapegoat king, who accepts the scepter
knowing that he will be killed during some riotous saturnalia in
which all authority is mocked. And consider the mocking of ultimate religious authority in the crucifixion of God's son, Jesus.
When, in Handel's *Messiah*, we refer to Him who is reviled of
men and scorned and spat upon, we are acting out an archetypal
rite in which mankind expresses its age-old contempt, which is
vicariously accepted by the figure on the cross. The expression of
our disdain and mocking—indeed, of all these so-called negative

and destructive emotions—enables us then to see and experience more clearly the positive side of religious conviction. We can change the *forms* of these positive and negative sides of human nature, but we cannot change the *fact* of them without amputating parts of human experience and impoverishing ourselves.

Are not the excesses in American life—one of which is violence —related to this lack of Dionysian ritual? Detective stories, identification with the hero in gangster movies, apotheosing the criminal as in the postprohibition period in the 1930s—all are symptoms in part of a lack of sound opportunities to let out the "secret dreams of revenge on the society that thwarts and contains us."

> You cannot in fact bottle up these deep feelings of protest in a world as mechanical as ours and think that you will syphon them off casually in lacey thrillers and in little evasions of the forces of order. . . . Anti-social feelings in a hierarchic society like ours are first a power, then a commodity on which some unscrupulous leader can rise to fame, and become the spokesman for the dream of violence of all underdogs.[10]

The recognition of the value of the rebel would go a long way in channeling such daimonic forces in constructive directions.

For the rebel does what the rest of us would like to do but don't dare. Note that Christ *willingly* takes on Himself the sins and the scorn of men; He acts, lives, and dies, vicariously for the rest of us. This is what makes Him a rebel. The rebel and the savior then turn out to be the same figure. Through his rebellion the rebel saves us. We see here another demonstration of my previous thesis—that civilization needs the rebel.

3. THE ARTIST AS REBEL

Who, upon seeing them, has not been seized by wonder and perplexity at the gargoyles leering from their perches just below the roofs of Notre Dame in Paris? These half-animal, half-human creatures eating other animals alive, these satanic figures with their tongues stuck out at the hordes of people in the city square below, with expressions of contempt carved in stone, who sit watch in broad daylight over Paris—are they in some way the devil's hostages? No such evasive answer is possible. They are expressions of a tension that exists in all of us, a dialectic between light and darkness, good and evil. These expressions of the daimonic are critically important to the fact that this French nation could construct cathedrals that emanate such beauty. For the artist who lights up our world, as those sculptors did, lives and breathes with the daimonic. What we used to call beauty (a word we should not use very often in our day, Auden reminds us) is impossible if we cut loose our connection with this nether world.

The artist faces an ancient and powerful interdiction in the second of the Ten Commandments: "Thou shalt not make unto thee any graven image, or any likeness of anything that is in heaven above, or that is in the earth beneath, or that is in the water under the earth." This is an interdiction against the worship of idols. It is also a prohibition of magic placed upon the ancient Hebrews, an interdiction of the primitive way of getting power over an animal or a person by drawing his likeness in the sand. Peasants around the Mediterranean are to this day skittish about having their snapshots taken—apparently a carry-over of the early feeling that if you got their image by means of camera or crayon or paint, you captured part of their soul. The "graven image" must relate to the *form* of the person, something that he experiences as crucial to his autonomy. I cited this as a "primitive" idea, but it is a sophisticated insight as well. For the portrait as drawn or painted by any competent artist is related not so much to the appearance of the subject but rather to what the artist *sees* in the subject, which will be something of the latter's underlying form. However one phrases the problem, it is a sign of courage that a person commits himself to becoming an artist in the first place. He has to have considerable rebelliousness to set himself against the archetypal prohibition.

Art is a substitute for violence. The same impulses that drive some persons to violence—the hunger for meaning, the need for ecstasy, the impulse to risk all—drive the artist to create. He is by nature our archrebel. I am not speaking of art as social protest: it can be that, as it was with Delacroix, and artists are almost always in the front line of social causes. I mean rather that his whole work is a rebellion against the status quo of the society—that which would make the society banal, conformist, stagnant. Often this takes the form of rebellion against the academic tradition in art it-self—*vide* van Gogh, Cézanne, Picasso. But the essence of the re-bellion is in the new way of seeing nature and life. The art consists of the discovery and expression of this new way of seeing, which in turn is related to the artist's originality, his sense of newness and freshness, his criticism of the past and present in the light of future possibilities.

Alfred Adler used to say that the artist teaches mankind to see. But the artist teaches us the possibilities of new forms as well. He shows us new options of perceiving and responding to the world and each other which did not exist before he saw them and pointed them out. He does not *impose* form on a chaotic world as the thinker does; he *exists in this form*. Hence it becomes "sig-nificant form," to use Clive Bell's expression in his essays on Cézanne.

As long as the artist can create, he does not have to resort to vi-olence. As a person he is generally an unbellicose, unaggressive type and exists by the live-and-let-live code, although we find that in heated discussions he can be stubborn and reach heights of passion which in someone else would be expressed in violence.

Hence the artist has a proportionately harder time in periods of transition like ours—harder, say, than the doctor, whose subject (the human body) remains relatively constant even in periods of social upheaval.[11] Contemporary artists may feel this difficulty keenly, as they will reveal in conversation. A few years ago Robert Motherwell could state that this is the first age in which the artist had to create his own community. But some artists now say that there is *no* meaningful society into which they can fit. They have no community. Society *appears* to worship the artist, but this is pretense; actually contemporary society buys and sells him, and any individual with money can buy up all an artist's canvases and dump them into a big hole in a field.

Society can enthrone the artist—very much like they did in the case of the scapegoat king that Bronowski talked about. This happened to Jackson Pollock. He appeared on the cover of *Life* magazine—the highest "throne" in those days of the beginning of mass communication—with the caption, "Is Pollock the Greatest American Painter?" He was acknowledged a great public success, and such acknowledgment is very hard to take. Shortly afterward he ended his life by driving his car off the road. Mark Rothko became financially successful and then committed suicide. These and other artists' suicides may mean many things. But they also seem to support my artist-friends' claim that society only pretends to value the artist. The artist is actually a second-class citizen; he is accepted as the "frosting" and not the bread of life. The age admires art as a financial investment, then goes merrily on its way with technological gimmicks. To see this we need not look far. The skyline of New York, once one of the wonders of the modern world, has been progressively ruined by the conglomerate, haphazard erection of skyscrapers thrown together with no reference at all to an over-all form or vision. Yes, they are built with glass and glistening aluminum and all sorts of other interesting materials. One can build a cesspool out of interesting materials.

The contemporary artist finds himself in a strange bind and is tempted to fall into despair. Some of them say that Mondrian, for example, went as far as anyone could in rebellion, and his rebellion has had precious little effect on anyone. They also point out that the war in Vietnam is too vivid, with the bombing of villages and the defoliation of the land, all of which is accepted apathetically by the citizenry. How can you force people to see—which is the artist's function—with such competition? However much one may talk of how Charles Manson was groomed for his later violence by the "postgraduate training" in crime he received during his thirteen years in prison, his satanic cult illustrates how actual murder can be recorded by the murderers themselves on film and in music as an artistic experience.

One can and must note these things. True, my concept of the artist as rebel can be exaggerated to the degree of pathology, especially when it occurs in a technological civilization characterized by built-in violence on the roads and in actual motor cars and in imaginary TV programs of violence in any city on any day. But the fact that something can be pushed to a pathological extreme does not make it the norm, nor is it any argument against the norm. Sex crimes are no argument against the healthy experience of sexual love.

These disturbing facts make the thesis of the artist as rebel more serious and more real. The artist as rebel is a gadfly to the culture. His task is still to follow his talent of perceiving and showing us the new forms in which we, too, can see and experience the world around us. We must pay attention to him if we wish to learn what the spiritual content of our new world will be.

4. THE LIMITS OF THE REBEL

Most people are surprised to learn that the rebel operates with built-in restraints. Indeed, that is his chief distinction from the revolutionary who, concerned as he is with political change, experiences only outer restraints. But the rebel, who is concerned with people's attitudes and motives, has inner limits. He is restrained by the boundaries inherent in the order he proposes. In describing these limits, I shall speak in ideal terms to clarify my point.

The first is the universality of the rebel's vision. His ideal of life, which gives birth to his rebellion in the first place, applies not just to himself but to others as well; and these others must include his enemies. To pursue the metaphor I employed earlier, if the slave kills the master he has no choice but to usurp the master's throne and be killed himself; and we have round after round of meaningless bloodshed, like the sultans' murders in the seraglio. The excitement of the ego trip is secondary to the rebel; he is concerned chiefly with his vision. In this vision of the world are present the restraints upon his actions. Socrates is restrained from making a secret deal with Sparta not by the Athenians, who condemned him to death, but by the requirements of his own personally chosen ethics. Jesus could not take up the sword without betraying His own vision of the world.

The rebel scorns as a motive personal revenge (actually the nursing of feelings of rejection, of his own hurt pride—authentic enough but not the basis for a genuine rebellion). He does not have the right to demand revenge, and furthermore there is no time to do so. The essential characteristic of the rebel is his capacity to transcend his own particular hurt pride in identification with his people and with his universal ideal.

Another limit is the rebel's *compassion*. As we noted in the case of Daniel Ellsberg, the compassion of the rebel is one of the things that makes him a rebel in the first place. He identifies with people who suffer and feels a passionate desire to do something about this suffering. This arises from his sensitivity and empathy for other people which inform his vision. True, the rebel is sometimes so absorbed in the universal application of his ideal that he neglects his own family. Well, like us all, he remains a human being of both good and bad traits. His capacity for empathy makes him more compassionate for peoples—if not always for the members of his family—and enables him to form his vision.

The limits also come from the fact that *the rebel's mind meets other minds.* The others' views of reality restrain and sharpen his; and in encounter between them, they work out something of greater value for both. This is why dialogue is so important for the rebel. Dialogue includes all the tangling of emotions, temperament, and diverse goals which occurs in any real interchange. The authentic rebel knows that the silencing of all his adversaries is the last thing on earth he wishes: their extermination would deprive him and whoever else remains alive from the uniqueness, the originality, and the capacity for insight that these enemies—being human—also have and could share with him. If we wish the death of our enemies, we cannot talk about the community of man. In the losing of the chance for dialogue with our enemies, we are the poorer. We would lose not only our enemies' good ideas, but the restraints they give us as well.

The rebel is committed to giving a form and pattern to the world. It is a pattern born of the indomitable thrust of the human mind, the mind which makes out of the mass of meaningless data in the world an order and a form. "Born as we are out of chaos," writes Witold Gombrowicz, Polish novelist, "why can we never establish contact with it? No sooner do we look at it than order, pattern, shape is born under our eyes." [12] This is not only true of the novelist, but of the painter, the engineer, and the intellectual as well—indeed, true of us all. The forming of the world begins with the simple act of perception, which arranges things in a Gestalt that has meaning for us. *We* institute the order. It is a product of the human mind's continual search for meaning in a world in which meaning does not exist apart from our minds. True, nature does have rhythm in its day and night; it does have balance and harmony, summer and winter. I give away the quality of the human mind when I write "summer and winter"; without our patterns, the functions are blind and meaninglessly repetitive. But no sooner does the human mind look at this chaos than order is born. Out of the meeting of the human mind and the chaos of nature some meaning is established by which we can orient ourselves.

The rebel is he who can grasp this meaning with a clarity that reaches beyond that of the masses of people. "An act of rebellion on [the rebel's] part seems like a demand for clarity and unity," writes Camus. "The most elementary form of rebellion, paradoxically, expresses an aspiration to order." [13] Those who hold political power may not trust the rebel's vision and may hang on to their power to oppose it. But in this new vision, this very pattern and order, there are present the restraining factors on the rebel himself. When one writes a sonnet or any other kind of poetry, the chosen form exercises a restraint upon the poet just as the banks restrain a river. Otherwise creativity flows off absurdly in every direction and the river is lost in the sand.

There are even limits to such a personal aim as self-actualization. The human potential movement has fallen heir to the form of innocence prevalent in America, namely that we grow toward greater and greater moral perfection. Trying to be good all the time will make one not into an ethical giant but into a prig.[14] We should grow, rather, toward greater sensitivity to *both* evil and good. The moral life is a dialectic between good and evil.

Especially in the understanding of violence is it necessary to be aware of the good and evil in each of us. As Camus again puts it:

> Whatever we may do, excess will always keep its place in the heart of man, in the place where solitude is found. We all carry within us our places of exile, our crimes and our ravages. But our task is not to unleash them on the world; it is to fight them in ourselves and in others. Rebellion, the secular will not to surrender . . . is still today at the basis of the struggle. Origin of form, source of real life, it keeps us always erect in the savage, formless movement of history.[15]

The fact that good and evil are present in all of us prohibits anyone from moral arrogance. No one can insist on his own moral supremacy. It is out of this sense of restraint that the possibility of forgiveness arises.

TWELVE

TOWARD
NEW COMMUNITY

We cannot avoid
Using power,
Cannot escape the compulsion
To afflict the world,
So let us, cautious in diction
And mighty in contradiction,
Love powerfully.

—Martin Buber,
from "Power and Love"

1. FAREWELL TO INNOCENCE

If we hope to mitigate violence, we must deal with it on a level commensurate with the problem. Why do most proposals for alleviating violence strike us as superficial when compared with the problem itself?

Take, for example, the common cry that TV is the culprit. The most vocal representative of this argument is the psychiatrist Frederic Wertham, who believes that violence is "socially conditioned and socially preventable." [1] He holds the mass media largely responsible for the spread of violence since they stimulate children to think violently, acclimatize people to violence, and create a generation of "hard" Americans who are competitive and insensitive and who accept violence as a way of life.

But this argument assumes that violence is a relatively recent arrival on the American scene, born fifty years ago with mass media, which is far from the truth. The problem of violence has been present in America all along: ask one of the few remaining Indians or any of the frontiersmen who took the law into their own hands and lived by brute force. Would Dr. Wertham prefer that the Vietnam war no longer be covered on TV? The evil is surely not TV, but the war itself. Mass communication holds a mirror up to ourselves, and would those who argue, like Dr. Wertham, break the mirror so that we can remain blissfully innocent of our own destructiveness? "The whole idea is that of 'original innocence,' " writes Hedy Bookin, in criticizing Dr. Wertham's view. "Man would never be so evil if the serpent of the mass media hadn't tempted him with the forbidden fruit of violence." [2]

Wertham's argument would be stronger if it were made against the *passive* character of television, for a steady diet of TV cultivates not the participation but the spectator role of the viewer. In this way it may cultivate a real feeling of impotence, and this impotence may well contribute to violence.

Other practical suggestions that have been offered often impress one as being good but failing to go deeply enough. Konrad Lorenz's recommendation of holding more international sports contests in order to drain off international competition is sound in itself. But it again deals mainly with a symptom. The ping-pong matches between the United States and China were more a result of a change in attitude between the two countries—they occurred after President Nixon had already planned his trip to China. There is also merit in Anthony Storr's proposals for greater effort toward birth control and in his acceptance of euthanasia, both aimed at lessening the pressure of the world's burgeoning populations and the latter at permitting old people to pass out of life with some dignity. But, again, the problem is already upon us, and we must search for ways of dealing with the aggression and violence already present in the Western world.

Violence is a symptom. The disease is variously powerlessness, insignificance, injustice—in short, a conviction that I am less than human and I am homeless in the world. For a convenient short-hand I have called the disease impotence, fully recognizing that violence also requires for its triggering some promise, a despair combined with the hope that conditions cannot but be bettered by one's own pain or death.

To strike the disease at its core requires that we deal with the impotence. Ideally, we must find ways of sharing and distributing power so that every person, in whatever realm of our bureaucratic society, can feel that he too counts, that he too makes a difference to his fellows and is not cast out on the dunghill of indifference as a nonperson.

Power is the birthright of every human being. It is the source of his self-esteem and the root of his conviction that he is inter-personally significant. Whether a person is black or a woman or a convict or a patient in a mental hospital or a student facing anni-hilation in Vietnam or confronting overpopulation and pollu-tion, the problem is roughly the same—to enable the individual to feel that he will be counted, that he has a valuable function, that "attention will be paid." I do not speak of external opportu-nities for men to be individuals—the last two hundred years of inventions have steadily liberated human beings. I speak rather of the inward conviction of significance, the individual's psychologi-cal and spiritual valuing by himself and by his fellows.

I wish to illustrate how this distribution of power is possible and how it alleviates violence. The University of Oklahoma was able to avoid riots—and in a creative rather than suppressive way

—when most other universities were torn by violence. In September, 1967, under the newly appointed president, J. Herbert Holloman, there was instituted a plan to survey the whole educational project and reconstruct the university. To that end twenty-three committees were set up, comprising all groups affected by the university. This included faculty, students, administrators, private citizens, alumni, and legislators. For students this was no token representation. Their opinion was an essential part of the study.

When riots swept over the colleges and universities at the time of the Kent State shooting, Oklahoma had its uproar but no violence. Those in the best position to know at Oklahoma stated that it was this giving the students an integral part of the reconstruction that was responsible for their freedom from violence. It was *power distributed*—not paternalistically, but authentically. The students' judgment was valued, desired, and utilized—as, indeed, it would have to be if such a reconstruction was to be effective. It was power *with responsibility* in accord with the level of development of the persons (i.e., students) involved.[3] Responsibility was commensurate with the power. When the threats did come, they did not escalate into violence. Why should the students become violent? They were not impotent; it had already been demonstrated that they had their voice in the direction of the university.

An interesting event occurred which shows the changed mood at this university. In the days immediately following the Kent State shooting, a group of radical students carrying North Vietnamese flags rode motorcycles through the lines of parading ROTC. Then they picketed the ROTC building. Tension was high and dangerously near the boiling point. The colonel in charge of ROTC felt this tension, as did everyone else; it was the taut state that called either for action or explosion into violence. What to do! His eye lighted on a large coffee urn in his office. He got this out and with the aid of a few helpers he served coffee to the picketers. This "blew my mind" said one of the nearby faculty members; and it so impressed the picketers that tension was greatly reduced without violence. Thus communication became possible.

This colonel, as I later talked to him, was not an especially imaginative man, and he disclaimed any intention of a nonviolent or altruistic strategy or even any conscious hope that his act would have any effect. He felt only that he had to *do* something, and the coffee urn was the one thing at hand. It is an interesting illustration of the build-up of energy almost to the breaking point and its rechanneling before its outbreak in a constructive rather than destructive direction.

2. ''IF I COULD HAVE FOUND MY TONGUE''

Power is required for communication. To stand up before an indifferent or hostile group and have one's say, or to speak honestly to a friend truths which go deep and hurt—these require self-affirmation, self-assertion, and even at times aggression. This point is so self-evident that it is generally overlooked. Hence Buber adjures us to be "mighty in contradiction." My experience in psychotherapy convinces me that the act which requires the most courage is the simple truthful communication, unpropelled by rage or anger, of one's deepest thoughts to another. We generally communicate most openly only to those who are our equals in power.

Violence itself is a kind of communication. This is particularly true with members of the proletarian class, who are described in the person of Billy Budd: they cannot communicate with the tongue, so they strike in violence. But it is still a language, however rudimentary or primitive, appropriate in certain conditions, and necessary in others.

The blacks in Africa are violent because they do not possess the self-esteem necessary for communication. They cannot stand and deliver themselves of their feelings in relation to the colonists;

indeed, unable to formulate them, they are unsure of what their feelings really are. The sooner the colonial whites turn their minds away from exploiting Africans for financial gain and become concerned with the rights of the blacks as human beings, the sooner the violence will be mitigated.

Frantz Fanon points out that there is something more important for the powerful nations to send to the weaker ones than food and arms. This is the *poets*. For the poets (and writers in general) are the ones skilled in communication. They can speak in universal forms which will be understood by people of whatever color or nationality. They speak the language of consciousness, of dignity, regardless of race or color; they can cultivate the integrity of the blacks and the other characteristics that are essential to being human. For they know that communication makes community, and community is the possibility of human beings living together for their mutual psychological, physical, and spiritual nourishment.

What did Billy Budd mean when he said, standing there in the captain's office as he was being tried by the ship's officers for murder, that he would not have killed Claggart if he could have spoken? What is this "tongue" that he could not find? Obviously not *mere* talk—which can be meaningless chatter, a filling up of emptiness to keep people from being afraid. Melville must refer, through Billy's statement, to that kind of communication that overcomes the impulse to violence and that binds persons to each other. This kind of talking is conciliatory and restorative.

In psychotherapy we find that the difficulties experienced by a man and wife in a relationship can be gauged roughly by how much trouble they have in communicating with each other. When there is difficulty understanding what the other is talking (or not talking) about, we can assume an estrangement. Then the person is simply not (or perhaps does not want to be) tuned in on the wave length of the other. Intellectualizing or talking abstractly is a symptom of the same thing—a desire not to communicate one's real feelings, a blocking-off of one's total self. As hostility grows, projection increases also; there is apt to be a good deal of allegations and an increase in distance, all of which is indicative of growing hostility. We know that we shall get to the stage of violence ere long. Psychotherapy is reversing that process so that the persons can talk on the same wave length. Even if the couple decides to divorce, at least *they* decide it together, and the process has that much more community in it.

Communication recovers the original "we-ness" of the human being on a new level. Authentic communication depends on authentic language. Authentic talk is organic—the speaker communicates not merely with words but with his body also; his gestures, his movements, his expression, his tone of voice communicate the same thing as his words. He speaks not as a disembodied voice but as one organic totality to another.

We would not communicate unless we valued the other, considered him worth talking to, worth the effort to make our ideas clear. This is communicating without talking down, without patronizing. Communication implies the presence of what Alfred Adler calls "social interest." You have to have an interest in the other to make it worthwhile to hear him. This means one relates to another not as receptacle for the expression of one's sexuality, or as a being to be exploited for the assuaging of one's own loneliness, or in any other way as an object, but as a human being in the full meaning of that term. Communication leads to community—that is, to understanding, intimacy, and the mutual valuing that was previously lacking.

Community can be defined simply as a group in which free conversation can take place. Community is where I can share my innermost thoughts, bring out the depths of my own feelings, and know they will be understood. These days there is a great search for community, partly because our human experience of community has largely evaporated and we are lonely. The term *community* gives birth to a rich cluster of words, all of which have powerful connotations. There is *commune*, a relatively new word with a positive ring; and *communion*, an old word with new meaning that has for many of us a still more positive tone. But we come then to a cognate which is taken negatively by many people—namely *communism*. All of these words have the same root.

Community is destroyed by destructive violence. If I, like Cain, commit murder, I must flee into the desert, driven by my guilt at having taken the life of my brother Abel; a cleavage now exists between me and the other members of my erstwhile community. In this sense I shrink my world and thus kill part of myself.

I need my enemy in my community. He keeps me alert, vital. I need his criticism. Strange to say, I need him to posit myself against. Lessing once said: "I would walk twenty miles to see my worst enemy if I could learn something from him." But beyond what we specifically learn from our enemies, we need them emotionally: our psychic economy cannot get along well without them. Persons often remark that, curiously to them, they feel a singular emptiness when their enemy dies or is incapacitated. All of which indicates that our enemy is as necessary for us as is our friends. Both together are part of authentic community.

Community is where I can accept my own loneliness, distinguishing between that part of it which can be overcome and that part of it which is inescapable. Community is the group in which I can depend upon my fellows to support me; it is partially the source of my physical courage in that, knowing I can depend on others, I guarantee that they also can depend on me. It is where my moral courage, consisting of standing against members of my own community, is supported even by those I stand against.

3. LOVE AND POWER

When Priscilla remarked to me that a man in her home town would not have committed suicide if "one person had known him," what was she saying? I believe she was saying that this man had no person to whom he could open himself up, no one who was interested enough in him to listen, to pay attention to him. She was saying that he lacked someone who had compassion for him, a compassion which would be the basis of his self-esteem. If he had had such a person, he would have counted himself too valuable to wipe out.

She was also saying, although she did not know it, that the line between knowing and loving is impossible to draw. One merges into the other. If I know someone well I will tend to have compassion for him; and as I have compassion for him I will try to know him well. This is why it is next to impossible, when somebody you dislike is talking, to listen to him, take in what you hear, and let it form itself into a comprehensible structure in your mind. The tendency is to close off our minds, if not our ears; to block out the person we do not like.

The development of power is a prerequisite for compassion just as it is for communication. At the beginning of psychotherapy persons are normally so bereft of power in interpersonal relationships that they have very little compassion to give. Priscilla was unable to orient herself enough to give to others. Compassion requires that one have some security, some position of power from which he can give concern to another. Lack of self-esteem and self-affirmation makes it very difficult to have anything left over for others; an individual must have something with which to "prime the pump" before he can give to others.

I cannot agree with some of my colleagues who hold that there are two kinds of people: those who operate by love, and those who operate by power. I believe this is a dichotomy which leaves the way open for the illusion of the past, namely that one can have "powerless love" and another (generally a person one does not like) "loveless power."

At this point I would take my stand with Martin Buber when he says: "Do not protest, 'Let love alone rule!'" He continues;

> Can you prove it true?
> But resolve: Every morning
> I shall concern myself anew about the boundary
> Between the love-deed-Yes and the power-deed-No
> And pressing forward honor reality.[4]

If we are to "honor reality," we must be aware that power and love can have a dialectical relationship, each feeding and nourishing the other. We must turn our attention to the interplay between love and power, and the fact that love needs power if it is to be more than sentimentality and that power needs love if it is not to slide into manipulation. Power without charity ends up in cruelty. The destructive kind of power generally comes from persons who have suffered radical deprivation, like when Oliver, despairing over the lack of effect his protests had in Washington, fantasied shooting all the old ladies in the supermarket. The constructive forms of power, such as nutrient power and integrative power, come only when there has already been built up within the individual some self-esteem and self-affirmation.

Having established the relationship between power and love, let me now state that there is an experience in which love does transcend power. This is shown in Goethe's drama in which Faust has made his compact with Mephistopheles to gain infinite knowledge and infinite sensual experience. Mephistopheles can give him only power, and that he does. Faust has loved Margarete and Helen of Troy and thinks he will leave them easily and casually behind. But when Faust experiences the moment when his soul should logically be surrendered to the devil, he is saved by Margarete's love for him. The "mothers" re-enter the drama, carrying with them the ties that every man has with nature and with mankind.

This allegory of love conquering power reveals an archetype of human experience that speaks to us all in diverse ways. We can understand again what Buber means when he writes in the same poem:

> I do not know what would remain to us
> Were love not transfigured power
> And power not straying love.

We are the creatures whose love is continually straying into power, and whose power is occasionally transfigured by love. I would deny Buber's contention only if it is used as a way of escaping the reality of power and avoiding the fact that we all participate in some way or other in the power structure of our society.

Compassion is the name of that form of love which is based on our knowing and our understanding each other. Compassion is the awareness that we are all in the same boat and that we all shall either sink or swim together. *Compassion arises from the recognition of community.* It realizes that all men and women are brothers and sisters, even though a disciplining of our own instincts is necessary for us even to begin to carry out that belief in our actions. Compassion is the tie felt for another not because he "fulfills his potentialities" (as if anyone ever did!). Compassion is felt toward another as much because he *doesn't* fulfill his potentialities—in other words, he is human, like you or me, forever engaged in the struggle between fulfillment and nonfulfillment. We then surrender the demand that we be divine in order to join mankind in its suffering and its destiny. As Jacob Bronowski says:

"We are all lonely. . . . We've learnt to pity one another for being alone. And we've learnt that nothing remains to be discovered except compassion." [5]

Compassion is the acceptance of the conviction that nothing human is foreign to me. I can then understand that if my enemy is killed, humanity is reduced that much. Even if the sum total of cruelty has not greatly diminished in the last twenty centuries —children still suffer for things for which they have not the slightest responsibility—we shall not require a token success. It is in the confronting of this dilemma—fighting cruelty without regard for tangible success—that man discovers what he is in the depth of his personality.

Compassion gives us a basis for arriving at the humanistic position which will include both power and love. Compassion occupies a position opposite to violence; as violence projects hostile images on the opponent, compassion accepts such daimonic impulses in one's self. It gives us the basis for judging someone without condemning him. Although loving one's enemies requires grace, compassion for one's enemies is a human possibility.

Will our compassion be, as Daniel Ellsberg's was, ignited by the war in Vietnam? Many of us have had no way out of our despair at being unable to stop this cruel holocaust, nothing effective to do, struggle as we might with the viable alternatives. Almost universally this war is hated, and most people would like to forget it if they could. Regardless of all our protests, it goes on and on, with the steady attrition of our sense of honesty, credulity, and even language. But, even as we continue all efforts to end the war as soon as is humanly possible, it may be that Vietnam will be, in the long run, of service—if one may speak that way without blasphemy—to America. With all its evil Vietnam may, daimonically indeed, represent an occasion in which America could achieve an insight into life that will be essential to its future. This could come about by our gaining a tragic sense, an awareness of our own complicity in evil, our own participation in automatized,

dehumanized destructiveness. What two world wars failed to do
may be accomplished by the little country so decisively inferior
to our power but able to continue its self-assertion despite all
the sufferings we inflict. The guilt we feel is surely a normal guilt
and may be the beginning of America's transformation from an
adolescent posturing to the maturity of a responsible nation. So
far we have kept our innocence, despite all lessons to the contrary.
Let us hope that this sad event will constitute a farewell to innocence.

4. TOWARD A NEW ETHIC

The argument of Part III of this book leads us toward a new
ethic, an ethic which will be relevant to the new age into which
we are moving. Put simply, it is an ethic of intention. It is based
on the assumption that each man is responsible for the *effects* of
his own actions.

The real tragic flaw in Billy Budd can now be stated: he blocked
off his own awareness of the effect he was having on Claggart,
despite the endeavors of the old sailor, Dansker, to point out
Claggart's growing hostility toward him. Billy sought to preserve
his own innocence. Indeed, his innocence was precisely the defense against this crucial awareness—it was a shield behind which
he nursed his own childlikeness. His unawareness made the killing of Claggart and his own hanging inevitable.

The ultimate evil in our day, similarly, is inherent in situations
in which the person is prevented from taking such responsibility
—as in that involving our hypothetical national guardsman, or
the members of the battalions in Vietnam who were ordered to
shoot innocent noncombatants. The triumph of good over evil is
shown in individuals like the American soldier who landed a
helicopter at Mylai and turned his gun on Lieutenant Calley to
shoot him if Calley continued the massacre.

The future lies with the man or woman who can live as an individual, conscious *within* the solidarity of the human race. He then uses the tension between individuality and solidarity as the source of his ethical creativity. So far we have been taught to do one or the other. We have learned to accept responsibility for our convictions; but that is not enough. We have learned to accept responsibility for the sincerity of our actions; but that, too, is not enough. These are both individualistic—both part of the ethic which had its roots in the Renaissance. It is worth reminding ourselves that one can be entirely sincere and firm in one's convictions—and entirely wrong. We must accept responsibility for whether we *are* right or wrong. It is to be hoped that one can learn to do that without the guilt on his hands of the killing of the mathematician in the bombing of the building at Madison or the killing of hundreds of thousands of innocent people in Vietnam.

We can, in a splurge of individualism, live by our own integrity; or we can, in a splurge of solidarity, identify ourselves with a group or party that takes over our decisions for us and decides by its own rules. Either way leads us into error if it neglects the other. Held in balance, however, they constitute the two sources of ethical choice. From the first should be preserved the element of the consciousness of the individual, necessary to all ethics; and from the second, the element of interpersonal responsibility, also a necessary source of all ethics.

Let us compare this ethic with that orientation most popular among psychologists—the ethics of growth. Man's "unlimited potential" is a term one hears often, and we are adjured to "fulfill it" as much as possible. But what tends to be missing is the recognition that this potential never functions except as it is experienced within its own limits. The error is in treating potential as if it had no limits at all, as though life's course were perpetually "onward and upward." The illusion that we become "good" by progressing a little more each day is a doctrine bootlegged from technology and made into a dogma in ethics where it does not fit. This *is* the course in technology; but in ethics, in aesthetics, in other matters of the spirit, the term *progress* in that sense has no place. Modern man is not ethically superior to Socrates and the Greeks, and although we build buildings differently, we do not make them more beautiful than the Parthenon.

Bulletins of the encounter-group movement, where this error is seen most often, lists such courses as "Creative Encounter," followed in the next bulletin by "Advanced Creative Encounter." Or "Joy," and in the next issue, "More Joy." And where do you go from there? As though human life were a Roman candle onto which you can hang to be carried higher and higher into the stratosphere, up, up, forever. But soon the Roman candle bursts, and then where are you? It is completely forgotten that joy increases to the extent that the capacity for woe does also. Forgotten is the wisdom of William Blake:

> Man was made for joy and Woe;
> And when this we rightly know
> Thro' the world we safely go,
> Joy & Woe are woven fine,
> A Clothing for the Soul divine.[6]

The awareness that human existence is both joy and woe is prerequisite to accepting responsibility for the effect of one's intentions. My intentions will sometimes be evil—the dragon or the Sphinx in me will often be clamoring and will sometimes be expressed—but I ought to do my best to accept it as part of myself rather than to project it on you.

Growth cannot be a basis for ethics, for growth is evil as well as good. Each day we grow toward infirmity and death. Many a neurotic sees this better than the rest of us: he fears growing into greater maturity because he recognizes, in a neurotic way of course, that each step upward brings him nearer to death. Cancer is a growth. It is a disproportionate growth where some cells run wild growing. The sun is generally good for the body, but when one has tuberculosis, it is disproportionately better for the t.b. bacilli, and therefore the affected parts have to be shielded. Whenever we find we have to balance one element against another, we find that we need other, more profound criteria than the one-dimensional ethic of growth.

The question will arise: What is the relation of the ethic suggested here to our present ethical system in Christianity? Christianity has to be taken realistically, in terms of what it has become rather than what was ideally meant by Jesus. The Christian ethic evolved from the "an eye for an eye and a tooth for a tooth" system of justice present at the beginning of the Old Testament —i.e., the concept of justice attained by the balance of evils. The Christian and Hebrew ethic then shifted its focus to the inner attitudes: "As a man thinketh in his heart, so is he." The ethic of love ultimately became the criterion, even to the extent of the ideal commandment: "Love your enemies."

But in the course of this development it was forgotten that love for one's enemies is a matter of grace. It is, in Reinhold Niebuhr's phrase, "a possible impossibility," never to be realized in a real sense except by an act of grace. It would require grace for me to love Hitler—a grace for which I have no inclination to apply at the present moment. When the element of grace is omitted the commandment of loving one's enemies becomes moralistic: it is advocated as a state an individual can achieve by working on his own character, a result of moral effort. Then we have something very different: an oversimplified, hypocritical form of ethical pretense. This leads to those moral calisthenics that are based on a blocking-off of one's awareness of reality and that prevent the actually valuable actions one could make for social betterment. The innocent person in religion, the one who lacks the "wisdom of serpents," can do considerable harm without knowing it.

We also tend consistently to forget the presence of the daimonic all the way through the Old Testament. Speaking of Jeremiah, Daniel Berrigan beautifully expresses my point:

> "To pluck up and break down, to destroy and overthrow, to build and to plant." Such words sound strangely "destructive" to modern ears. But the words spoken to Jeremiah are an enemy to all gradualism, all theories of history based upon the escalation of goodness. . . .
>
> Can it be true that God is not a Niagara of Pablum, spilling His childish comfort upon the morally and humanly neutral, whose faces are raised blankly to partake of that infantile nourishment? . . . "Therefore I will contend with you" [says God to Jeremiah]. It is at once the highest compliment of God and a guaranty of the dramatic and abrasive quality of life.[7]

Another thing that occurred in cultural evolution is that the ethic of Christianity in our time became allied, especially in the last five centuries, with the individualism which emerged in the Renaissance. This increasingly became the ethics of the isolated individual, standing bravely in his lonely situation of self-enclosed integrity. The emphasis was on being true to one's own convictions. This was true especially in American sectarian Protestantism, strongly aided by the individualism cultivated by our life on the frontier. Hence the great emphasis in America on *sincerity* as one lived by one's own convictions. We idealized men such as Thoreau, who supposedly did that. Hence also the emphasis on one's own character development, which in America seems always to have a moral connotation. Woodrow Wilson called this "the character that makes one intolerable to other men." Ethics and religion became largely a matter of Sunday, the weekdays being relegated to making money—which one always did by ways that kept one's own character impeccable. We had then the curious situation of the man of impeccable character directing a factory that unconscionably exploited its thousands of employees. It is interesting that fundamentalism, that form of Protestantism which puts most emphasis on the individualistic habits of character, tends to be also the most nationalistic and war-minded of the sects, and the most rabid against any form of international understanding with China or Russia.

A central criticism of this ethical development is that it omitted any real inclusion of the *solidarity* of the human kind. The "crowd," as it was called, was important in one's moral development only as something one stood against, as something one trained one's self not to be influenced by. We bought our own "ethical" achievement as solitary creatures, interested in helping others only by giving from our own abundance—tithing. And since this "character development" fitted the capitalistic system and the habits that went into making money, one rose socially, never forgetting one's duty to share with the "less fortunate." But this rarely fooled the less fortunate, and it never got us out of our individualistic shell.

What is lacking is an authentic empathy with others, an identification with the woes and the joys of those bereft of power—the blacks, the convicts, the poor. Naturally the Marxist concern with solidarity, geared to the proletariat in contrast to the self-involved middle and upper classes, achieved a vast following. It is no wonder that the Marxist emphasis on internationalism, brotherhood, and comradeship caught the imagination and emotions of a world which thirsted for just that.

We need not—indeed, we must not—surrender our concern with integrity and our valuing of the individual. I am proposing that our individualistic gains since the Renaissance be set in balance with our new solidarity, our willingly assumed responsibility for our fellow men and women. In these days of mass communication, we can no longer be oblivious to their needs; and to ignore them is to express our hatred. Understanding, in contrast to ideal love, is a human possibility—understanding for our enemies as well as our friends. There is in understanding the beginnings of compassion, of pity, and of charity.

Granted that human potentialities are not fulfilled by a movement upward but by an increase in scope downward as well. As

Daniel Berrigan says: "Every step forward also digs the depths to which one can likewise go." No longer shall we feel that virtues are to be gained merely by leaving behind vices; the distance up the ladder ethically is not to be defined in terms of what we have left behind. Otherwise goodness is no longer good but self-righteous pride in one's own character. Evil also, if it is not balanced by capacities for good, becomes insipid, banal, gutless, and apathetic. Actually we become more *sensitive* to both good and evil each day; and this dialectic is essential for our creativity.

To admit frankly, our capacity for evil hinges on our breaking through our pseudoinnocence. So long as we preserve our one-dimensional thinking, we can cover up our deeds by pleading innocent. This anti-diluvian escape from conscience is no longer possible. We are responsible for the effect of our actions, and we are also responsible for becoming as aware as we can of these effects.

It is especially hard for the person in psychotherapy to accept his or her increased potentiality for evil which goes along with the capacity for good. Patients have been so used to assuming their own powerlessness—whether truly powerless, as in the case of Priscilla, or a necessary strategy as in the case of Oliver. Any direct awareness of power throws their orientation to life off balance, and they don't know what they would do *if* they were to admit their own evil. That she could actually hurt other people, and me, her therapist, seemed an unthinkable thing to Priscilla; she had been always used to being hurt by others. Mercedes had been able to hurt others only when, as a child, she worked herself into a frenzy on the ghetto streets, as in fighting or hysteria, or when she got insanely mad at her husband. But frenzy and hysteria are exactly ways of not being conscious of what one is doing.

It is a considerable boon for a person to realize that he has his negative side like everyone else, that the daimonic works in potentiality for both good and evil, and that he can neither disown it nor live without it. It is similarly beneficial when he also comes to see that much of his achievement is bound up with the very conflicts this daimonic impulse engenders. This is the seat of the experience that life is a mixture of good and evil; that there is no such thing as *pure* good; and that if the evil weren't there as a potentiality, the good would not be either. Life consists of achieving good not apart from evil but *in spite of it.*

NOTES

ONE Madness and Powerlessness

[1] Harry Stack Sullivan, *Conceptions of Modern Psychiatry* (New York: W. W. Norton, 1953), p. 6: ". . . one must consider especially the states characterized by the feeling of ability or power. This is ordinarily much more important in the human being than are the impulses resulting from a feeling of hunger or thirst. . . . We seem to be born, however, with something of this power motive in us."

[2] Arthur M. Schlesinger, Jr., "The Spirit of '70," *Newsweek*, July 6, 1970, pp. 20–34.

[3] Hans Morgenthau, in the *New York Times*, May 29, 1969.

[4] Kenneth B. Clark, presidential address to the American Psychological Association, Washington, D.C., Sept. 4, 1971.

[5] David McClellan, "The Two Faces of Power," *Journal of International Affairs*, XXIV/1 (1970), 44.

[6] Edgar Z. Friedenberg, *Coming of Age in America* (New York: Random House, 1965), pp. 47–48.

[7] Quoted by Kenneth B. Clark, *Dark Ghetto: Dilemmas of Social Power* (New York: Harper & Row, 1965), p. 4.

[8] Hans Toch, *Violent Men: An Inquiry into the Psychology of Violence* (Chicago: Aldine, 1969), p. vii. In his study of men in prison, Toch uses other prisoners, specially trained, to interview the inmates, rightly thinking that in this way he will get truer accounts. The reports of the policemen who did the arresting and the men in prison are given and then analyzed in terms of understanding the violent incident and what makes the violent personality. In this book Toch is remarkably fair to both police and incarcerated men.

[9] *Ibid.*, p. 125.

[10] *Ibid.*, p. 220.

[11] *Ibid.*, p. 240. Allan Berman's unpublished study of applicants for the position of guard at state prisons, entitled "MMPI Characteristics of Correctional Officers," presented at the April 16, 1971, meeting of the Eastern Psychological Association which took place in New York, bears out the same thing: ". . . correctional officer candidates, like inmates, show emotional shallowness, alienation from social customs, and relative inability to profit from social sanctions" (p. 4). Also, Berman's findings indicate that "both the officer candidates and the inmates seem to be about equal in their feelings of aggressiveness, hostility, resentment, suspicion and desire to act out assaultatively" (p. 6).

[12] Here, we shall refer to the anesthetizing drugs, specifically heroin. The hallucinogenic drugs, such as LSD, also do violence to the mind in the sense of forcing the individual out of his present state of being, but in a different way.

[13] These words are from Dr. George De Leon, a psychologist who works with addicts. Most of the material in this section comes from conversations with Dr. De Leon, and the sexual material comes specifically from an unpublished paper by him and his colleague, Harry K. Wexler, entitled, "Heroin Addiction: Its Relation to Sexual Behavior and Sexual Experience." They studied the relationship between sexuality and addiction in twenty-eight postaddicts and addicts in treatment at Phoenix House in New York. The sexual activity—defined as masturbation, night emissions, length of time till ejaculation in intercourse, degree of feeling in intercourse, and so on—was studied through answers given to various questions by individuals and groups of five (the latter taking advantage of the encounter form at Phoenix House—i.e., using the psychological pressure of the group to make the individual completely honest). The pattern of sexuality that emerged is (1) before addiction, impotence and lack of sexual competence; (2) during addiction, lack of sexual feeling so the addict is not bothered by sexual desire, or if he does have intercourse, he can go on interminably. Often his difficulty is in having an orgasm; and (3) after getting over the addiction, generally more competence and sexual desire than before addiction. Heroin, it is pointed out, is a profound anesthetic, shutting off all feelings; hence, one of the reasons it is taken is because the individual cannot take the total feeling of ejaculation.

[14] Herbert Hendin, "A Psychoanalyst Looks at Student Revolutionaries," *New York Times Magazine*, Feb. 14, 1971, p. 24.

[15] In the movie *La Dolce Vita*, the opening scene, a kind of prelude to the entire film, is of an upper middle-class man caught inside his car in a traffic jam at the opening to a tunnel. He frantically tries to get his locked windows open but cannot budge them, and he panics more and more. A bus at his side is stopped in the traffic while going the other way, so close to him that the people inside could have touched his car windows; but each person in the bus is preoccupied in his own reverie, and as the man gets more and more frantic they show no sign whatever that he even exists. One gets the eerie feeling of living in an insane world—as, indeed, in many ways it is.

It is a stroke of genius to begin this film of our times with such a prelude. For what happens in this film about the upper middle class is a continuous grasping for sensual stimulation to give some simulation of contact in a world in which *no one can hear or see* any other person. The only ones in the movie who have a sense of significance are the children who see the vision of the Holy Mother, which turns out to be a fraud, and the organist, who later commits suicide, and his small family.

16 Richard Maxwell Brown, "Historical Patterns of Violence in America," in *The History of Violence in America: Historical and Comparative Perspectives*, A Report Submitted to the National Commission on the Causes and Prevention of Violence, ed. Hugh Davis Graham and Ted Robert Gurr (New York: Praeger, 1969), p. 75.

17 *Ibid.*, p. 76.

18 I describe here the simplest form of violence; other forms, such as when one incites others, are described in Chapter Nine.

19 Clark, p. 10. As another black put it: "A lot of times, when I'm working, I become despondent as hell and I feel like crying. I'm not a man, none of us are men! I don't own anything. I'm not man enough to own a store; none of us are."

TWO Innocence and the End of an Era

1 Hugh Davis Graham and Ted Robert Gurr, Conclusion, in *The History of Violence in America: Historical and Comparative Perspectives*, A Report Submitted to the National Commission on the Causes and Prevention of Violence, ed Hugh Davis Graham and Ted Robert Gurr (New York: Praeger, 1969), p. 792.

2 Richard Hofstadter quotes this remark and then adds: "There seems to be more truth than we care to admit in the dictum of D. H. Lawrence" ("Spontaneous, Sporadic and Disorganized," *New York Times Magazine*, April 28, 1968). I do not wish to seem to tar the nation with a black brush; I am only trying to clarify the facts in order to reach below them to psychological causes.

3 John Lukacs, "America's Malady Is Not Violence but Savagery," in *Violence in America: A Historical and Contemporary Reader*, ed. Thomas Rose (New York: Vintage, 1970).

4 Henry Steele Commager, *The American Mind: An Interpretation of American Thought and Character since the 1880's* (New Haven: Yale University Press, 1950).

5 Charles Reich, *The Greening of America: The Coming of a New Consciousness and the Rebirth of a Future* (New York: Random House, 1970), p. 348.

6 *Ibid.*, p. 357.

7 Hannah Arendt, *On Violence* (New York: Harcourt Brace Javonovich, 1969), p. 14.

8 This is a second way the younger generation absorbs the prejudices of the older generation; the first is the belief that history is irrelevant.

9 Arendt, p. 7.

[10] Werner Heisenberg, "The Representation of Nature in Contemporary Physics," in *Symbolism in Religion and Literature*, ed. Rollo May (New York: Braziller, 1960), p. 225.

THREE Language: The First Casualty

[1] Harry Stack Sullivan, "Basic Conceptions," in *Conceptions of Modern Psychiatry* (New York: W. W. Norton, 1953), p. 15.

[2] Richard Abrams, George Vickers, and Richard Weiss, Postscript, in *Dialogue on Violence*, ed. Robert Theobald (New York: Bobbs-Merrill, 1968), p. 90.

[3] I do not speak of the kind of aggression known as "lover's quarrels," where the aggression is really an expression of a desire to come together again. This is on the side of "love" rather than the opposite of it; we still want to talk, and such a state can be stimulating. I speak of the real opposite of love—animosity, a state in which one wants to get as far away from the other person as possible, which deadens language, deadens the capacity to speak, to communicate. A difficult problem, somewhat different from the above, is that the hatred which results in violence must always be related in some way to love; otherwise it would lose its energy and wouldn't be worth fighting over. Anything we fight over has the ambivalence of hate-love, the love side being repressed and thus giving dynamic to the hatred by virtue of its repression.

[4] I received many letters telling me that to read my book *Love and Will* was like being "touched" continuously, that I seemed "to be an immediate presence" to the reader—although the writer of the letter may never have met me and actually was thousands of miles away. This was usually followed by congratulations on my capacity for presence in the *now*. What was not realized by most correspondents was that the experience of *being* was the result of eight years of writing and rewriting. The writing and rewriting would not give the experience of "touching" the reader by itself, nor would my sense of presence accomplish it by itself. Both are necessary.

[5] Alan Levy, "Ezra Pound's Voice of Silence," *New York Times Magazine*, Jan. 9, 1972.

[6] Especially when Rubin himself strains through every kind of punctuation and printing device to give his book effects that he cannot get by the power of writing itself. Jerry Rubin, *Do It: A Revolutionary Manifesto* (New York: Simon & Schuster, 1970), p. 109.

[7] In France even today the sexual meaning is referred to when someone asks whether you have had "experience."

[8] "Talk with Konrad Lorenz," *New York Times Magazine*, July 5, 1970, p. 4.

[9] *Ibid.*, p. 5.

FOUR Black and Impotent: The Life of Mercedes

[1] This phenomenon is not at all limited to blacks; it is universal. In our present age, when people of all classes feel impotent and despondent, there is a symptomatic increase in preoccupation with astrology and the occult

(not to mention actual witchcraft). Our magical tendencies are shown in our grasping for utopias. There is, paradoxically enough, an element of magic in our reliance on science, regardless of the character of the science itself. In the contemporary interest in operant conditioning, there is also a magic element: "When we are all controlled by the conditioners, we'll get along fine."

FIVE The Meaning of Power

1 Freud's concept of "libido" has some elements of ontology in it in that it is the force that causes the life process to continue. But for our purposes here, Freud never fully saw the social aspect of life, and hence the word *strength* can be used more accurately for libido than power.

2 Those who turn to psychology for help with the problem of power, we must add, are bound to be disappointed. Psychologists have shared in the general avoidance of the topic that, as we shall see below, has characterized all intellectuals. Several years ago I went through the card catalogue of the Harvard library and could find no book about power written by a psychologist except *Dark Ghetto*, a study of Harlem, by black psychologist Kenneth Clark, about an area of powerlessness where he could not escape the problem. My secretary found the same situation in the library at Columbia. The only research of moment on power I know of in psychology has been the work of David McClelland and his students on achievement motivation and power motivation. I am aware that in psychology, power has been subsumed under other terms like *will*, but even that is eschewed by academic psychologists.

The psychotherapists are, of course, a different matter. Working with suffering people, they cannot help confronting powerlessness and the effects of power. Alfred Adler's work, for example, is centrally based on power needs in individuals.

3 Quoted by Thomas Rose, "How Violence Occurs," in *Violence in America: A Historical and Contemporary Reader*, ed. Thomas Rose (New York: Vintage, 1970), p. 34.

4 Paul Tillich (*Love, Power and Justice: Ontological Analyses and Ethical Applications* [New York: Oxford University Press, 1960]) goes somewhat further than I am able to. He states that power "actualizes itself through force and compulsion. But power is neither one nor the other. It uses and abuses compulsion in order to overcome the threat of non-being. . . . It is not compulsion that is bad, but a compulsion which does not express the power of being in the name of which it is applied" (pp. 47–48). This last statement means, I take it, that the bearers of the power must be honest with themselves and with others about their motives for the application of force.

5 Peter Nettl, "Power and the Intellectuals," in *Power and Consciousness*, ed. Conner Cruise O'Brien and William Dean Vanech (New York: New York University Press, 1969), p. 16.

6 *Ibid.*, p. 15.

7 *Ibid.*, p. 17.

8 In his book *Society and Power* (New York: Random House, 1960), Prof. Richard A. Schermerhorn has listed eight kinds of influence and power. In

every case except one—"mutual friendship"—influence and power are identical.

9 "I know of no country in which there is so little independence of mind and real freedom of discussion as in America" (de Tocqueville, quoted in Schermerhorn, p. 44).

10 This idea was formulated by Anthony Athos in a private conversation with me.

11 Nettl, p. 25.

12 It is this con-man behavior in ethics, with its pretense and dishonesty, which young people now turn radically against.

13 Quoted by Kenneth B. Clark, *Dark Ghetto: Dilemmas of Social Power* (New York: Harper & Row, 1965), p. 183.

14 M. E. Wolfgang, "Who Kills Whom?," *Psychology Today* (Oct. 3, 1969), 55. Also see Elton B. McNeil, "Violence Today," *Pastoral Psychology* (Sept., 1971), 21–31.

15 Rollo May, *Love and Will* (New York: W. W. Norton, 1969), p. 147.

16 "It was misinterpretation which induced the philosopher of the will-to-power (i.e., Nietzsche), to reject radically the Christian idea of love. And it is the same misinterpretation which induces the Christian theologicans to reject Nietzsche's philosophy of the 'will-to-power' in the name of the Christian idea of love" (Tillich, p. 11). Tillich also argues that there could be no Christian social ethics or effective work for social justice on the basis of the separation of love and power.

six The Power to Be

1 Clara M. Thompson, *Interpersonal Psychoanalysis*, ed. Maurice R. Green (New York: Basic Books, 1964), p. 179.

2 D. W. Winnicott, "Aggression in Relation to Emotional Development," in *Collected Papers through Paediatrics to Psychoanalysis* (London: Tavistock, 1958), p. 204.

3 Anthony Storr, *Human Aggression* (New York: Atheneum, 1968), p. 41.

4 Anna Freud said, in her address to the International Congress of Psychoanalysis in Vienna, 1971, that aggression precedes defense in its origin: a child will take another's toys, and when the other comes to retrieve them, the first child will run and hide behind his mother's skirt. This interesting observation ought to be seen in the context of our culture.

5 Storr, p. 43.

6 *Ibid.*, p. 46.

7 Note B. F. Skinner's fondness for using the word *control* in *Beyond Freedom and Dignity* (New York: Knopf, 1971).

8 The remark invites special psychoanalytic interpretation for those interested. This young man's basic problem is his relationship with his mother, who always bought him too many groceries. Such old women are prototypes of *his* establishment and the ones he is going to have to kill symbolically (Oresteslike) if he is to attain psychological freedom and autonomy.

9 "Every being affirms his own being," writes Paul Tillich. "Its life is its

self-affirmation—even if the self-affirmation has the form of self-surrender" (*The Courage to Be* [New Haven: Yale University Press, 1952], p. 39).

[10] Charlotte Buhler, "The Four Basic Tendencies as Existential Characteristics," to be published.

[11] Tillich, p. 4.

[12] Walter Kaufman, *Nietzche: Philosopher, Psychologist, Antichrist* (Princeton: Princeton University Press, 1950), p. 183.

[13] *Ibid.*, p. 214.

SEVEN Aggression

[1] Walter B. Cannon, "Voodoo Death," *American Anthropologist*, XLIV/2 (April, 1942), 169–81.

[2] Anthony Storr, *Human Aggression* (New York: Atheneum, 1968), p. 16. In *The Meaning of Anxiety* (New York: Ronald, 1950), I have noted the similarity that exists between the endocrine secretions of sex and those of fighting. Alfred C. Kinsey has also noted that there are fourteen physiological changes that are identical in sexual arousal and in aggressive arousal (*Sexual Behavior in the Human Female* [Philadelphia: Saunders, 1953], p. 704).

[3] Sigmund Freud, "Instincts and Their Vicissitudes," in *Dora: An Analysis of a Case of Hysteria*, vol. IV of *Collected Papers of Sigmund Freud* (New York: Macmillan, 1963), p. 82.

[4] Anna Freud, at the International Congress of Psychoanalysis, Vienna (July, 1971).

[5] Konrad Lorenz, *On Aggression*, trans. Marjorie K. Wilson (New York: Harcourt Brace Javonovich, 1966).

[6] I am indebted to Dr. S. S. Tomkins for much of what follows here. Tomkins, however, was interested in the *commitment* of these men, while I am interested in the meaning of their aggression. Silvan S. Tomkins, "The Constructive Role of Violence and Suffering for the Individual and for His Society," in *Affect, Cognition and Personality*, eds. S. S. Tomkins and C. E. Izard (New York: Springer, 1965).

[7] *Ibid.*, p. 165.

[8] *Ibid.*, p. 166.

[9] *Ibid.*, p. 165.

[10] *Ibid.*, p. 163.

[11] *Ibid.*, pp. 163–64.

[12] *Ibid.*, p. 165.

[13] *Ibid.*, p. 166.

[14] *Ibid.*, p. 167.

EIGHT Ecstasy and Violence

[1] Jerry Rubin, *Do It: A Revolutionary Manifesto* (New York: Simon & Schuster, 1970), p. 36.

[2] One watches with a mixture of emotions the gyrations that various TV networks go through to "clean up" the violence in programs. This effort, I am sorry to say, adds up chiefly to a greater repression of the violence, a

greater subtlety in presenting it, and, unfortunately, a greater dishonesty in keeping out all its grime, dirt, and ugliness. In the long run, this amounts not to being on the side of nonviolence, but to hypocrisy and pretense.

3 Rollo May, *Love and Will* (New York: W. W. Norton, 1969), p. 99.

4 Actually, the opposite turned out to be truer. A few years after I graduated college, Hitler capitalized precisely on our faculty in this country for playing ostrich. Not willing to face the degree of evil of which certain men, particularly Hitler, were capable, we thus became accomplices of that evil.

5 William James, "The Moral Equivalent of War," in *Pragmatism and Other Essays*, ed. J. L. Blau (New York: Washington Square Press, 1963), pp. 290–96.

6 According to one compendium of contemporary history (Louis L. Snyder, *The World in the Twentieth Century*, rev. ed. [Gloucester, Mass.: Peter Smith, 1964], p. 138), we have had seventy-four wars in Europe during the first thirty years of this century, which is more than in the previous eight hundred years. With allowances made for all obvious points, such as increased density of population and the frequency of smaller wars (although who can deny our large ones also!), this fact still casts radical doubt on the comforting assumptions that as man grows more rational, he will fight less; or as his weapons grow more lethal, he will use them less. Such assumptions are whistling in the dark. Meditating on *Homo sapiens*, Pascal expressed our problem admirably with his simple sigh: "If reason were only reasonable!"

7 I will except the war in Vietnam from the following analysis. Our interest here is in aggression and violence; the Vietnam war seems to represent more the problem of dehumanization. In any case, since it is still going on, we shall not speak of it but of the world wars and those prior.

8 J. Glenn Gray, *The Warriors* (New York: Harper & Row, 1967).

9 *Ibid.*, p. 28.

10 *Ibid.*, p. 44.

11 *Ibid.*, p. 28.

12 *Ibid.*

13 I find a parallel here with the riots that occurred among the blacks in Watts, Detroit, and Newark. What we are here seeking to discover is the element of fascination in every situation *in extremis*. Wars and riots put the individual participant "on the line" in an ultimate sense. Our problem is: If modern warfare becomes impossible, what situations are going to be open to those people who need such living *in extremis*? This is not at all a question of war being inevitable and necessary; it is a statement that we must be concerned with correcting the needs from which that war comes and to which it ministers.

14 Gray, p. 51.

15 *Ibid.*, p. 217.

16 *Ibid.*

NINE The Anatomy of Violence

1 I am indebted to Dr. Gerald Chrzanowski for his discussion of these points.

2 See Walter Cannon's *The Wisdom of the Body* (New York: W. W. Norton, 1963).

3 These are the familiar workings of the sympathetic division of the autonomic nervous system, which I have described in *The Meaning of Anxiety* (New York: Ronald, 1950), pp. 62–63.

4 Harry Stack Sullivan, *Conceptions of Modern Psychiatry* (New York: W. W. Norton, 1953), p. 4.

5 J. William Fulbright, "In Thrall to Fear," *New Yorker*, Jan. 8, 1972, pp. 41–62.

6 Frantz Fanon, *The Wretched of the Earth* (New York: Grove Press, 1965), pp. 204–5.

TEN Innocence and Murder

1 Rainer Maria Rilke, *Letters to a Young Poet*, trans. M. D. Herter Norton (New York: W. W. Norton, 1934), p. 35.

2 Albert Camus, *The Rebel* (New York: Harcourt Brace Javonovich, 1970), pp. 6–7.

3 In the *New York Times*, May 19, 1970.

4 Obvious homosexual elements enter the picture, but they are not primary and it would be a gross oversimplification to make them so. I take them as one aspect of a general inability of Claggart to tolerate Billy Budd in his world, of which there are other aspects as well.

5 A phrase Melville gets from Plato. I suggest the reader not get trapped into futile arguments as to whether or not it is really "born with him and innate," which obviously goes against much that is taught in contemporary psychology. Rather, let us think of "evil nature" as archetypal, not to be dealt with adequately by a mere change of environment.

6 Jacob Bronowski, in *The Face of Violence: An Essay with a Play*, new and enlarged ed. (Cleveland: World, 1967), p. 2, also makes this point.

7 *Ibid.*, p. 2.

8 *Ibid.*, p. 3.

9 *Ibid.*, p. 166.

ELEVEN The Humanity of the Rebel

1 The core of my idea in this chapter is affirmed by various psychologists. Take the following from Frank X. Barron (*Creativity and Psychological Health: Origins of Personal Vitality and Creative Freedom* [Princeton: Van Nostrand, 1963], p. 144):

> . . . rebellion—resistance to accultural, refusal to "adjust," adamant insistence on the importance of the self and of individuality—is very often the mark of the healthy character. If the rules deprive you of some part of yourself, then it is better to be unruly. The socially disapproved expression of this is delinquency, and most delinquency certainly is just plain confusion or blind and harmful striking out at the wrong enemy; but some delinquency has affirmation behind it, and we should not be too hasty in giving a bad name to what gives us a

bad time. The great givers to humanity often have proud refusal in their souls, and they are aroused to wrath at the shoddy, the meretricious, and the unjust, which society seems to produce in appalling volume. Society is tough in its way, and it's no wonder that those who fight it tooth and nail are "tough guys." I think that much of the research and of the social action in relation to delinquency would be wiser if it recognized the potential value of the wayward characters who make its business for it. A person who is neither shy nor rebellious in his youth is not likely to be worth a farthing to himself nor to anyone else in the years of his physical maturity.

2 The definitions are from *Webster's Third New International Dictionary* (Springfield, Mass.: G. & C. Merriam, 1961).

3 Thomas Jefferson's "I have sworn upon the altar of God, eternal hostility against every form of tyranny over the mind of man" is almost the password for admission to the rebels.

4 In *The Rebel*, Albert Camus has written powerfully and insightfully on this distinction. The central idea of my illustration of the slaves is borrowed from him.

5 Dylan Thomas, *Collected Poems* (New York: New Directions, 1939), p. 128.

6 Jacob Bronowski, *The Face of Violence: An Essay with a Play*, new and enlarged ed. (Cleveland: World, 1967), p. 4.

7 Albert Camus, *The Rebel* (New York: Vintage, 1956), p. 295.

8 Hannah Arendt, *On Violence* (New York: Harcourt Brace Javonovich, 1970), p. 10.

9 When reading about these experiments, I can never get over the feeling that much more is going on than meets the eye of the experimenter. What about the interpersonal relationship between the subject and the experimenter—the trust the subject has in the experimenter and the responsibility the former automatically hands over to the latter? The fact that the subject enters such an experiment in the first place says something about his checking his responsibility at the door. I recall when I was a senior in college I participated in a psychological experiment in which I was told to do various things. I gave myself temporarily over to the experimenter, but I had a hundred and one private thoughts about *his* experiment. To find out what is really happening in contrast to what appears to be going on, one would need to know all of these subjective items.

10 Bronowski, pp. 64, 65.

11 I am obviously not referring to the values or difficulties of the doctor's work as contrasted with that of the artist. I am only saying that physiology is relatively constant, whereas the community and its forms—the subjects of the artist—are in radical upheaval.

12 Quoted by Peter Nettl, "Power and the Intellectuals," in *Power and Consciousness*, ed. Conner Cruise O'Brien and William Dean Vanech (New York: New York University Press, 1969), p. 32.

13 Camus, p. 23.

14 This moral arrogance was present in the early days of psychoanalysis; "We fortunate few have chosen the right track" was often stated or implied by the novitiates.

15 Camus, p. 301.

TWELVE Toward New Community

1 Quoted by Hedy Bookin, "The Medium Is the Mirror," in *Dialogue on Violence*, ed. Robert Theobald (New York: Bobbs-Merrill, 1968), p. 58.

2 *Ibid.*

3 University of Oklahoma Executive Planning Committee, *The Future of the University: A Report to the People*, ed. Gordon A. Christenson (Norman, Okla.: University of Oklahoma Press, 1969). These committees had a very interesting plan in that each committee studied not its own particular area in the university, such as liberal arts or law, but another. The organizers believed that groups could best deal with subjects that they did not have to defend. Thus they took a good deal of the competitiveness out of the power.

4 Martin Buber, "Power and Love," in *A Believing Humanism* (New York: Simon and Schuster, 1967), p. 45.

5 Jacob Bronowski, *The Face of Violence: An Essay with a Play*, new and enlarged ed. (Cleveland: World, 1967), pp. 161–62. He adds: "At the end of years of despair, there is nothing to grow in you as tall as a blade of grass except your own humanity."

6 From *Complete Poetry and Selected Prose of John Donne and Complete Poetry of William Blake* (New York: Modern Library, 1941), p. 598.

7 Daniel Berrigan, *No Bars to Manhood* (New York: Bantam Books, 1971), p. 97.

INDEX

Abolitionist movement, 158–63
Abraham, 225
Action therapies, 34, 69–70, 255
Adam and Eve myth, 222–23
Adler, Alfred, 35, 123, 154, 156, 233, 247
Aeschylus, 108, 224
Aggression
  animal behavior studies and, 141
  in art, 147–48, 153–54
  constructive, 158–63
  destructive, 156–57
  failure-of-nerve theories and, 22–23
  love and, 118
  meaning of, 148–52
  moral condemnation of, 149
  nature *v.* nurture question, 37–38, 123
  object-related, 183
  origins and development of, 123–26
  positive and negative aspects of, 151–52
  potential levels of power and, 42
  psychology of, Adlerian, 154–56; Freudian, 154–55; frustration and, 155–56
  psychotherapeutic approach to, 44–45, 93

  self-affirmation and, 138
  varieties of, 152–54; creative, 153–54; indirect, 152–53; self-directed, 153
  see also Violence; *all related entries*
Agnew, Spiro, 67
Altamont, 54
American Legion, 178
"America's Malady Is Not Violence but Savagery" (Lukacs) 52
Anderson, Maxwell, 111
Antigone (Sophocles), 172
Anxiety
  aggression and, 151–52
  apathy and, 162
  courage as triumph over, 159
  potentialities of power and, 122
Arendt, Hannah, 23, 35, 59, 227
Aristotle, 171
Art
  aggression and violence in, 147–48, 153–54, 170–72, 233
  rebel as artist, 231–35
Athos, Anthony, 104
Attica uprising, 32, 54
Auden, W. H., 21, 65, 232

Baptism, 92
Bazelon, David, 13, 106
Beckett, Samuel, 68, 104